This book must be returned on or before the above date.
Fines will be charged on all overdue items.
This item may be renewed twice:
Phone : 0161 484 6625

Confession   *s Years*
(1993). I   988) and
The Queen

by the same author

Plays

The Great Celestial Cow
Ten Tiny Fingers, Nine Tiny Toes
The Secret Diary of Adrian Mole Aged 13¾ – The Play
The Queen and I – The Play
Bazaar & Rummage, Groping for Words, Womberang

Fiction

The Secret Diary of Adrian Mole Aged 13¾
The Growing Pains of Adrian Mole
The True Confessions of Adrian Albert Mole, Margaret Hilda Roberts and
Susan Lilian Townsend
Rebuilding Coventry
The Queen and I
Adrian Mole: The Wilderness Years

Songs

The Secret Diary of Adrian Mole Songbook
(*in collaboration with Ken Howard and Alan Blaikley*)

SUE TOWNSEND

Plays: 1

Womberang

Bazaar & Rummage

Groping for Words

The Great Celestial Cow

The Secret Diary of Adrian Mole Aged 13¾ – The Play
with songs by Ken Howard and Alan Blaikley

Methuen Drama

METHUEN CONTEMPORARY DRAMATISTS

3 5 7 9 10 8 6 4

This edition first published in Great Britain 1996
by Methuen Drama
Random House UK Limited
20 Vauxhall Bridge Road, London SW1 2SA
and Australia, New Zealand and South Africa

Random House UK Limited Reg. No. 954000

Bazaar & Rummage, Groping for Words, Womberang first published in Great
Britain in one volume in 1984 as a Methuen Paperback; revised and reissued
in the Methuen Modern Plays series in 1990
Bazaar & Rummage copyright © 1984, 1990 by Sue Townsend
Groping for Words copyright © 1984, 1990 by Sue Townsend
Womberang copyright © 1984, 1990 by Sue Townsend
The Great Celestial Cow first published in Great Britain in 1984 as a Methuen
Paperback in association with the Royal Court Theatre; revised and reissued
in the Methuen Modern Plays series in 1990. Copyright © 1984, 1990 by
Sue Townsend
The Secret Diary of Adrian Mole Aged 13¾ – The Play first published in Great
Britain in 1985 as a Methuen Paperback. Play copyright © 1985 by Sue
Townsend. Music and lyrics copyright © 1985 by Ken Howard and Alan
Blaikley, Axle Music Ltd

Copyright in the Introduction © 1996 by Sue Townsend
The author has asserted her moral rights

ISBN 0–413–70250–2

A CIP catalogue record for this book
is available at the British Library

Typeset by Wilmaset Ltd, Birkenhead, Wirral
Printed and bound in Great Britain by Cox & Wyman Ltd, Reading, Berkshire

Caution

Contents

Sue Townsend:
A Chronology

PLAYS

1979   *In the Club and Up the Spout* touring production.
Womberang produced at the Soho Poly Theatre Club, London, and won the Thames Television bursary competition.

1981   *The Ghost of Daniel Lambert* (music by Rick Lloyd) produced at the Phoenix Arts Centre, Leicester.
Dayroom produced at the Croydon Warehouse Theatre.

1982   *Womberang* produced as *The Waiting Room* at the Phoenix Arts Centre, Leicester.
Bazaar & Rummage produced at the Royal Court Theatre Upstairs, London.

1983   *Bazaar & Rummage* produced on BBC TV.
Groping for Words produced at the Croydon Warehouse Theatre.
Clients produced at the Croydon Warehouse Theatre.

1984   *The Great Celestial Cow* first presented by Joint Stock Theatre Company at the Leicester Haymarket Studio, then toured before opening at the Royal Court Theatre, London.
The Secret Diary of Adrian Mole Aged 13¾ – The Play (with songs by Ken Howard and Alan Blaikley) produced at the Phoenix Arts Centre, Leicester, and subsequently at Wyndham's Theatre, London.

1986   *Groping for Words* produced in a revised version as *Are You Sitting Comfortably?* at the Palace Theatre, Watford.

1989   *Ear, Nose and Throat* produced at the Chichester Festival Theatre.
Ten Tiny Fingers, Nine Tiny Toes produced at the Library Theatre, Manchester.

1990   *Disneyland It Ain't* produced at the Royal Court Theatre Upstairs, London.

1991   *The Ashes*, a radio play, presented on BBC Radio 4.

1994   *The Queen and I* produced by Out of Joint, Leicester
       Haymarket Theatre and the Royal Court Theatre, London
       (with songs by Ian Dury and Mickey Gallagher).
       Subsequently played at the Vaudeville Theatre, London.
       Bodies, part of a series on Englishness, presented on BBC2.

FICTION

The Secret Diary of Adrian Mole Aged 13¾ (Methuen, 1982)
The Growing Pains of Adrian Mole (Methuen, 1984)
Rebuilding Coventry: A Tale of Two Cities (Methuen, 1988)
*The True Confessions of Adrian Albert Mole, Margaret Hilda Roberts and
   Susan Lilian Townsend* (Methuen, 1989)
Mr Bevan's Dream (Chatto and Windus, 1989)
Adrian Mole from Minor to Major (incorporating *The Secret Diary of
   Adrian Mole Aged 13¾, The Growing Pains of Adrian Mole, True
   Confessions of Adrian Albert Mole* and *Adrian Mole and the Small
   Amphibians,* Methuen, 1991)
The Queen and I (Methuen, 1992)
Adrian Mole: The Wilderness Years (Methuen, 1993)

Introduction

I left school one week before my fifteenth birthday. They were glad to see the back of me. I was not disruptive but if I'd been in the army I would have been charged many times with 'dumb insolence'. I was addicted to print, and I would smuggle books into lessons. I was once given an order mark for reading Malcolm Lowry's *Under the Volcano* during a (Religious Instruction) lesson.

There was a good English teacher, a pale, reserved woman, called Miss Morris. She was passionate about clean fingernails, William Blake and Oscar Wilde. Miss Morris praised my writing but pointed out that 'clouds like cotton wool' was a horrible cliché. Her criticism was invaluable, to this day I am very wary of adjectives and clichés. When I left school I missed Miss Morris and I also missed writing my weekly composition. So I started to write at home, in my bedroom. It was the usual mawkish adolescent stuff and I knew better than to leave it lying around, so I hid it and I continued to hide it for twenty years – a period which encompassed my first marriage and the birth of three of my four children.

Miss Morris formed the Orpheans Drama Group and I became an active member. I was Jesus in Miss Morris' passion play, and I dragged a wooden cross around mental hospitals and churches in Leicester and in various religious establishments in Holland. I was Gertrude in Wilde's *The Importance of Being Ernest* in many village halls, but I stopped acting after a boyfriend came to see me as Lady Bracknell in a festival of drama. 'You looked bloody stupid,' he said. I was seventeen before I saw a professional theatrical production. It was *A Streetcar Named Desire* and I wept with rage and jealousy as the audience filed out at the end of the performance. I didn't want to be in the audience, I wanted to be on the stage or backstage or *involved* in some way.

I wrote my first play in a cheap exercise book using a black felt-tip pen. I have never learnt to type, I have a strong antipathy to pressing those keys down. I much prefer making scratchy noises on paper. The play was a pantomime for the Youth Club I worked in three nights a week.

My second play was also a pantomime, this time for an adventure playground, 'The Pied Piper'. On the day of the performance the Pied Piper himself had to be dragged from a bus stop where he was waiting to catch a bus into town with his mother to buy a pair of school trousers. He'd been too ashamed to tell his mother he was the star of our long-rehearsed play. He was frogmarched from the bus stop at 2.15, at 2.30 p.m. he was in his green tights performing in front of over a hundred invited guests. His mother never forgave me.

The vast majority of the audience had never been to the theatre before, they enjoyed the pantomime so much that they demanded an immediate repeat performance; so we did it again. This time several unruly toddlers ran onto the acting area and stole the rats and quite a few mothers and fathers, who were drunk both on pride and alcohol, distracted their children by shouting out words of encouragement. I was very moved by this experience, but my heart sank when the parents and children asked me for another scripted play.

The process of getting the play on had been exhausting enough. Rehearsing twenty-five young people, most of whom couldn't read (the abysmal local secondary school was closed down by Leicestershire County Council), was extremely difficult – at one time I had a deputation of young men asking me if I could write a scene where the Pied Piper had a knife fight with the citizens of Hamelin. Then there were the costumes to be made. The scenery to be built and painted, the songs to be rehearsed. Chairs had to be found for the audience. Invitations – printed by hand by the children – to be given out. The hall had to be cleaned of the evidence of adventure play and disguised as a theatre. Volunteers had to be found to serve refreshments during the interval. It was the best introduction to working in the professional theatre I could have had.

From then on 'plays' became a daily activity on the

playground, but they were improvised plays. I trawled charity shops for dressing-up clothes and props. The children and young people would fight over my spoils, then lock themselves into a room, and, with much violent argument and tearful scuffles, begin to devise a play. Their plays invariably had big themes: Justice, Love, Death etc. We had many courtroom dramas, and more knife fights than I care to remember. Their outdoor version of *West Side Story* will always be remembered by those who saw it for its spectacular opening scene, when the rival gangs, the Jets and the Sharks, made their entrances by running from behind the trees and jumping over a fiercely burning bonfire.

Most of the youngsters are parents themselves now. I still live in Leicester so I see them quite often, and we talk and laugh about the days when 'we made plays'. Shortly after my fourth child was born I confessed to my second husband that I was a secret writer and he urged me to join the Phoenix Writers Group. I did join and thanks to Ian Giles, the director of the Phoenix, six months later I had been shortlisted for a Thames Television Playwrights Bursary. I borrowed my mother's clothes and went to London for the first time in my adult life. I entered a room and saw John Mortimer, Michael Billington, Sir Hugh Carlton Greene and other such luminaries. John Mortimer read aloud from my play *Womberang* and made them laugh. When I got home to Leicester I found a telegram on the doormat to say I had won. The newspaper, *The Stage*, reported my win, but also reported that 'it had been a bad year'.

My prize was £2000, to be paid in quarterly payments of £500, and the job of resident writer at the Phoenix. I was terrified, so terrified that I overcompensated like mad, I wrote twelve pieces of drama in that year, including a play called 'The Ghost of Daniel Lambert' which had eleven actors, but forty-two speaking and singing parts.

I have been commissioned ever since, but I still don't know how to write a play. I am now on the panel of the Thames Television Playwrights Scheme, and I take my duties very carefully indeed.

People need drama, like they need water, air and food, it

sustains us and comforts us, and reminds us that we are not
totally alone.

Womberang

This was my first play. Originally it lasted only half an hour
but it had ten characters. As I said, it was my first play. I
didn't know that I was breaking all the theatrical rules. It
has been extended but is still quite short and runs without an
interval.

I wrote *Womberang* because I spent a great deal of time
hanging about in gynaecological waiting rooms (I have four
children). I was a meek creature then and did as I was told
but I used to fantasise about changing the furniture round,
complaining and generally carrying on as my heroine, Rita,
does. This play is the result of my fantasies.

My daughter, when she was about to have a baby, told me
that the waiting rooms are still the same (though they are
now painted pink and grey). The magazines are still four
years old and the doctors' hands are still cold.

Bazaar & Rummage

Agoraphobia forces you to act in the most ridiculous fashion.
I once suffered from it for three weeks and during that time I
would hang my washing out in the garden at midnight. I was
lucky in that I analysed the cause of my agoraphobia: I
hated where I lived. So there was a simple solution. Move. I
did move and as soon as the decision was made the
agoraphobia went.

Some agoraphobics haven't left their houses for twenty
years, others can only move within a very small territory. All
of them suffer great anxiety at the thought of going out. It is
very sad but most of the sufferers can and will laugh about
their experiences.

Bazaar & Rummage is also about the nature of 'caring' and
the sometimes parasitic stranglehold that carers have on
those they are supposed to be caring for. Who needs whom?

I think that agoraphobia is only an outward symptom of other deeper problems. And, something more sinister perhaps, it often suits husbands and children to have their wives and mothers at home all day every day and if the sufferer talks about seeking a cure this will be seen almost as an act of betrayal.

This play is a comedy, and so, like all comedy, it should not be played for laughs. It should be played for the truth in the lines. The laughs will come.

Groping for Words

I wrote *Groping for Words* because I was angry about the high level of illiteracy in this country. I couldn't understand (and still can't) why so many young people were leaving school unable to read or write properly after *eleven years* of compulsory education. I daydreamed about a world in which everyone was fully literate. What would happen if we all demanded a university education? A career? A skilled job? The conclusion I came to was that failure is built into our education system: our present political and social organisations would be unable to cope with a highly educated and demanding workforce.

I once worked on an adventure playground on a so-called 'problem' housing estate. The level of illiteracy was frighteningly high but the children were very intelligent, quick witted and ashamed of their inability to fill in a simple form or read a story to a younger child.

But there is always hope. A friend of mine, Beryl Lawrence, went to literacy classes for four years. Then, at the age of fifty-one she wrote a short book called *Me*. At the age of fifty-two she wrote a longer book called *Me Again*. She is now studying for French GCSE.

The Great Celestial Cow

I started to write *The Great Celestial Cow* after seeing Four Asian women laughing in a street in Leicester. They were leaving a factory and were obviously happy to be out in the fresh air for a while until their household duties claimed them.

When I say that I started to 'write' the play, I don't mean that I rushed home grabbed a pen and wrote there and then. What I mean is that I started to think about the lives of Asian women in Leicester.

Many of these women come from rural backgrounds. It is common for their husbands to come to Leicester, find a job, establish a home and then send for their wives and children. Consequently, during their husbands' absence, the women enjoy a certain autonomy. I thought how difficult it must be to transplant yourself to a cold urban environment with a different set of rules and customs, where the language is foreign and where suddenly your status is reduced.

I put myself in their place and knew that, were our positions to be reversed, I would go quietly mad.

The play was commissioned by the Joint Stock Theatre Company and performed after a period of research, a ten-week writing gap and four weeks' rehearsal during which the actors and director Carole Hayman contributed to the final performance script. It is their play as well as mine.

The Great Celestial Cow was the cause of much heated debate amongst the (mostly male) Asian community in Leicester. There was resentment because I was a white woman writer. How dare I criticise the Asian family. Yet I watched many of our critics laughing (and sometimes obviously moved) as they watched the play, only to raise their voices in anger during the discussions after the show.

I noticed my first grey hairs during the research period. More appeared in the ten weeks of writing and by the time the play had finished its tour and was at the Royal Court I was reaching for the hair dye. Yet *The Great Celestial Cow* remains my favourite play. It was difficult to write and is difficult to stage but it can be quite magical when it works.

The Secret Diary of Adrian Mole Aged 13¾

I wrote *The Secret Diary of Adrian Mole – The Play* for Graham Watkins, the then director of the Phoenix Arts Theatre in

Leicester. He was convinced (unlike me) that the play would be a huge success, and that the subsequent box office revenue would put the Phoenix on a firmer financial footing.

Graham was right, and I was wrong. The 'House Full' sign had to be searched for and dusted down. People queued around the block for returned tickets, and a millionaire, Eddie Kulukundis, flew to Leicester in a helicopter and said he would like to produce *Adrian Mole* in the West End. The play ran for over two years at Wyndham's Theatre on the Charing Cross Road.

The structure of the play is in diary form, and is therefore episodic. It demands a great deal from the young man who is to play Adrian Mole: a lot of lines to learn and moves to remember. We were lucky to find a superb young actor, Simon Schatzberger, to play the first Adrian Mole. The play is set in Leicester and works best with East Midlands or Northern accents. The citizens of Leicester were outraged when *Mole* was televised and most of the actors spoke with Birmingham accents. God knows how they would have reacted to the Flemish, surrealist version of *Mole* I saw in Belgium, complete with nudity and atonal music. This was the only time I have ever been dragged onto the stage (fully clothed) and made to take a bow before the audience. It was rather nice.

Sue Townsend
Leicester, 1996

Womberang

Womberang was first presented at the Soho Poly Theatre Club, London, on 20 October 1979, with the following cast:

Rita	Joan Morrow
Clerk	Carolyn Pickles
Dolly	Trudie Goodwin
Mrs Conelly	Fanny Carby
Mrs Lovett	Sheila Collins
James	Kit Jackson
Audrey	Fleure Chandler
Lynda	Carolyn Pickles
Mrs Cornwallis	Carolyn Pickles
Mr Riley	Kit Jackson

Directed by Sue Pomeroy
Designed by Dee Greenwood

A hospital outpatients' waiting room. The afternoon gynaecological clinic is in progress. A **Clerk** *at a desk faces padded benches, one of which has a pile of tatty magazines stacked on it. On the wall is a large ticking clock surrounded by the usual notices. Blood-donor and anti-smoking posters predominate. A large sign simply says 'No Smoking'.*

A row of curtained cubicles stands next to the **Doctor**'s *door. Two large free-standing ashtrays complete the furnishing of this 'room'.*

A hospital smell would help the atmosphere.

Mrs Lovett *and* **Mrs Conelly** *sit on the front bench,* **Audrey Lemon** *and* **James Lemon** *sit on the bench behind them.*

There must be a long pause before **Rita** *and* **Dolly** *enter. Everyone sitting looks up, stares.* **Rita** *stares back,* **Sitters** *drop eyes.* **Rita** *and* **Dolly** *go to* **Clerk**'s *desk.* **Clerk** *is writing, ignoring the* **Sitters**. **Sitters** *cough, shuffle and after thirty seconds* **Rita** *brings bell from large bag and rings it. There is an immediate result. The* **Clerk** *looks up and the* **Sitters** *are riveted by the interruption to the sluggish afternoon.*

Rita About bleedin' time! Don't you know it's very bad manners to ignore people? Writing can wait – you're only writing lists of names aren't you?

Clerk You should have said!

Rita You knew we were here! (*To* **Sitters**.) I ring it in shops now when they keep me waiting for nothing. Teaches them a lesson. They don't expect it.

Clerk Have you got an appointment?

Rita Yes, for half-past two, it is now two-fifteen by my watch, so in a quarter of an hour I shall be expecting to see Dr Riley.

Clerk Well, we're running very late, you may have to wait a bit longer than half-past two.

Rita I have a plane to catch at Heathrow Airport. It is crucial that my appointment is on time. You will have to tell Dr Riley to get his finger out, perhaps literally get his finger out.

Rita *and* **Dolly** *laugh,* **Mrs Lovett**, *a* **Sitter**, *sniggers.*

Clerk Can I have your name?

Rita If you like, but you might change your name when you hear it. It's Rita Onions, or if you prefer O-nions.

Clerk Is that Miss or Mrs O-nions?

Rita Divorced Rita O-nions, put what you like. Mr would be more suitable, short for mother.

Clerk Would you take a seat?

Rita Where to?

Dolly *laughs.*

Clerk Will you sit down?

Rita Tidier that way aren't we?

Dolly C'mon, Reet, my feet are killin' me with walking round town. Let's sit down.

The two sit down on the front bench, **Dolly** *next to* **Mrs Lovett.**

Rita Shall we have a fag?

Dolly No, it's no smokin', Reet!

Rita Look, in a quarter of an hour I could find out I've got six months to live, if I don't need a fag now, when do I?

Both light up.

James Lemon *is shocked.*

Clerk I'm afraid there's no smoking.

Rita Then why provide ashtrays? Bloody hypocrites!

Clerk The smoke may be offensive to other patients!

James Lemon *coughs.*

Rita I'll ask them! (*To other* **Sitters.**) This smoke bothering anyone?

No one reacts.

Rita (*stands, enunciates clearly*) I said, is this smoke bothering anyone? No? Good. Hands up who likes the smell of hospitals.

No one reacts.

Rita The smoke wins by a clear (*To* **Clerk.**) if not devastating majority.

Mrs Conelly *gets up from the bench and goes to the desk.*

Conelly (*in a loud whisper*) I'm very sorry, dear, but I've forgotten to bring a sample of water.

Clerk Were you definitely told to bring one at your last consultation?

Conelly Yes, I'm sorry, but with all the worry . . .

Clerk Well *I'm* sorry but the hospital can't be expected to provide containers, that's why you're told to bring them from home.

Conelly What shall I do then?

Clerk I'd better make you another appointment. Will a fortnight today be all right, at the same time?

Rita (*standing*) No it will not. (*To* **Conelly**.) Don't worry, love, I'll sort you out. (*To all.*) Who's got a bottle or jar – anything waterproof? They only need a drop of pee for Christ's sake?

Dolly Will this do, Reet? (*She holds up a Tic-Tac box.*)

Rita No it will not, Dolly, this lady can't pee into a Tic-Tac box and neither could Olga Korvet . . . Somebody must have a bottle, come with me, duck, we'll find something.

Rita *takes* **Mrs Conelly** *out into the corridor.*

Lovett (*to* **Dolly**) You a friend of hers?

Dolly (*proudly*) I'm her best friend.

Lovett Does she always carry on like that, or is she in a bad mood?

Dolly She's always the same nowadays, it's not a bad mood, it's more . . . now then, she did tell me, I've forgotten the word . . . it's quite a long one, not one you use every day . . . one of those.

Lovett Paranoia?

Dolly No, it doesn't begin with a P, although that's the type of word. Are you educated then?

Lovett Not properly, who is? No, I used to clean for a doctor. He used to let me take some of his books home to read. Then one of my neighbours went funny during the change – you know. She thought everyone was talkin' about her, saying her house smelt.

I looked it up and it was called paranoia, it sort of stuck in my mind. (*Pause.*) Between you and me, her house did smell.

Dolly I wish I could remember that word, still, Reet will be back soon, she'll tell you.

Lovett It's quiet in here again without her. She's like a one-woman show.

Dolly Yes, she's a case isn't she? You wouldn't have known her last year. Her husband walked all over her, got so bad she wouldn't go out of the house, kids did all the shopping, she sat by the fire watching telly all day then cleaned the house over and over when the kids were in bed. Not normal is it?

Lovett shakes her head.

Anyway, her doctor sent her to the Towers, got an order from the court, she wouldn't go voluntary, wouldn't leave the kids. But oh, you should have seen her at the end, like a wild woman she was. *I* had to go in and feed the kids, do the washing and all that. She sat in a chair filthy, watching the telly, didn't speak a word to nobody, then one night one of the kids burnt themselves on the stove making some toast. Reet never moved, didn't turn her head. They took the kids away that night, in care they call it. I told them I'd have them, but they said we was already overcrowded anyway. Reet goes in the Towers like a zombie and comes out like you've seen her today.

Lovett Did she have the electric shock?

Dolly Yes, but it wasn't that, it was the therapy group. Therapy, that's where they all sit around and tell everyone in the group what they really think, really think! Like say if someone's got dirty teeth, they tell them . . .

*The **Sitters** all become teeth-conscious.*

. . . I think you should clean your teeth. Awful isn't it? Or if they've got a bogy in their nose . . . you tell them, you tell them all about when you were a kid. If your husband drives you mad when he's eating. Things you wouldn't normally tell nobody. Reet was quiet at first, didn't talk much, then somebody said her roots needed doing, she's not a natural blonde – but don't say anything. Well Reet went wild, called him everything from a pig to a cow. After that she's been the same as you saw her today, speaks her mind, does things instead of sitting quiet.

Lovett She's a bit much though, isn't she? Doesn't she show you up?

Dolly Yes she does, but she's a good friend to me. F'rinstance, my baker's been fiddling me for years. You know what they do, charge you for cakes you haven't had, leave bread you haven't ordered, it soon mounts up.

Mrs Lovett and **Audrey Lemon** *nod.*

Lovett I'd have told him first time it happened, you're daft to have put up with it.

Dolly Some can, some can't. I could never pluck up the courage. Reet made me tell him. She stood behind the door. I said, 'I shan't want no more bread.' He said, 'When, this week?' 'No, never,' I says and Reet shot from behind the door and says, 'And she won't be paying this week's bill neither, take it out of what you've fiddled from her over the years.' Well he never said a word, just got into his van and drove off. Oh, it was so lovely not having him call every day, but I did feel a bit sorry for him.

Lovett Serves the bugger right. (*She laughs.*) Who was it, Co-op?

Dolly Yes, how did you know? (*All the* **Women** *laugh.*)

Lovett What's she here for then?

Dolly (*dropping her voice*) She's not been right down below.

Lovett Waterworks?

Dolly Well near there, very near.

Lovett Baby trouble?

Dolly Not exactly baby trouble in that area.

Lovett Dropped has it?

Dolly Has what dropped?

Lovett Her womb!

Dolly I think it's more stuck than dropped.

Lovett Stuck eh! Never heard of that. I'm here for a drop. I'm expecting to have it all took away. Should have happened years ago. I suffered in silence for years, didn't think the family could spare me for going into hospital. Now I don't care if the selfish sods starve while I'm in, do 'em all good to do their own washing as well. If I don't have the operation soon, I'll cut my throat, that's how I feel.

Rita *enters.*

Rita Well, in this age of medical technology, an old age pensioner is peeing into a Coca-Cola bottle using a *Beano* comic as a funnel. Look good in the *Standard* wouldn't it, dear? (*She glares at the* **Clerk***.*) I can see the results of the test now: 'Mrs Conelly is suffering from Desperate Dan-itis and Beryl the Peril syndrome'.

Rita, Dolly, Lovett and **Audrey** *laugh.* **James** *silences* **Audrey.**

Dolly I was telling this lady about you, Reet, since your therapy.

Rita Oh yes? She'll be thinking I'm a loony, Dolly, all I do is speak my mind and tell the truth. It's good for you, that's what therapy means, good for you. I bet most of us here are only imagining things wrong with us. If we had a talk I bet we'd walk out of here blooming with health.

Clerk Mrs Lovett, would you undress and go and sit in the cubicle on the right please, Mr Riley won't keep you long.

Mrs Lovett *stands.*

Rita Yes he will keep her long! He's just got his tea and biscuits, and he's lit up one of them small cigars. I just saw him through the crack in the door. Take your time Mrs Lovett, and another thing, don't put your feet in them stirrup things, let them learn to look at our faces first, instead of our bums. It's undignified for all concerned.

Clerk Mrs O-nions, I must ask you not to interfere with medical matters, you are not qualified to give advice to these ladies.

Rita You're not qualfied to give advice to me, you sweet little school leaver, making an old age pensioner piss into a Coca-Cola bottle!

Mrs Conelly *enters holding Coca-Cola bottle half full of pee.*

Conelly Here it is, dear, I couldn't manage much, is there enough?

Rita You can have some of mine if you like, that'll baffle the sods.

Clerk That's enough! Now sit down and shut up. You're getting all of this free you know! You shouldn't mock it, it's sacrilege! It's bad enough working with disgusting, ill people all day, without having them being rude to me as well. I've had enough. I'm off. I shall have to report you, Mrs O-nions.

*The **Clerk** exits.*

Dolly Now you've done it, Reet.

Rita She's not suited to the job is she? One day she might have a difficult patient to deal with, I'm only giving her a bit of training. Anyway, now she's gone, let's talk, all of us. Let's change the benches round so we can see each other properly. Light your fags up if you want to, Riley's in there smoking his cigar.

*The **Women** change the benches around, **James** and **Audrey** remain seated, they are pulled around by the other **Women**.*

Right, are we all comfy? Someone has to start the ball rolling . . . or the womb dropping. (*She laughs.*) *Remember?* That lady's fat isn't she, Mummy? Slap. (**Rita** *slaps her wrist.*) Uncle Ted, your ears stick out. (*She slaps herself.*) I expect you've done it to your own kids, teach them to tell the truth, then smack 'em round the ear'ole if they do. Right, shall I start?

*There are wary nods from **Dolly**, **Lovett** and **Conelly**.*

Mrs Conelly, dear, did you know your corsets show right through your dress? If I were you I'd wear a looser dress or throw the bloody corset away.

Conelly But I've always worn it. It keeps me in, it keeps me back straight. I shouldn't feel dressed without it.

Rita Group, what does she look like in it?

Silence.

Rita Come on, the truth now!

All women except Audrey Take it off. Awful. You can see every whalebone.

Rita Go on, take it off, Mrs Conelly. Let it all hang out.

Conelly I'll think about it, promise. I'll give it some thought.

Rita Good. Right, who's next?

The **Group** *becomes uncomfortable.*

Rita (*to* **James**) Who are you? Not waiting to see the gynaecologist are you? Don't want a sex change?

James *is reading* Watchtower.

James I'm accompanying my wife, and I'd rather you didn't include either of us in your game.

Rita Oh. It isn't a game, duck, it's serious. Go on, let yourself go. You're as wound up as a milkman's alarm clock. Anyway perhaps your wife does want to take part?

Audrey *shakes her head after looking at* **James**.

Rita Don't ask him! Do you want to take part?

Audrey *shakes her head.*

Rita Are you mute, dear? Are you lip-reading? If so I will speak very clearly. One – more – time – do – you – want – to – take – part – question – mark.

Audrey (*clearing her throat*) I can speak. (*She looks at* **James**.) But if my husband doesn't want me to take part, then I won't.

James *pats* **Audrey**'*s arm.*

Rita Do my ears deceive me? You've just put Women's Liberation back ten years. I bet Christabel . . . wotsit is whirling in her grave.

Lovett Pankhurt. Christabel Pankhurst.

Rita Thanks, dear. (*To* **Audrey**.) Now you can tell me what your name is, can't you, or will your hubby mind?

James *whispers to* **Audrey**.

Audrey It's Mrs Audrey Lemon.

Rita We make a right pair, don't we? Onions and Lemons. Like the kid's song: (*She sings.*) Onions and Lemons.

Lovett Oranges! (*She gets no response.*) It's oranges (*To herself.*)

Audrey *laughs.*

James *stands.*

James I forbid you to speak another word to my wife, she leads a very sheltered life, she has an extremely nervous disposition.

Dolly I get nerves. (*She sees* **Rita**'s *glance.*) Now . . . and again. (*Her voice fades.*)

Rita Audrey, does he always speak to you like this?

Audrey Mm. I suppose he does.

Rita Today will be the last day, Audrey, you have my word.

Audrey It doesn't bother me, not really.

Rita It bothers me, dear.

James Audrey needs a firm hand, she *can* be headstrong.

Rita By the look of it she needs a firm something. Why are you here, Audrey, something wrong?

James Audrey!

Rita Go on, love.

Audrey We've been married five years and . . .

James Audrey!

Audrey James has been waiting for kiddies to come along and they haven't, so I've got to have some tests –

James Audrey! I won't tell you again, you will not discuss our private life with this woman!

Audrey *looks at* **Rita** *who gives her an encouraging gesture.*

Audrey James, Mrs Onions is quite right, I ought to be allowed to speak if I want to.

James I'm warning you, Audrey, open your mouth one more time and I'm off. You can face the doctor on your own.

Audrey Please, James, it can't do any harm.

James Have you gone mad? I've just told you to keep your mouth shut.

Audrey Well I won't!

James Shut it!

Audrey No!

James Shut your mouth!

Audrey Piss off!

James Audrey, you swore.

Audrey I might swear again.

James Think of your mother.

Audrey Bugger!

James Audrey!

Audrey I might say the really bad word!

James God help you, Audrey.

Audrey You need his help more than I do!

James I'll have to report you to the brethren.

Audrey You can tell them to piss off too. I'm sick of seeing their miserable faces, no smoking, no drinking, no Christmas, not even a blood transfusion.

James You've lost your faith!

Audrey I've never had it, James. Every week trudging around preaching the message no one wants to hear. You've seen their faces change when they realise who we are, and James, I don't believe we'll be saved at Armageddon, if it ever comes we'll die like the rest.

James You're condemned to everlasting death now, you realise that don't you? You're past saving now, I'll have to leave . . . you're unclean. (*To* **Rita**.) You're an agent of the Devil with your bleached hair and cigarettes.

Rita I'm a natural blonde! I'll show you my armpits if you like.

James *rushes out.*

Dolly Oh God! You've really done it now, Reet.

Rita Me! What did I do? She did it all herself. Good girl! Been waiting long to tell him all that?

Audrey Five years!

Rita Feel better now?

Audrey Much better.

Lovett He looked like a right miserable sod to me, you're well rid of him. You a Jehovah's Witness then?

Audrey I was, until a few moments ago. I hope he never comes back, never, if he goes home today, I shall go and get a job. Start again.

Lovett Well good luck to you, gal, I say.

Rita What about the doctor? Will you still see him?

Audrey There's no point. There's nothing wrong with me. It's just that some men don't know about certain things.

Rita What kind of certain things?

Audrey Well, intimate things . . .

Lovett She means sex.

Conelly Some men don't know how to go on, my husband was a bit slow coming forward. We had to practise quite a lot.

Rita Are you telling me your husband's brought you down here for a check up and really it's him who doesn't know how to go on?

Audrey Yes, he wasn't doing it right.

Rita How was he doing it?

Dolly Reet!

Rita Is he one of them perverts?

Dolly Reet!

Audrey No. Nothing like that. It's just that instead of putting it in here (*She indicates her groin.*) he was putting it there. (*She indicates her navel.*)

Rita What! In your belly button?

Audrey *nods.*

Rita Not so much making love as a bleeding naval exercise! Why didn't you tell him?

Audrey I just couldn't, he wouldn't allow any talk about sex, he'd walk out of the room if I tried to talk. I never once saw him undressed – and he never saw me. He'd close his eyes. It's his mother's fault, she brought him up to think that women were dirty. Perhaps she told him babies were born out of your tummy button.

Lovett He must have been going around with his eyes and ears shut for years. Like them Japanese that think the war's still on.

Rita It's sad really, just think what he's missing.

Lovett I shouldn't miss it. I've had no rockets firing or bells ringing for me. It's a quick grope when the club shuts on Sunday afternoon. He's stinking of beer and I've got an Oxo cube in me hand and I'm lying there smelling meat burning in the oven.

Dolly I'm all right there, I've got one of those pre-timers, my meat switches itself off.

Rita All right! All right! Before we get bogged down with self-cleaning ovens and bloody washing-machines, let's get back to Audrey. So you think it's all over do you, love? Starting out on your own? Join the club, it can be done, can't it Dolly? We're both on our own, we have a good laugh. No shirts to wash and iron, none of them big slimy handkerchiefs to wash, no dinner to be on the table dead on six.

Dolly I sometimes miss my John, late at night, when Reet's gone home. The kids miss him, they're always asking when he's coming home. I have to keep on thinking up new excuses. At the moment he's supposed to be drilling for oil in Bahrain.

Rita That's a laugh, couldn't fill his lighter without spilling it all over the place.

Lovett If he's gone for good, you should tell the kids, it's not fair to keep them hoping.

Rita Dolly thinks he will come back, don't you Dolly? She thinks he'll leave his posh flat and his page-three bird to come back to his council house, three screaming kids and Raquel Welch here.

Dolly Honestly, Reet, sometimes you can be so cruel.

Dolly *is almost in tears.*

Rita I'm cruel to be kind, Dolly, you know that.

Audrey I think I'll go now, I've got a lot to do. I'm that excited, it's like being born again! I can please myself, do as I like. I can't wait to start.

Group Good luck! Mind how you go!

Audrey *gathers her bags, smiles at the door, waves and leaves.*

Audrey Bye! Bye!

Rita I'll give her six months before she finds a bloke from the Divine Light Mission or one of them Moonies. She's a natural victim that one.

Conelly She seemed a really nice girl.

Rita They always are.

Lovett Anyway, who's next?

Rita *sighs – a deep sigh of satisfaction, stretches her body on the seat and sits with her hands behind her head, the epitome of relaxation.*

Rita You don't do it like that, there has to be a general discussion, then it gets more personal. Let's talk about politics.

Group Oh no. I don't know anything . . .

Rita All right then, we won't talk about politics, we'll talk about Mrs Thatcher.

Dolly Oh she dresses lovely! And her hair always looks nice as well, just as if she's stepped out of the hairdresser's.

Rita That's because she has, Dolly. But do you think she's a good Prime Minister?

Conelly Well I've noticed that her voice has got deeper since she started, it must be all that talking.

Rita That's only on the telly and for speeches, I'll bet she talks different at home.

She gives a Thatcher impression.

Denis! Denis! Come and empty this filthy ashtray.

All the **Women** *laugh.*

Lovett I've got nothing to thank her for. The night my husband came home and told me that he'd been laid-off I could have strangled her. He'd been crying on his way home, he'd been there twenty years. All his mates were there. He still gets up at the same time, sometimes he forgets and puts his boots on. It's a habit you see, going to work.

Rita What makes me laugh is how nobody admits to voting for her.

Dolly (*blushing*) Did you read in *Woman* that Mrs Thatcher has never asked her husband about his first wife?

Lovett Oh, I didn't know he'd been married before.

Rita You mean they don't talk about his first wife?

Dolly No, they've never talked about her, not once!

Lovett Not natural is it? I should have wanted all the details, what she liked for breakfast, did she have her own teeth, everything.

Rita Politicians are not normal though are they? I spoke to one at a Christmas Bazaar. He said, 'Do you live round here?' I said, 'Yes.' He said, 'How lovely. How lovely!' I said, 'It's not lovely, it's where they put all the bad tenants.' But his eyes glazed over and he walked off.

Conelly I saw William Whitelaw once when he came to our Community Centre. He's got bad teeth.

Rita What did he say?

Conelly He didn't say anything, he made a speech.

Lovett I saw Len Fairclough when he opened Wilkinson's Hardware. He's shorter than you think. Looks as if he needs to eat more greens.

Lynda *enters clutching her belly.*

Lynda (*startled*) Oh! Am I in the right place?

Rita Yes, and at the right time by the look of you. When's it due?

Lynda On the twenty-ninth. I'm overdue.

Lovett It won't be long, it's dropped.

Lynda Has it?

Lovett You've got a boy in there. It's all at the front. I've never been wrong yet. You could bet a million pounds on it. I hope you want a boy because that's what you've got – a boy.

Lynda I don't mind what it is . . .

All As long as it's all right.

Lynda I think they're going to induce me.

Rita Oh they will. Babies aren't allowed to be born late nowadays.

Lovett Or at weekends.

Dolly Or late at night.

Conelly Except on Christmas Eve.

Rita Or New Year's Day, so they can get in the paper. What's your name, love?

Lynda Lynda with a Y.

Dolly I was induced with one of mine. (*She adds in a comforting manner.*) But don't worry, it's all right.

Rita Don't tell bloody lies, Dolly! You told me it was a nightmare, you screamed your bloody head off.

Dolly Reet!

Rita I won't take part in this conspiracy, Dolly. True, some women have 'em like shelling peas, but for some it's painful, even agonising. Scream your head off, love, that way they fill you so full of Pethidene you won't care if they drive a steamroller over you.

Lynda Oh, it won't be like that for me, I've been to relaxation classes, there's no need for it to be painful, after all it's a natural process.

Rita So is toothache a natural process.

Lynda But there's no need to have a toothache if you take care of your teeth and go the dentist regularly.

Rita And you do?

Lynda Of course.

Rita I bet you bake your own bread, don't you? Brown bread with all them nasty bits in it. Am I right?

Lynda Yes, how did you know?

Rita I saw the *Guardian* in your bag. My social worker's wife reads the *Guardian*. She looks a bit like you. She bakes her own bread. I know because when he gets round my house all them nasty bits are stuck between his teeth.

Lynda The whole grain.

Rita He goes on at me to try it but quite honestly I think you must be a bit mental to go to all that trouble when you can nip out and buy a sliced loaf.

Conelly I think she's right, dear. I remember *having* to bake the bread. I'd be there all day mixing, kneading, keeping it out of the draughts. Then watching the oven, and nine times out of ten it turned out wrong.

Everyone laughs.

Lovett Like the dolly tub and the washing. Some used to swear that it got your sheets whiter than the machines. So what? I say, bung it in the machine and have the time to yourself, I say.

Rita I bet you're on a lot of committees, aren't you? Preserving things?

Lynda Not many. Mostly jam now. (*She gives a little laugh.*)

Rita You look healthy. I bet you take your iron tablets every day.

Lynda Yes.

Rita Grow your own vegetables?

Lynda Yes.

Rita You make your own clothes too by the look of them, don't you?

Lynda Yes.

Rita And shop at Sainsbury's?

Dolly *You* shop at Sainsbury's, Reet!

Rita But I don't buy yoghurt, Dolly!

Lynda Nor do I. I make my own.

Rita See! See! I knew it! She would wouldn't she? I bet your library books are never overdue. What are you calling the baby?

Lynda If it's a girl, Florrie.

The **Women** *giggle.*

Lynda If it's a boy, Hereward.

The **Women** *laugh.*

Rita Hereward! Poor little sod!

Lynda They are both very old English names.

Lovett I had a dog called Florrie, she got distemper from the ferrets. We had to have her put down.

Rita When he gets to school, they'll kill Hereward, have you thought about that?

Lynda Our child will be taught to tolerate the ignorance of others.

Rita Teach him boxing at the same time then, do him more good.

Lynda *gasps and clutches her belly.*

Rita Are you all right, love?

Dolly She looks awful!

Lynda I feel as if I've wet myself.

Rita Is it a lot?

Lynda It's still coming! I can't stop it!

Lynda *grows very very slowly hysterical. She makes no loud sounds but her breathing attempts a pattern, then fails.*

Rita You don't need your fancy breathing yet, it's only a show. You're not in proper labour yet.

Dolly It's her waters broken, Reet.

Lynda (*moans*) Help me! Help me!

She falls to the floor and rolls around.

Dolly Undo her bra!

Rita Shut up, Dolly!

Lovett We'd better fetch a nurse.

Rita She'll have to calm down first, they'll think she's a loony. Lynda, calm down and shut up, or I'll smack you round the chops.

Lynda *carries on.*

Lynda, I'll give you three, then I'll smack you. One – two – three.

Rita *smacks* **Lynda**'s *face; there is instant silence.*

Dolly, go and fetch a wheelchair, I'll take her up to maternity. All right now, love? Good girl.

Dolly *leaves.*

Lynda I'm so sorry. It took me by surprise. I'm so frightened though. Is it true it's so painful?

Rita Yes it's true. But you'll have a baby at the end of it. *I* think it's worth it.

Conelly I've had two boys and I hardly felt a thing, you might be like me.

Lynda Oh yes, I might! Thank you.

Dolly *returns pushing a wheelchair.*

Dolly I got it from the X-ray department next door.

Rita Right, let's have you in it, Lynda.

The **Women** *help* **Lynda** *into the wheelchair.*

Conelly You'll be all right, my love. I shall be thinking of you.

Lynda Thank you.

Rita Comfy?

Lynda *nods*.

Rita Right, we're off.

Group Good luck! Best of luck!

Rita *wheels* **Lynda** *out*.

Lovett Well what a to-do! And all over the waters breaking! She looked such a nice girl as well. Nicely spoken too.

Conelly Won't be long before Florrie or Hereward's here then, will it?

All the **Women** *laugh*.

Dolly Anyone want a drink? I don't usually in the day but it's my birthday tomorrow.

Lovett I'll have one, what is it, gin?

Dolly *hands over half a bottle of gin*.

Conelly Not for me thanks, gin goes straight to my head. Last time I had gin I made a fool of myself. I did a dance in my corsets, using me teeth as castanets. It was five years ago at Christmas, at our Edna's party. I'd only had a couple of glasses. So I shan't, thank you anyway.

Lovett Go on, have one. A swig won't hurt you.

Dolly Go on, keep us company.

Conelly Oh all right, just a small one though, have we got a glass?

Lovett Just swig it out of the bottle, nobody's looking. Go on.

Conelly *swigs heavily*.

Lovett Hey! Steady on! You've still to see the doctor remember. You can't go in there *stinking* of gin.

Conelly It wouldn't matter if I didn't go in, I only come to hear his voice, he's got such a lovely voice, so gentle and kind. Is he Scots?

Lovett No, he's Irish, from Dublin. I asked him once. His first

name is Declan. I steamed a letter open he'd written to my
doctor, it was signed 'yours Declan'.

Rita *enters.*

Rita I see Dolly's at the gin again.

Dolly (*hurriedly*) How is she, Reet?

Rita I took her straight up to the Labour ward in the lift. They
weren't very pleased. It's probably thrown their whole schedule
out, having a baby born in its own time. What you been talking
about then?

Conelly I was just saying I only come to hear Dr Riley's voice. I
don't need to come, I know what's wrong with me.

Lovett What's wrong then, duck?

Conelly It's not very nice to talk about it, people don't like it.
You won't.

Lovett You can tell us anything, we won't mind.

Conelly All right.

Pause.

Rita Go on, love.

Conelly I've got carcinoma of the womb.

Dolly Oh, it sounds awful. What is it?

Rita It's cancer by a posh name. But it's cancer. (*Slight pause.*)
Can they do anything? Are you having treatment?

Conelly I've had an operation and I've had treatment, but
when my hair started falling out I stopped it. I'm not dying
bald. I've always had nice hair. I take tablets for the pain and
when it gets too bad to bear I shall take the lot and finish myself
off. I come to see Dr Riley to find out how long I've got.

Rita Does he tell you?

Conelly As near as he can.

Rita How long have you got then?

Conelly I should have been dead last week, according to him.

She indicates **Riley**'s *door. There is a slight pause, then they all laugh.*

Conelly Let's have another drink, Rita do you want one? You've not had one yet.

Rita Yes, I'll have one. (*She takes a swig.*) Here's to you, love. I hope you enjoy what time you've got left. What's your name?

Conelly Mrs Conelly.

Rita Not your *husband*'s name, your name.

Conelly It's Evelyn.

Group Nice, pretty name.

Rita I'd like to propose a toast to Evelyn. Let's hope the rest of your life is happy.

Rita *drinks and passes the bottle round.*

Conelly Thank you everyone. I wish I could say I've had a happy life. (*She shows no self-pity – there is more surprise.*) But I can't think of anything really . . . apart from the war, but then everyone was happy in the war. It was nice when the boys were small and I'll miss not seeing my grandchildren grow up but that's all. Makes you wonder why you're put on this earth.

Dolly *I've* often wondered that, have you, Reet?

Rita We're here to provide the next generation, that's all.

Lovett There must be more to it than that!

Conelly Well, if it's what Rita says about the next generation, I've done that. We lived in a rough area but my boys grew up nice – never any trouble with the police. They've both got good jobs as well, one's got his own office.

Rita There you are then, you've done your bit. More than I have. My kids are in care, but I'm getting them out as soon as I'm properly discharged from the Towers. I see 'em three times a week, don't I, Dolly? Every time I see them they ask, 'Can we come home today, Mum?'

Pause.

Conelly Oh it's so hot in here, you know, I think I'll take these corsets off. (*She giggles.*) That gin's gone straight to my head. I've had nothing to eat today. (*She stands.*) These corsets have been a torment to me all my life. I'll take them off, I'll go into one of the cubicles. If Dr Riley wants me, tell him I shan't bother. Besides I've had too much to drink, I shouldn't keep a straight face.

Everyone laughs.

Conelly *goes into a cubicle.*

Rita Do you want some help?

Conelly Can you undo the laces at the back? It'll save me the struggling?

Rita Come out here then, there's not much room in there.

Conelly What if somebody comes?

Rita They can't lock you up for taking your corsets off. (*Undressing* **Conelly**.) This is a nice dress.

Conelly I got it from a rummage sale at Hampstead. It's worth the extra bus fare – everything is so clean.

Rita We get our stuff from War on Want, don't we Dolly?

Dolly Not everything, not underwear.

Rita *has to help* **Conelly** *off with her cardigan, dress, long petticoat, until she is standing in her hat, corsets and shoes.*

Lovett Christ! It's terrible. How do you get it on and off?

Conelly I'm used to it, it doesn't take long.

Rita (*laughing*) What *do* you look like?

Conelly I don't care, I once did a dance in me corsets at a party, I'd had a few drinks, I was telling Dolly and Mrs Lovett just now.

Lovett I wish I'd seen that.

Rita Show us your dance, do it now.

Dolly No Reet, not here, not in a hospital.

Lovett Why not? Go on, do it, Evelyn. We'll clap, won't we?

Rita Go on, Evelyn, it's all yours.

Conelly I have to take my teeth out first.

The **Women** *are laughing and excited.*

Conelly (*turns back, takes out her teeth*) Right give me some room!

She sings 'Viva Espana', dances around the room, climbs with help on to a bench, dances and clacks her false teeth.

Come on, join in.

The **Women** *join in, dancing flamenco-style.*

James Lemon *and a woman,* **Mrs Cornwallis**, *who is the* **Assistant Hospital Administrator** *enter, and stand and stare at the scene in front of them.*

James (*pointing to* **Rita**) That's her!

The **Women** *stop dancing.* **Conelly** *remains standing on the bench.*

Mrs Cornwallis You are Mrs Rita O-nions?

Rita Rita Onions, yes.

Mrs Cornwallis I am the Assistant Hospital Administrator. I have received two complaints about your conduct in this waiting room. You are alleged to have smoked, used bad language, changed the furniture around, abused patients and interfered in medical matters and now I see you're drinking gin! Do you know it smells like a public bar in here?

Rita No, I use the lounge myself.

James Has my wife seen the doctor yet?

Rita, Lovett and **Dolly** *laugh.*

Rita No, she didn't need to. It's you that needs to, he'll tell you the correct position for sexual intercourse.

James Stop it! Tell her to stop it! (*He puts his hands over his ears.*)

Mrs Cornwallis Mr Lemon, you're overwrought. Go to my office. You take the lift to the basement, then once out of the lift it's the second corridor on the left, carry straight down until you see a door marked mortuary. My office is opposite. Go in and make yourself a cup of tea. The teabags are in the second drawer down in my desk. The key to the drawer is on the back of the door marked with a two. Please lock the drawer and replace the key when you have finished your tea. Here's the key to the office.

James *leaves.*

Mrs Cornwallis Mrs O-nions, please leave now!

Rita I'll go when I've seen Dr Riley.

Mrs Cornwallis It's *Mr* Riley, he is a consultant.

Rita Marvellous isn't it, they sweat for seven years to get the Dr in front of their names, then sweat again for God knows how long to get it taken off.

Mrs Cornwallis I'm a very busy person Mrs Onions. If you will leave now, I will make you another appointment for next week.

Dolly *stands.*

Rita When I've seen the doctor. Sit down, Dolly, we're not going anywhere!

Dolly *sits.*

Mrs Cornwallis Why is this lady in her underwear?

Rita She was changing to see the doctor.

Mrs Cornwallis Why has she got her teeth in her hand?

Rita Ask her, she's not deaf and dumb.

Conelly *tries to reply, but breaks into laughter.* **Lovett, Rita** *and* **Dolly** *join in.*

She thought she might have to have an emergency operation. (*She laughs.*) She should have been dead last week.

There is a great gust of laughter, from **Rita, Dolly, Lovett** *and* **Conelly** *who all clutch each other.*

Mrs Cornwallis How sick! All four of you are drunk. You can come back next week at the same time, I'll make sure we have extra staff to cope. Leave now before I call the police.

Rita *lights a fag.*

Mrs Cornwallis The notice! (*She points to the No Smoking sign.*)

Rita The ashray! (*She points to the ashtray*)

There is a pause – **Rita** *and the* **Assistant Hospital Administrator** *eye each other up for five seconds.*

Mrs Cornwallis (*to Mrs Conelly*) For goodness' sake, woman, get dressed! Go into a cubicle and get out of my sight, an old woman like you! You should be ashamed! What if your family found out? Perhaps they ought to know what you get up to.

Mrs Conelly *goes into a cubicle.*

Rita You carry on talking like that and I'll break your ugly, fat neck.

Mrs Cornwallis You're obviously an unstable personality. I won't allow you to roam this hospital at will. You have threatened *me* with violence, *me*! I trained in the Towers, I recognise an unstable personality when I see one.

Dolly No! She's better now, they got her better, she –

Rita Dolly, shut it!

Mrs Cornwallis You've been in the Towers?

Rita Yes.

Mrs Cornwallis Were you a voluntary patient?

Rita I'm not answering any more questions. I'll sit here and wait to see the doctor.

Mrs Cornwallis I'm going to ring the Towers. I'll find out about you, Mrs Onions, and they'll find out just how you've been conducting yourself since your release. They may want you back for an assessment. Who's your consultant at the Towers?

Rita *doesn't reply.*

Mrs Cornwallis I'll find out quickly enough, you may as well tell me.

Rita I can't pronounce it, it's full of k's and z's, he's Polish. He's barmy as well, he washes his hands the whole time he's talking to the patients. He's frightened their madness will contaminate him. He thinks it's catching.

Mrs Cornwallis It's probably Dr Zedeweski you're referring to. Like all brilliant men he has his own harmless eccentricities.

Rita He's just plain barmy, everyone knows it, they've been trying to get rid of him for years. And there he still is, in charge of all those unhappy people. Just wait until I'm properly discharged, I'll get rid of the mad old bugger.

Mrs Cornwallis So you're not properly discharged?

Rita Community care they call it. I'm supposed to slot back into society without a ripple. I'm in the charge of a social worker. He's a nice bloke, means well, but his marriage is breaking up, so he's a bit preoccupied. He's having an affair with a lady policeman. He's told me all about it. *He* wanted *my* advice, should he leave his wife and kids? So who's looking after who?

Mrs Cornwallis (*patronising*) Come with me to my office, Mrs O-nions. It's quite cosy with its rubber plants and electric coal fire. I'll make you a nice cup of tea.

Rita No thank you, by the time time you've unlocked the teabags I shouldn't be thirsty.

Mrs Cornwallis You're obviously overwrought, your libido isn't quite ticking over at the right speed is it? I completely understand. The stresses and strains of the urban environment take their toll on us all. Escalating VAT . . .

Lovett Milk's going up. It's the Common Market.

All turn to **Mrs Lovett**, *all turn back.*

Mrs Cornwallis After the last porters' strike I was a mere shell of my former self. How much easier life was when we were all in the caves. (*She puts an arm around* **Rita**'s *shoulder.*)

Rita Please take your arm off my shoulders.

Mrs Cornwallis A little support, that's all, dearie.

Rita My bra gives me all the support I want. Take your bleedin' arm off my shoulders!

The **Assistant Hospital Administrator** *grabs* **Rita**'s *wrist. They struggle.*

Conelly Leave her alone, it's a few years since I smacked anyone round the ear 'ole, but I haven't forgotten how it's done.

Lovett I'll join in an' all, let go of her!

Mrs Cornwallis This woman is potentially dangerous, it's more than my job's worth to let her loose again in this hospital.

Dolly (*to* **Mrs Cornwallis**) I shouldn't make her mad, she's been to night school for Kung Fu, she's ever so good.

Rita *struggles free and goes into Kung Fu attitude.*

Rita I can see the headlines in the *Standard* now, four inches high – 'Old Age Pensioner Degraded, Shock Birth in Waiting Room'. By the time the *Sun* gets hold of it it'll be 'Old Age Pensioner Gives Birth in a Bottle'.

Dolly But that wouldn't be true, Reet!

Rita That doesn't matter in newspapers, honestly sometimes you're as thick as two short planks!

Mrs Cornwallis Violence is the last resort of the ignorant, Mrs O-nions. I will not be intimidated by *it* or *you*.

Mrs Cornwallis *cowers as* **Rita** *forces her around the room.*

A good common sense talk like good common sense people, that's what we need Mrs O-nions.

Rita I'm not a common sense person thank Christ! I'd sooner be a raving lunatic than have common sense.

Audrey Lemon *enters, she is wearing some symbol of independence.*

Audrey Oh hello! What are you doing now? Is it charades?

Lovett It's judo I think. *One* of them.

Conelly It's Kung Fu. They're fighting. She (*She points to* **Mrs Cornwallis**.) Wants Rita to go for a cup of tea. And Rita doesn't want one.

Audrey (*doubtfully*) Oh I see, can I interrupt a weeny mo? Does anyone know where my husband is? He's got all the keys, I can't get into the house, silly aren't I?

Lovett Rita made him cry. He's in her office drinking tea. We'll all be in there soon at this rate.

Conelly Shall I fetch him? I enjoy walking without me corsets.

Audrey Would you mind? I'd rather see him with Rita here, he's got a violent tongue.

Rita Nobody was ever *licked* to death, Audrey, shout back. You've done it once.

Mrs Cornwallis Would you fetch some porters, Mrs Conelly, and ask somebody to telephone the police. Reason has failed, it's time for the civil authorities. Will you do that for me, dear?

Conelly No, I don't feel like it!

Conelly *goes out.*

Mrs Cornwallis This is too much, when even old age pensioners won't do as they're told! It's anarchy, anarchy, and who will attend to the drains? Ask yourselves that, I can feel a small breakdown coming on, do you mind if I sit down?

She sits.

Dolly Do you want a drink? You look awful.

Rita Go on, humanise yourself.

The **Assistant Hospital Administrator** *drinks from the gin bottle.*

Mrs Cornwallis This is the climax of a disastrous day. I was five crates short of prunes in the kitchen supplies this morning. Then I discovered that the date stamps on the disposable enema packs ran out yesterday, and being the *Assistant* Administrator I get all the blame. *He's* always in a meeting. (*Bitterly.*) Now the patients are talking back, it's never happened before.

Audrey Are you going to cry? I've got some tissues if you are.

Mrs Cornwallis If you've got them handy I may as well.

Mrs Cornwallis *cries quietly.*

Rita You can't help feeling sorry for her, can you? It's like seeing a hot-air balloon being let down.

Dolly Aah! Be fair, Rita, she has got a hard job.

Rita Yes, where would the hospital be without its prunes and enemas?

Lovett Bunged up for a start.

Everyone laughs except **Mrs Cornwallis**.

Conelly (*self-importantly enters*) He says he won't come in if Rita's here. He says she's mad.

Rita Where is he?

Conelly Outside the door, he's listening.

Rita (*shouting to* **James**) Get in here! There's somebody needs spiritual guidance!

James Is it Audrey?

Rita *pulls* **James** *in, shuts the door and leans on it.*

Rita No it's me. I want you to tell me something.

There is a pause. She walks about.

Where do I go to catch the ark?

James You don't catch it, it isn't a bus.

Lovett It's a boat!

Rita I know that. Will it sail up the canal? And how will all your people get in it?

James The Lord Jehovah will make provision for all his saved souls. Audrey won't be amongst them of course.

Audrey I don't *like* boats, I get seasick.

Rita How big will this ark be?

James Big.

Lovett How will it get down the canals and through all them locks?

James It will sail over the inland waterways. It will sail over your sinful bodies and we, the saved, will lean over the side and watch the sinners and unbelievers gasping their last breaths in the foaming waters.

Conelly He's got a lovely turn of phrase hasn't he?

Lovett Will it go to London?

James It will save all who repent and put their souls in the hands of Jehovah, God.

Lovett Yes, but will it go to London?

James Yes, I expect so, once it's toured the provinces.

Lovett Only I've got a cousin in London that's a Jehovah's Witness, she'll be disappointed if you forgot her. She's a miserable sod like you.

Conelly (*to* **James**) Audrey wants the keys.

Audrey Yes James, could I have the keys?

James No, I'm the householder, they are *my* keys.

Audrey My clothes are in the house, give me the keys.

James I bought your clothes with my money, they're *my* clothes.

Audrey You'd look silly in my clothes, James. They'd be too small. Now give me the keys.

James No!

Audrey Give me the sodding keys!

James Don't swear, Audrey, think of your mother!

Audrey *makes a deep throaty noise of anger and lunges at* **James***'s trouser pocket. She pulls him to the floor, they wrestle over the keys.*

Mrs Cornwallis Oh my God! Now there's a fight! I can't cope on my own. I need a man. Where's Mr Riley?

Lovett I haven't seen him all afternoon.

Rita I haven't seen anyone with medical qualifications since I stepped foot in the place.

Mrs Cornwallis The hospital is on accident alert, there's a disturbance at the Job Centre.

Rita Knock on his door, Evelyn, see if he's still in there.

Conelly Oh I daren't.

Rita He's only a man.

Conelly No he's not, he's a doctor.

Lovett I'll go.

She knocks on **Riley***'s door. There is no answer. She knocks again and puts her head round the door.*

He's asleep! Shush!

Mrs Cornwallis He can't be asleep, doctors don't sleep!

Lovett He must be dead then.

Dolly Dead. Oh my God, the doctor's dead!

Mrs Cornwallis Mr Riley's manners are impeccable. He wouldn't die in a National Health hospital.

Lovett He's not moving.

Mrs Cornwallis They'll blame me! It's all the clerk's fault. She should have stayed at her post, instead of coming whining to me. Her job is to protect the doctor from his patients, now they've killed him! I'll get the blame, I always do.

Mrs Cornwallis *cries loudly. The telephone rings on the* **Clerk**'s *desk. Everyone stops for three seconds, then carries on. The Assistant Hospital Administrator answers it.*

(*Giving phone to* **Rita**) It's for you. You'll be thinking you own the hospital next.

Rita I do! Me and sixty million others. (*She speaks into the phone.*) Hello!

Pause.

Hang on a minute. (*She speaks to the* **Group** *who are making a terrible row.*) Shut the bleedin' row, I'm on the phone.

The **Group** *is silent.*

(*She speaks to the* **Group**) Lynda's had her baby. It's a girl!

The **Group** *cheer.*

Lovett, Conelly, Audrey, Dolly Oh! How lovely! How much does it weigh? (*Etc.*)

Rita (*into phone*) My middle name? Mary . . . Oh that's nice, tell her I'll be up to see her when she's had a sleep. (*She puts the phone down and speaks to the* **Group**.) She's calling her baby Mary, that's my middle name.

Lovett Isn't that nice. It's quite an honour as how they're posh and that.

Conelly Quick with it, wasn't she? It must have been all that yoghurt.

Audrey *and* **James**'s *fighting has turned to passionate embraces.*

Audrey James!

James Audrey!

They make their way into a cubicle.

Dolly She'll be a Libra.

Lovett Who will?

Dolly The baby – Mary. That's a nice sign that is. I wonder what her stars say. I'm a Libra. We're home-lovers and we . . .

Rita I'm Aries.

Dolly They're bossy and can't settle to nothing.

Rita It's a load of rubbish.

Dolly It's not, Rita, it's been proved.

Lovett I think it's rubbish. The day my husband was laid-off his stars said 'Job prospects look good'.

Conelly I like reading my stars. Once it said 'Your finances will improve' and I found ten pence in the street.

Dolly There you are you see.

Conelly But I lost a pound the day after.

Dolly I bet you're a Leo aren't you, Evelyn?

Rita Shut up, Dolly, you're always wrong.

Dolly I think I'm right this time.

Conelly No I'm Capricorn.

Dolly Oh well . . . Let's see what your stars say for the week. Here it is: 'You are embarking on a most exciting period. The future has never looked better.'

Conelly It looks like I'm going to have more fun dead than alive.

Mrs Cornwallis How can you joke about such a painful subject? There are people in the process of dying upstairs. I find your merriment strangely inappropriate.

Conelly Well, I'm in the process of dying down here. (*She laughs.*) If you can prove to me that lauging is harmful, then I'll stop. But until then I'll laugh as much as I like!

Rita Let's have a toast to Mary . . . I hope she has a bleedin' good laugh all her life.

Dolly I wish that she's good-looking and that she ends up with a nice bloke.

Lovett To Mary, I hope that she's clever, got brains y'know.

Conelly I wish her good health and a long life.

Rita (*to* **Mrs Cornwallis**) It's your turn.

Mrs Cornwallis I wish the child well certainly.

To the refrain of Stevie Wonder's 'Happy Birthday To You' **Riley** *enters.* **Riley** *comes in yawning. He looks at his watch then stands and stares at the scene in front of him.* **Mrs Cornwallis** *is holding the gin bottle.* **Dolly** *is reading* Woman *with her feet on the* **Clerk**'s *desk. Everyone else is watching* **Audrey** *and* **James**'s *feet in the curtained cubicle.* **Mrs Lovett** *is laughing,* **Audrey** *and* **James** *are oblivious to everything.* **Rita** *is handing out the patients' confidential files.*

Rita Here, read your own file.

Dolly (*seeing* **Riley**) Hello, we thought you were dead!

Riley I wish I was.

Rita Do you feel better for that sleep?

Riley *crosses to the cubicle and looks over the top, indicating* **James** *and* **Audrey**.

Riley Is that Mrs Lemon in there?

Lovett Yes, with Mr Lemon.

Rita Well, they started fighting over a bunch of keys. Here, Mrs Conelly.

Rita *passes* **Conelly** *her file.*

Conelly Thanks, Rita.

Mrs Cornwallis Oh! Mr Riley, you're alive!

Riley Only just, Mrs Cornwallis, only just. Is it wise to be seen carrying a bottle of gin around the hospital Mrs Cornwallis?

Rita Why don't you go and water your rubber plants? I'll get you out of trouble, I don't bear grudges. Here you are Mrs Lovett.

She gives **Lovett** *her file.*

Lovett Thanks, I've been dying to get me hands on this.

She reads the file avidly.

Mrs Cornwallis Doctor, the patients are rebelling, they won't keep still or quiet.

Riley They do seem unusually animated. I'm used to seeing them in rows like dead sheep. Go and tidy up, Mrs Cornwallis. Your eyelashes are falling off.

Conelly Hello, Mr Riley, are you all right now?

Riley Hello, my dear, still here then?

Conelly Yes, I've had a lovely afternoon.

Riley Are you coming to see me?

Lovett Ooh 'ya bugger, I think he fancies you, Evelyn.

Conelly I think he's got a bet on how long I've got left. The Irish *are* betting men.

Rita Can we start the clinic now, doctor?

Riley There should be a list. Where's the clerk?

Dolly Oh *she* ran off ages ago.

Rita *sorts out her file.*

Rita Well if nobody minds, I'll go first. Then we'll all go up and see Lynda's baby later on.

Dolly It's not visiting time, Rita, and they only let close family see the baby. They're ever so strict in maternity.

Rita According to her file, Dr Riley's Lynda's consultant. So we'll all go up with him, won't we Dr Riley?

Riley Will you?

Rita You've got alcohol on your breath, Dr Riley.

Riley Just a taint dear, just a taint.

Rita *guides* **Riley** *into his room.*

Rita You warm your hands on the radiator, Declan, I won't be long. (*She speaks to the* **Group***.*) Don't let her mess you about. (*She indicates* **Mrs Cornwallis***.*) Dolly, take a collection, we'll buy Lynda some flowers.

Pause.

Wish me luck.

Rita *lights a cigarette.*

Dolly I'm sure it's not serious, Reet. You'll be all right.

Group Good luck. See you soon.

Rita *goes into the consulting room.*

Dolly Well er . . . Does anybody want to start the collection?

Lovett I'd like to but I've only got my bus fare home. We're a bit short right now.

Dolly *You* don't work then?

Lovett I *was* a school dinner lady.

Dolly Oh . . . that's a shame.

Conelly I'll put twenty pence in it for you. I got my pension today.

Lovett No. I'd sooner walk home than take money from a pensioner.

Conelly No, let me! I can afford it. I don't need money any more do I? My insurance is all paid up. (*She laughs.*) It's nice to help somebody for a change.

Lovett All right then, but I'll give it back, give me your address before you go.

Dolly (*to* **Mrs Cornwallis**) Will you put some money in?

Mrs Cornwallis I hardly think it's apposite. If I sent flowers to every patient in this hospital I'd be a pauper.

Lovett You've drunk more than twenty p's worth of gin, so you can give Dolly twenty pence and then Dolly can put it in.

There is an ecstatic groan.

Dolly What are they doing in there? (*She indicates the cubicle.*)

Lovett Each other by the sound of it.

Dolly (*clearing her throat and approaching the cubicle*) Excuse me. Excuse me.

Lovett Throw a bucket of water over them!

James *and* **Audrey** *fall out of the cubicle.*

Dolly I'm collecting some money for some flowers for Lynda, would you like to . . .

Mrs Cornwallis Mr Lemon, I have no wish to see your underwear. Please adjust the opening of your trousers.

Lovett I bet this is the first time she's seen a bloke's underwear . . . with a bloke in it.

Mrs Cornwallis I heard that. I fail to see the humour in a man disporting himself in public. Quite frankly I'm disgusted with you, Mr Lemon. I think you must have some perverse sense of social decorum.

Lovett That's the second time you've been called a pervert.

Audrey James is a perfectly normal man. And if anyone says one more word about him being a pervert, I shall have to scratch their eyes out.

James Audrey darling!

They embrace.

Mrs Cornwallis That's enough, Mr Lemon. Pull yourself together and move these benches back. We require a man's strength.

James, *with a passionate look at his wife, does as he is told.*

What has happened this afternoon will never happen again. Is that clear? So we're going to start by sitting down and keeping quiet. And you can give me those files back. They are private and confidential.

Lovett I've read mine.

Mrs Cornwallis Quiet!

There is a long pause as everyone settles back to normal.

Dolly I've remembered that word.

Lovett What, Rita's word?

Dolly Yes. It's activist, she's an activist.

Lovett Never heard of it.

Blackout.

Bazaar & Rummage

Bazaar & Rummage was first presented in the Royal Court Theatre Upstairs on 10 May 1982, with the following cast:

Margaret, *a working-class vulgarian, agoraphobic for fifteen years*	Polly Hemingway
Bell-Bell, *an obsessionally clean agoraphobic, who plays the piano*	Liz Kean
Fliss, *a youngish trainee social worker*	Carol Leader
Gwenda, *a middle-aged volunteer social worker, an ex-agoraphobic*	Janette Legge
Katrina, *an agoraphobic, ex-variety 'songstress'*	Lou Wakefield
WPC, *a woman who is terrified of community policing*	Janette Legge

Directed by Carole Hayman
Music by Liz Kean
Decor by Amanda Fisk
Lighting by Val Claus
Sound by Patrick Bridgeman

Act One

A multi-purpose hall in Acton. A pair of double doors are flanked by two stained-glass windows. Missing panes of glass have been replaced by pieces of coloured cellophane. A garish crucifix hangs over the doors. Trestle tables and folding chairs are stacked against a wall. A piano and a small table complete the furnishings. An internal door leads to the lavatory and kitchen.

Gwenda *and* **Fliss** *enter,* **Gwenda** *is wearing a Crimplene two-piece with a nylon roll-neck sweater underneath.* **Fliss** *is wearing ragged dungarees (though her boots and shoulder bag are expensive-looking). They are both carrying a cardboard box under one arm and a black plastic bag under the other.* **Gwenda**'s *box slides and falls, books fall out and scatter on the floor.*

Gwenda (*with a small scream*) I said we were overloaded!

She stands in confusion.

Fliss No problem.

Gwenda Here take this. (*She hands the plastic bag to* **Fliss** *who is now overloaded.*)

Fliss (*calmly*) Gwenda, take the bag from me and put it on the floor.

Gwenda (*scrabbling on the floor picking up books*) Have you read *Dr Zhivago*? (*She holds a book up.*) I started it but Russian names are so confusing. I tried calling them Smith and Jones. But even so . . . (*She looks through the book.*)

Fliss Gwenda, is there anything breakable in this bag?

Gwenda Did you see the film? I loved the music. (*She sings the* Dr Zhivago *theme.*) What was his name? You know the one, he's rather good at cards.

Fliss (*drops bags and throws down box; there is a tiny breaking sound as if breakables were in the bag*) Omar Sharif, and he's a compulsive gambler.

Gwenda Oh the poor man! Is he having treatment?

Fliss I expect he's having a ball. It's only a problem when the money runs out.

Gwenda Do you know him?

Fliss No, but we did compulsive gambling at college last week. It's all tied up with orgasm.

Gwenda Lack of?

Fliss Well of course lack of, it's compensation.

Gwenda Surely not in his case, Fliss! He's such an attractive man!

Fliss To you he may be, to me he's a boring old Egyptian fart.

Gwenda You're so unkind, Fliss. So uncharitable.

Fliss I save my charity for those deserving it.

Gwenda I don't understand why you want to be a social worker. You don't seem to like anything or anybody, apart from dirty old tramps and delinquent Rastafarians. You'll end up catching a contractable disease from one or other of them. You mark my words.

Fliss *laughs*.

And here's me who absolutely adores people in crisis and I can't even get on the Social Work Training Course. It's so unfair!

Fliss You do it because you want to do it.

Gwenda I do it because these poor women need me. There's something in my personality that they respond to.

Fliss It's the fellowship that one hunted animal feels for another.

Gwenda What do you mean by that? I'm not used to people who speak in riddles. Some of us missed university unfortunately.

Fliss Unfortunately I didn't.

Gwenda So that's another thing you don't like. Your parents must be so disappointed in you.

Fliss My parents are incapable of feeling any emotion; they're dead people.

Gwenda Oh, I'm sorry, dear, I didn't know.

Fliss I mean they live in Reading. I couldn't breathe when I lived at home. I was stifled.

Gwenda I was asthmatic when I was a girl, I never once held a hockey stick or a netball. I just stood on the sidelines holding the armbands and blowing the whistle at half-time. (*She sighs with self-pity.*)

Fliss Oh sod it! What's the point? (*She goes out angrily.*)

Gwenda (*unaware that* **Fliss** *has gone, she continues stacking the books into paperback and hardback piles*) I read a lot when I was a girl. Asthmatics are usually well-read, have you noticed? I had Enid Blyton's complete works. Complete. My father brought one home every Friday night without fail. My mother had a quarter pound of Mint Imperials, father had two ounces of Shag and I had my new Enid Blyton. I'm sure that's why I'm quite without racial prejudice you know. Golly, Wog and Nigger were always my favourites, they were naughty to the other toys, but they always took their punishment well. (*She finds* Black Beauty.) *Black Beauty*! I could go on *Mastermind* with *Black Beauty* as my main subject. (*Quickly.*) What was Black Beauty's mother's name? (*Carefully.*) Duchess. (*Quickly.*) Who was the first man to break Black Beauty in? (*Carefully.*) Squire Gordon. (*Quickly.*) What lesson did Squire Gordon teach Black Beauty? (*Softly.*) You must never start at what you see, nor bite nor kick, nor have any will of your own. But always do your master's will, even though you may be very tired or hungry. That was more or less what father taught me. It's kept me in good stead, service first self second.

Fliss (*enters carrying more plastic bags and a standard lamp, the floral lampshade is on her head*) That's everything out of the car. (*She dumps the bag down.*)

Gwenda Fliss! You look lovely in that lampshade, it really suits you. Look in the mirror.

Fliss Don't be ridiculous, Gwenda. It's hideous.

Gwenda No, really. It's the first time I've seen you in anything feminine. You're usually such a scruff-bag. Of course, I know it's *de rigueur* to dress *à la* bohemian at college but . . .

Fliss Actually it isn't. (*She takes the lampshade off.*)

Gwenda The ladies like to see us dressed well, it makes them feel secure.

Fliss Has research been done on it?

Gwenda I don't know, I expect the Americans have looked into it.

Fliss I fail to see the correlation.

Gwenda Well then I shall have to be blunt. (*She takes a deep breath.*) Felicity . . .

Fliss Fliss.

Gwenda If I were an agoraphobic who'd been shut in the house for years, I would not be tempted into the big wide yonder by somebody who looked like you!

Fliss And I wouldn't be enticed out by somebody clad from head to foot in sodding man-made fibres!

Gwenda Let's keep it on a professional level, Felicity. They're quick to dry and non-iron, they suit my life-style. I'm a very busy woman. The polyesters have done untold service for women's emancipation. The denims might demonstrate but it's the bri-nylons in the background that enable them to.

Gwenda *starts to assemble the standard lamp. She is upset, her movements are jerky. It should be obvious that she is carrying on an internal dialogue.*

Fliss I locked the boot. (*She hands* **Gwenda** *the keys.*)

Gwenda I prefer the boot *unlocked*. (*They stare at each other.*) Disadvantaged working-class criminals have forced their way into my boot twice. I've lost two jacks and a tin of Gun-gum. (*She takes a light bulb out of her bag.*)

Fliss Well, I'll go and *unlock* the boot. (*Pause.*) Would you like me to open all four doors and turn the radio on?

Gwenda No thank you. The car's interior is protected by technology.

Gwenda *hands the keys back and* **Fliss** *goes out.*

Gwenda (*sings*) Would you like your lamp on, Daddy? Is the pain bad? Nurse will be here soon. Daddy don't be sad. Please don't look like that, Daddy, don't apologise. I'm putting on your lamp now, Daddy. Close your eyes. (*She screws the light bulb in,* *switches the lamp on and looks at it.*) Yes, I'll ask three pounds for you.

Fliss (*enters*) Katrina's outside.

Gwenda (*in a panic*) Oh! Where?

Fliss She's sitting in the car working up to an anxiety attack.

Gwenda Is Maurice there?

Fliss Of course, when is he not?

Gwenda I'd better go to her.

Fliss Oh give her a chance. The deal was that she'd walk unaided up the path and through that door. She knows you're here.

Gwenda Is it a serious attack?

Fliss It's hard to tell with Katrina isn't it? She's either giving an Oscar-winning performance as Our Lady of Lourdes or punishing Maurice for forgetting her *Woman's Own*. If I had my way, she'd be permanently wired up to a lie detector.

Gwenda Oh yes? An expert on agoraphobia are you now, Felicity?

Fliss Fliss.

Gwenda Know all about it, do you?

Fliss (*through gritted teeth*) No.

Gwenda No. But I do! Professional cowards, and it takes one to know one, I'm an ex-aggie myself.

Fliss If I were a leper, I wouldn't want an ex-leper to treat me. I'd want a consultant in tropical medicine.

Gwenda Who said anything about leprosy? I run a self-help group for agoraphobics.

Fliss You can't call them a group. They've never met!

Gwenda They're in telephone contact!

Fliss I hope that oily creep Maurice isn't staying.

Gwenda He's been a tower of strength to Katrina. I don't know what she'd have done without him.

Fliss (*quietly*) I do.

Katrina *enters. She leans on the door jamb. She is a pretty woman in her early thirties.*

Katrina Maurice says to tell you I'm having an anxiety attack.

Gwenda (*in a panic*) Katrina! Where's Maurice? Have you taken a pill? Sit down. (**Katrina** *sits.*) Now start breathing! In . . . out . . . in . . . out . . . in . . . out . . . Relax, relax!

Fliss For Christ's sake, Gwenda, calm down!

Gwenda Don't interfere, Felicity, carry on breathing, Katrina. In out, in out, in out, relax, float. Shall I sing your song?

Katrina No, don't bother. (**Katrina** *escapes from* **Gwenda**.)

Fliss Gwenda, she's all right.

Katrina (*to* **Fliss**) Let her sing, it calms her down. (*She smiles.*)

Gwenda (*sings*) If you're happy and you know it, clap your hands.

Katrina (*walks slowly around the room touching surfaces, accustoming herself to the strange environment*) She can't sing as well as I can. Did you know I was a singer?

Fliss Yes, you told me.

Katrina When?

Fliss I've been to your house a couple of times. I'm training to be a social worker.

Katrina Did you see my photographs?

Fliss Yes, you showed them to me.

Katrina Did you see the one of me and Hughie Green?

Fliss Yes.

Katrina I was a songstress.

Fliss Sorry, I . . . ?

Katrina That's what they called me in the *Stage*. Have you heard of the *Stage*? It's a newspaper.

Fliss Heard of it, yes.

Katrina I was nearly on *Crackerjack*.

Fliss I'm very pleased you came today. Are you pleased?

Katrina No. I'd rather be at home.

Fliss Why?

Katrina East west, home's best.

They both turn to **Gwenda** *who is finishing her song.*

Gwenda There! It always does the trick. You look much better now, Kat. Oh I do think you're a big brave girl coming here on your own. (*She hugs* **Katrina**.)

Katrina I didn't come on my own. Maurice brought me in the car.

Fliss But you walked up the path on your own, didn't you?

Katrina No, Maurice brought me to the door. (*To* **Fliss**.) I can't go out on my own. I'm an agoraphobic.

Gwenda Has Maurice gone now?

Katrina No, he's waiting for me in case I have to go home. He's sulking because he's not allowed to come in.

Gwenda Oh dear! I'd better have a word with him. Felicity will look after you. I'll only be in the car park if you need . . .

Gwenda *rushes out. There is a short pause.*

Katrina I can't stand her, can you?

Fliss She's all right. She means well.

Katrina She's in love with Maurice.

Fliss Is Maurice in love with her?

Katrina No. He doesn't like neurotic women. And anyway he loves me.

Fliss *drags out a trestle table.*

Fliss And how do you feel about him?

Katrina Oh I can't *stand* him! (*She giggles nervously.*)

Fliss Would you help me with this table.

Katrina Is it heavy?

Fliss Quite heavy.

Katrina I'd better not, I'm not allowed to lift anything heavy.

Fliss *sets up the table.*

Fliss Are you pregnant?

Katrina (*loudly*) No! (*Normally.*) I don't like sex, do you?

Fliss I like it very much.

Katrina I'm repressed. Gwenda and Maurice told me.

Fliss What don't you like about it?

Katrina Ugh! Well everything! His horrible *thing*, the noises he makes. I don't like him twiddling my knobs. You know (*She holds her breasts.*) but worst of all is the wetness, ugh. And he's such a weight! I felt half squashed to death by the time he'd finished. I don't see why people rave about it. I'd sooner do a jigsaw.

Fliss How does Maurice feel about it?

Katrina I don't know, I never ask him. We don't do it any more so it never comes up. (*Pause.*) He seems cheerful. (*Pause.*) He spends a lot of time in the bathroom.

Gwenda *enters nearly hidden under a pile of showbiz-style dresses. She carries an Elvis Presley mirror under one arm and a Hula-Hoop is hung round her neck.*

Gwenda It's twenty-five past eleven already! I promised to pick the others up by half-past. (*She dumps the dresses.*) Where are my car keys? (*She stands still, trying to compose herself.*) Oh I'm so tired! I've been on the go since six; my Teas-made ejaculated prematurely.

Fliss (*handing over the keys*) Drive carefully. Don't kill them all on their first day out.

Gwenda Can you cope with Katrina? I won't be long. (*The Hula-Hoop is still round her neck.*)

Fliss Hadn't you better leave the Hula-Hoop?

Gwenda (*at the door, passes mirror to* **Fliss**; *to* **Katrina**) Oh! Maurice says if you need him, he'll be in Sainsbury's for the next hour, after that he'll be in the car wash, washing the car. He's written the numbers down. (*She pushes a scrap of paper into* **Katrina***'s hand.*) Bye! (*She rushes out.*)

Fliss How long is it since you were out of your house?

Katrina *starts to rip up the piece of paper.*

Katrina Without Maurice or Gwenda?

Fliss Yes. In your street for instance.

Katrina Well, Gwenda's been visiting for two and half years and I'd been in then for two so it's . . . Oh I don't know. (*She throws the pieces of paper over her shoulder.*)

Fliss Yes you do, what's two and half and two?

Katrina I don't like sums.

Fliss For Christ's sake, that's not a sum! What's two and a half and two?

Katrina Don't shout at me!

Fliss Add it up, go on. Two and a half and two.

Katrina You're shouting at me. I want to go home. Take me home.

Fliss I can't take you home. I haven't got a car.

Katrina I don't like it here, I want to go home.

Fliss (*loudly*) How many years is it since you came out of your house?

Katrina (*shouts*) Four and a half!

Fliss Thank you. (*Pause.*) Are these your things? (*She indicates the dresses and mirror.*)

Katrina Yes. They're for the rummage. Elvis used to be the one but then Maurice told me that he was a drug addict and wore nappies and that. So he had to go. It's Barry now. He's my inspiration to get better. I want to see him in the flesh.

Fliss Barry?

Katrina Yes. Ignorant people say he's ugly and laugh at his nose. But they're only jealous because he's rich and famous.

She pulls her jumper up to show her Barry Manilow T-shirt.

Fliss (*reading*) Oh! Barry Manilow the singer!

Katrina He's more than a singer! He's got a bigger fan club than he (*she indicates the crucifix.*) ever had. Still, if you're not a fan, you're not a fan.

Song about Barry Manilow.

Fliss *sets up the trestle tables. She speech-sings certain words.*

Fliss Why don't you hang your dresses up? They'll crumple if you don't. The sequins will get bent.

Katrina *hangs up the dresses.*

Katrina They were sewn on by hand you know.

Fliss (*ironic*) Really! How truly staggering.

Katrina Maurice made all my stagewear. He's very good with clothes. He chooses everything for me. Well, nearly everything. He wouldn't buy me my T-shirt so I sent away for it. The milkman posted the letter. Maurice doesn't know I've got it. I keep it in my sanitary-towel box next to Barry's picture. I wear it on Saturday mornings when Maurice is at Sainsbury's.

Gwenda *enters carrying a plastic bag and men's suits on hangers. She has one arm around* **Bell-Bell. Bell-Bell** *is a very neat, middle-class Scotswoman. She is carrying two boxes, one is full of knick-knacks, the other full of musical instruments.*

Gwenda Well, here we are. Safe and sound. This is Bell-Bell. (*To* **Bell-Bell**.) Do you remember Fliss? She's the social worker who came to your house.

Katrina She's not a proper one yet.

Fliss (*smiles*) Hello!

Gwenda And this is your telephone pal, Katrina. Say hello to Bell-Bell, Kat.

Katrina Hello.

Bell-Bell Hello.

Gwenda Why don't you sit down next to Kat, Bell-Bell? You two must have so much to say to each other.

Bell-Bell *sits down on the piano stool.* **Katrina** *gives her the once-over.*

Fliss Where's Margaret?

Gwenda (*lying*) She wouldn't answer the door. I knocked until my knuckles were literally raw.

Fliss But she promised she'd come! She was looking forward to it.

Gwenda I think we were a little optimistic with Margaret. She's a mass of neuroses.

Fliss But I phoned her this morning. She said she'd had her coat on since half-past seven.

Gwenda (*pleased*) There you are then, you see. That's not normal, is it?

Fliss I'll go round and fetch her.

Gwenda We've got to be ready for the public by two.

Fliss It won't take long! Can I borrow your car?

Gwenda No, I'm only third party.

Katrina You lent it to Maurice.

Gwenda Maurice is a knight of the road.

Fliss (*losing patience*) She's sitting at home waiting for us.

Gwenda But Margaret's so unpleasant! She'll only spoil things.

Katrina She's the one that swears, isn't she?

Gwenda Yes, constantly. And I won't tolerate it in public.

Fliss (*angrily*) I'm going to fetch her! Are you going to lend me the car or not?

There is no reply.

Do you expect her to walk here?

Gwenda (*throwing keys at* **Fliss**) Don't turn your back on that car once!

Fliss starts to leave.

Fliss Gwenda, I know you don't like Margaret but for Christ's sake make an effort will you? It's her first day out. She's been in longer than anyone else.

She goes out. The door slams.

Katrina She makes it sound as if she's been in prison. (*She laughs.*)

The **women** *stare at the door.*

I can't stand her, can you?

Gwenda (*grudgingly*) She's all right, she means well. She hasn't had our experience in life. It'll come in time.

Katrina (*to* **Bell-Bell**) Are you the one who's husband is dead?

Gwenda Don't remind Bell-Bell of her sad loss, Kat!

Katrina I won't, it's just that I thought she might be the one that's married to the Yugoslavian.

Gwenda No! That's Ruby! She's gone back in. Bell-Bell's husband originated from the Shetlands, didn't he Bell-Bell?

Bell-Bell The Hebrides.

Gwenda That's right; I knew it was something to do with sheep.

Katrina Which part of England's that in?

Bell-Bell The wet part.

There is a pause. **Bell-Bell** *plays a few notes in the piano.*

Katrina Are you having an anxiety attack?

Bell-Bell No, I'm playing the piano.

Katrina You've got a limited range, haven't you? (*She laughs.*)

Bell-Bell So have you.

Katrina *crosses to* **Gwenda.**

Katrina Gwenda, I think I've just been insulted.

Gwenda (*cuddling her*) Don't be paranoid, Kat. Bell-Bell's only adjusting her perspectives. She's normally a very placid woman, aren't you, Bell-Bell?

There is no response apart from a spectacular piano rag played by **Bell-Bell.**

(*Shocked*) How were you able to do that?

Bell-Bell Piano lessons. Two a week for nine years.

Gwenda I've got a little tune I can play. Move along, Bell-Bell.

Gwenda *sits at the piano and plays 'Chopsticks' badly. When she's finished, she looks at* **Bell-Bell** *and* **Katrina** *for approval, but both look steadily at her without speaking.*

What did you do with the children, Bell-Bell?

Bell-Bell They're at Derek's mother's, watching *Tiswas* in colour.

Katrina You're black and white are you?

Bell-Bell Yes, and proud of it.

Katrina Are you? I'd be ashamed to admit it.

Gwenda *crosses over and picks up* **Derek***'s suits.*

Gwenda Are all these Derek's ex-things?

Bell-Bell Yes.

Gwenda (*looking in boxes*) He seems to have been a man of taste judging by his consumer durables.

She picks over the wallet, shaving kit, travelling clock, gloves, binoculars etc.

Bell-Bell Yes, he always bought things to last.

Gwenda And in the end he was outrun by a quartz travelling alarm. (*She sighs.*) It's so sad.

Katrina (*looking at binoculars*) How much are you going to charge for these?

Bell-Bell I hadn't thought.

Katrina (*looking through binoculars*) Oh they're ever so good. I can see all the blackheads on your chin, Gwenda.

Gwenda You can't give Derek's belongings to a rummage sale, Bell-Bell, they're much too good.

Bell-Bell It's time I got rid of them. He's not coming back, is he?

Gwenda Not in this world no, but if I were you I'd hang on to them a bit longer. Until you're emotionally stronger.

Bell-Bell I feel stronger now. I don't want to take them home with me again.

Gwenda I'm sure I'm right, Bell-Bell, now put them back into the box.

Katrina You have to do as Gwenda says, she's in charge of us.

Bell-Bell I don't want his things in the house any more.

Gwenda Don't you think that's rather callous of you? He'd turn in his grave if he knew . . .

Bell-Bell He was cremated.

Gwenda Well his ashes would never settle. (*She opens the other box.*) Now you just can't give his musical instruments away!

Gwenda *takes out a mandolin;* **Bell-Bell** *takes it from her.*

Bell-Bell They're not his, they're mine.

Gwenda What a sly old thing you are. I didn't know you had any talents.

Bell-Bell I used to play before I got married.

Katrina You don't look musical.

Bell-Bell I don't play them much. It annoys the neighbours. The walls are so thin.

Katrina You're in a semi, are you?

Bell-Bell Yes.

Katrina We're in a detached with a separate garage and mature garden.

Gwenda And Bar-B-Q patio. Katrina's husband is a boutique owner.

Katrina He owns Katrina's Kabin in Shepherd's Bush. That's Kabin with a 'K'. Do you get it?

Gwenda Clever isn't it?

Katrina Maurice could get you a good price for your instruments; he's still got connections in the business.

Bell-Bell Maybe I should take them back home.

Gwenda No, Katrina's right. We'll let Maurice cast his semi-professional eye over them first.

Bell-Bell *strums the mandolin.*

Gwenda Do you mind, Bell-Bell? I've got an aversion to stringed instruments.

Bell-Bell *stops playing.*

I wonder if Maurice could get into Derek's suits.

Katrina (*looking at suits*) Maurice wouldn't be seen dead in anything like these! He likes things with charisma.

Gwenda Well you've certainly had a clear-out of Derek's belongings, Bell-Bell.

Bell-Bell I'll be needing extra room in the wardrobe soon. I've sent away for a fun fur.

Gwenda Oh! But what do you want a fun fur for? You never go outside. You're an agoraphobic.

Bell-Bell (*defensively*) I go to the dustbin and back.

Gwenda Well, I suppose you must get your fun where you can.

Gwenda *turns and shepherds* **Katrina** *over to the shoebox; they pair up old shoes.* **Bell-Bell** *sings her fun-fur song.*

After the song:

Katrina Have another go.

Reprise of song. **Katrina** *joins in with a tambourine and does a flamenco-type dance. She enjoys showing off her talent.* **Gwenda** *watches* **Katrina** *fondly.*

Gwenda Oh, while we three are together (*Conspiratorially.*) don't take too much notice of Felicity. She means well of course but she's got a lot of untried modern ideas about treatment.

Bell-Bell (*eagerly*) Is there a new treatment?

Gwenda No, of course not, nothing that works. I'd know about it if there was.

Bell-Bell But would you tell us?

Gwenda Of course, (*Pause.*) if I thought you were ready.

Bell-Bell I'm ready now, Gwenda, would you take me to the doctor's on Monday? I want to talk to him about my treatment.

Katrina What treatment?

Bell-Bell Well that's just it, I'm not having any.

Gwenda Bell-Bell, you know how overburdened Dr Patel is!

Bell-Bell I've been on tranquillisers since Derek died. It's time I got off them.

Katrina I've been on them for four and a half years and they've not done me any harm. (*She gives a vacant look.*)

Gwenda Yes. They're extremely effective on naughty children and unhappy women.

Bell-Bell I don't know if I'm unhappy any more and I won't know until I stop taking them.

Gwenda But if you don't use your clothes prop, what happens to the washing line?

Bell-Bell and **Katrina** *stare blankly at each other.*

Katrina I don't know, Maurice does the washing.

Gwenda It sags doesn't it. Ergo – we all need our prop and support. I'm very fortunate in having the Lord as mine. I do wish you'd give yourself up to the Lord, Bell-Bell. Katrina has.

Katrina He was very pleased when I joined, wasn't he, Gwenda?

Gwenda He was over the moon, Kat. I was cured by spiritual healing, did I tell you Bell-Bell?

Bell-Bell (*sarcastically*) Yes I think you mentioned it in passing. A million times or so.

Gwenda I was inside for years looking after Daddy. The doctor said he mustn't be left alone for one minute. They said that he could go at any time.

Katrina (*sings*) Tell me the old story.

Gwenda Katrina, I'm trying to talk! So naturally I did what any good daughter would do in the circumstances; gave my little job up. The girls in the office presented me with a crystal sherry decanter. Oh there were tears all round the afternoon I left, and

I must confess to feeling a little resentful myself. I did love my job.

Katrina *mouths a few words here and there. She has heard this story many times.*

Joan from the office called round a few times, but Daddy started to be rather difficult so she stopped coming. Then everyone stopped coming, it was just me and Daddy and the home help twice a week.

She drifts off into thought.

Katrina (*to* **Bell-Bell**) The next bit is about when he died.

Bell-Bell I know.

Katrina *undermines* **Gwenda**'s *story.*

Gwenda Then the poor old chap passed on and I had to force myself to go outside to the funeral. I fell into the grave you know. The other mourners thought I was grief-stricken but it wasn't that, my legs simply gave way with the terror I felt at being outside again. The vicar was a very modern chappie, wanted to be called Les. He called round to see me the next day and I made him a cup of Bovril. Then he stood up and said, 'Gwenda, I can't keep my hands off you, you're crying out for the touch of the Lord.' And I went down in front of him and he stroked my face and my neck and my shoulders and I felt this strange glow inside me, then I was racked by the most joyful physical sensation, and all at once I felt free.

Katrina It sounds to me as if the vicar touched you up.

Gwenda It was nothing like that! Nothing! Besides he was a card-carrying homosexual.

Bell-Bell Maybe you felt free because your father died.

Gwenda What an extraordinary thing to say! I loved Daddy more than life itself. No, I was spiritually healed. Dear Les. He's in Soweto now, the natives adore him.

Katrina Not long to go now – his brain went.

Gwenda Daddy left his money to the Queen Mother, but Clarence House wrote to our solicitor and graciously gave it back to his next of kin, which was me. I decided to devote myself to the poor and ignorant . . .

Katrina Cheek!

Gwenda . . . as a sort of memorial to Daddy.

Bell-Bell And you turned to religion?

Gwenda Oh, I could no more do without my religion than I could do without my continental quilt. (*Coaxingly*.) Bell-Bell, let me lay my hands on you.

Bell-Bell (*firmly*) No thanks. No mumbo-jumbo. That sort of thing doesn't last. I want to get out and stay out.

Gwenda How about you, Kat?

Katrina It didn't work last time.

Gwenda But I'm getting better all the time, Kat. Yesterday I found a broken-winged sparrow on my compost heap and do you know, within half an hour of my stroking its little fluttering wing, it had flown away over Acton as if it had never had a day's illness in its life.

Katrina All right you can do it, but don't press down so hard this time.

Katrina *kneels in front of* **Gwenda** *who throws back her head in rapture.* **Gwenda** *lays both hands on* **Katrina**'s *head.*

Gwenda Dear Lord. Thank you for allowing Katrina and Bell-Bell to leave their homes. They beg forgiveness for their sins . . .

Bell-Bell I certainly don't. (*She busies herself with rummage.*)

Gwenda I speak to you as a dear friend, a Christian, one of a despised minority. Yes, I'm a Christian, Lord and I'm proud of it, Lord.

Bell-Bell (*ironic*) Hallelujah!

Katrina Yes, Hallelujah!

Gwenda I'm no last-minute, death-bed convert.

Bell-Bell No, Sir!

Gwenda I'm a twenty-four hour, round-the-clock Christian!

Bell-Bell Yes, Siree!

Gwenda And Katrina's trying, Lord, she's trying.

Bell-Bell She's very trying, Lord.

Katrina Bell-Bell! This is *my* prayer!

Bell-Bell *laughs and turns back.*

Gwenda Heal her, Lord, heal her. Free her from this curse. Send down your all-powerful love.

Katrina Oh Barry!

Gwenda Enfold her in your all-powerful arms.

Katrina Barry, take me in your arms.

Gwenda Fill her with love.

Katrina Fill me, Barry.

Gwenda Take possession of her, Lord!

Katrina Possess me, Barry, possess me!

Gwenda I can feel it coming, Kat!

She makes one last effort as if passing a huge turd.

Katrina Gwenda! You're pulling my hair!

Fliss *enters and crosses to* **Bell-Bell.**

Fliss What's going on?

Bell-Bell Spiritual healing.

Fliss Acton's answer to Saint Francis of Assisi. (*She giggles.*) Gwenda! Gwenda!

Gwenda (*with a shuddering sigh, her body limp, arms hanging*) I'm sorry, Kat. It's no good I can't concentrate, not with an atheist in the room.

Fliss Gwenda, come and help me with Margaret. She can't get out of the car, she says her legs have gone.

Gwenda Then you'll have to take her home, we haven't got time to look after invalids.

Fliss She'll be fine in a few minute, she's just worked herself up into a state.

Gwenda *doesn't move.*

Come on Gwenda! She's feeling sick and she's sitting in your car, on your sheepskin seat covers!

Gwenda She's causing trouble before she's stepped foot in the place and we were having such a lovely time.

Fliss *and* **Gwenda** *go out. A siren is heard.* **Katrina** *and* **Bell-Bell** *stand at the door and look out.*

Katrina Have you met Margaret Gittings?

Bell-Bell Not face to face. We ring each other up.

Katrina Why don't you ring me up?

Bell-Bell I do, sometimes. Your phone's engaged a lot.

Katrina I know, I ring dial a disc until I've learn the words.

Pause. **Bell-Bell** *looks out of the door.*

Bell-Bell What do you think of the streets?

Katrina What streets?

Bell-Bell The streets outside.

Katrina I didn't look at them. I counted Maurice's dandruff instead. He makes me sit in the back of the car in case we have an accident.

Bell-Bell *(quietly)* The streets are awful – awful. I don't know how people can bear to walk about in them.

There is laughter offstage, shouts, then **Gwenda** *and* **Fliss** *enter carrying* **Margaret** *between them.* **Katrina** *sits down on the piano stool. She turns her back.* **Margaret** *is a working-class woman. She has a loud voice and an assertive manner.*

Margaret Which one is Bell-Bell?

Bell-Bell It's me.

Margaret Me bastard legs have gone, Bell-Bell. Thought I was doing all right.

Gwenda *raises her eyebrows.*

Put me down then!

Fliss Where do you want to be?

Margaret Floor'll do.

They put her down under the crucifix. She lies on her back, then sits up and sees the crucifix.

Christ Almighty, look at that! Puts the fear of God in you, don't it?

Gwenda It's meant to.

Margaret Well I did it! I bleedin' well did it!

Gwenda Did what?

Margaret Well, I did it! I bleedin' (*She starts to break down.*) I ain't been further than putting the milk bottles out for bleedin' years. Now here I am, half a mile away, at a bleedin' rummage sale. (*She tries to control herself.*)

Bell-Bell I'm glad to see you, Margaret. I couldn't have come without you.

Margaret Don't start me off, Bell-Bell. (*She cries.*) She always starts me off she does. It's a wonder I ain't been electrocuted before now. I only have to hear her voice on the phone and I'm off.

Katrina Phones don't run on electricity.

Margaret You're Katrina, ain't you?

Katrina What if I am?

Margaret You look like Shirley bleedin' Temple.

Gwenda Can you get up now, Margaret? We need the floor.

Margaret You ain't selling the floorboards, are you? (*She laughs.*)

Gwenda (*to* **Fliss**) What did I tell you?

Fliss (*laughing*) See if you can stand up, eh?

Bell-Bell and **Fliss** *help* **Margaret** *up until she stands with their support.*

Margaret I can't yet, not on my own. Put me down on a chair.

Fliss Gwenda.

Gwenda What?

Fliss A chair.

Gwenda (*fetching a chair*) Paralysis is quite common amongst hysterics.

Margaret Who's hysterical?

Gwenda You are.

Margaret Balls! If anybody's hysterical, it's you.

Gwenda I am *not* hysterical!

Margaret Well you make me laugh. (*She laughs loudly.*)

Gwenda Are you going to sit around all day?

Margaret I hope not, I want to have a good look through the rummage, get myself a new winter wardrobe together. Specially now I'm making public appearances. (*She looks at* **Katrina**'s *show-biz dresses.*) Them Shirley Bassey dresses for sale?

Katrina Only to good homes. They've been all over the country those dresses.

Gwenda But it's time you let them go, isn't it, Kat? After what happened in Leicester.

Margaret What happened in Leicester?

Katrina (*alarmed*) Gwenda, don't!

Katrina *and* **Gwenda** *look at each other.*

Margaret 'ere Fliss, will you bring my stuff in?

Fliss Yes. Katrina and Bell-Bell can help me. Come on.

Katrina We can't go outside.

Bell-Bell Is it just to the car?

Fliss It's only a few yards.

Bell-Bell Will you come with us?

Fliss I'll walk to the car with you and you can walk back together.

Bell-Bell All right.

Katrina I'm not going out there. (*She goes to* **Gwenda**.) I can only go outside with Maurice or Gwenda, nobody else.

Gwenda (*to* **Fliss**) It's early days yet.

Fliss Four and a half years is not early days! Come on, Katrina, you'll be with me and Bell-Bell.

Bell-Bell Isabel. (*She walks to the door.*)

Fliss You're not coming, Katrina?

Katrina No.

Bell-Bell Gwenda started calling me Bell-Bell, but it's not my name. It's Isabel.

Fliss *and* **Bell-Bell** *go out. There is a long pause.*

Margaret Why didn't you pick me up, Gwenda?

Gwenda I knocked three times.

Margaret You're a bleedin' liar! I stood at my window all morning waiting and you didn't come. I sent our Darren out to look for you, thought you might have been hijacked. Why didn't you want me to come?

Katrina It's because you're a troublemaker.

Margaret Look here, chocolate box, the only trouble I've caused for the last fifteen years has been to myself. I ain't been nowhere to cause trouble.

Gwenda Until today.

Margaret Yeah, until today.

Fliss *enters carrying carrier bags.*

Fliss Where did you get all these toys from, Margaret?

Margaret They're my Darren's. 'e ain't touched 'em for years. He's a hard little bleeder, now. It's all Doc Martins and tennis ball haircuts now. Still least he keeps himself clean. (*She sees* **Bell-Bell** *entering carrying a toy garage.*) Here's our Isabel! (*She slaps her legs.*) Come on you bleeders, move!

Gwenda Would you like me to lay my hands on you?

Margaret No thank you, I ain't bleedin' Lazarus. It's only me nerves.

Margaret *gets up to go to* **Bell-Bell** *and takes the garage off her.*

Congratulations, Isabel, on having the bottle to get out there on your own.

Bell-Bell It wasn't for long.

Margaret It's a start, innit?

Fliss Well done, Isabel.

Margaret Have a fag, Bell?

Bell-Bell I shouldn't – but I will.

Katrina It's no smoking in here by order of the church.

Margaret (*turning notice back to front*) Well smoking's allowed now by order of me. (*She looks at the crucifix.*) He wouldn't mind, dead neurotic he was, if fag's 'ad been around when he was alive, he'd 'ave been on sixty a day.

Gwenda Our Lord would not have allowed a cigarette to touch his lips. And he was *not* neurotic.

Margaret 'Course he was. Hearin' voices in his head. Wandering about in the bleedin' desert. They'd lock the poor bleeder up nowadays and give him electric shocks.

Gwenda Margaret, as a practising Christian . . .

Margaret Well keep on practising, Gwenda.

Gwenda I can't stand here and take that lying down! Our Lord –

Margaret (*cutting in*) He's your Lord, not mine.

Gwenda He'd be yours if you let him. We all need something.

Margaret Twenty fags and one good shit a day's all I need.

Fliss Margaret!

Margaret (*angrily*) Well, she's always on at me, always. I don't tell her what to think, do I? She's got one bleeder brainwashed – ain't that enough? (*Slight pause.*) An' if she tries to lay her hands on me one more time, I'm gonna lay my hands round her bleedin' neck.

Katrina That's a threat to your life, Gwenda.

Fliss I don't think Scotland Yard need to know, do you Katrina?

Bell-Bell We've got to get the sale ready, haven't we?

Bell-Bell *starts to put up the trestle table.*

Margaret I've had my say. It's better out than in, like farting.

Katrina You shouldn't talk about religion or politics or anything like that. It's bad manners.

Margaret *helps* **Bell-Bell.**

Margaret Well I ain't come out after fifteen years to talk about the fucking weather.

Gwenda Felicity, I can't stand in a room where obscene language is used. It makes me physically ill. I shall have to leave you in charge until I recover my equilibrium.

She puts her coat on.

Margaret Christ, you ain't on Librium 'n all are you, Gwenda? It's the blind leading the bleedin' blind, ain't it?

Margaret, Bell-Bell *and* **Fliss** *laugh.*

Fliss Don't be ridiculous, Gwenda, we need you to tell us what to do. None of us have run a Bazaar and Rummage before.

Margaret It's sixpence on the door ain't it, Gwenda?

Gwenda Sixpence! Where have you been since decimalisation?

Margaret At home.

Gwenda Sorry.

Margaret Don't matter. (*Pause.*) Come on then, let's get cracking! We're flogging rubbish to the poor, ain't we? Least we can do is set it out nice.

Fliss So what do we do, Gwenda? You're the rummage sale expert.

Gwenda If you'll gather round, I'll define your areas of responsibility. Felicity, you're academic, so you've got the literature section.

Fliss Literature! You can't call this dog-eared crap, literature! (*She stacks books on the table.*)

Gwenda Bell-Bell, or Isabel. Bell-Bell please pay attention! You're in charge of the bric-à-brac section.

Bell-Bell What's that?

Gwenda Bric-à-brac! Knick-knacks.

Margaret Give a dog a bone. This old man came rolling home. (*She laughs.*)

Fliss Do you know what you're selling now, Isabel?

Bell-Bell Is it all the hard things?

Fliss Yes, apart from the hard porn, I'm selling that.

Margaret *is riding on a child's tricycle,* **Bell-Bell** *takes a pair of rubber gloves from a bag and puts them on.*

Gwenda Margaret, toys for you I think. Please keep still, I can't concentrate. Now, you'll need to check the jigsaws, I don't want to contravene the Trade Descriptions Act. If it says five thousand pieces on the outside of the box, then the public will expect five thousand pieces to be on the inside of the box. No more, no less.

Margaret Fuck me. I ain't counting the bleeders. I'll be here until pissing midnight if I do.

Margaret *gets off the bike and stares moodily into a jigsaw box.*

Katrina What about me?

Gwenda You can help me. We've got clothing.

Katrina Ugh! All the smelly things! Can't I just sell my own dresses?

Gwenda All right. But decide how much to charge in advance. I don't want you haggling with the *hoi polloi*.

The **Women** *start to dress their own bit of table.*

And a few rummage sale ground rules: Number one, beware of the dealers. They're quite easy to spot. They all drive Bedford vans and wear secondhand fur coats. Number two, thieves are everywhere. So our own handbags and coats are piled into a heap, then hidden under a chair.

The **Women**'*s own coats are given to* **Gwenda.**

Rule three: do not quote low prices just because you feel sorry for them. The poor are the architects of their own misfortunes. Rule four: today you are representing the wider agoraphobic community. As such your behaviour and choice of language must be examplary.

Margaret What's she on about?

Fliss She wants you to stop swearing in front of the public.

Margaret Christ all bleedin' mighty! She'll 'ave us at pissing elocution classes next.

Gwenda (*raising her voice*) Rule five! You will also be given a float.

Margaret Why, we going swimming after? (*She laughs.*)

Gwenda Fifty pence each in a saucer! Margaret! Are you listening?

Katrina Margaret, listen to Gwenda, she's highly experienced at rummage sales. She's kept a guide dog in Pedigree Chum for a year.

Gwenda Yes. And I've supplied half a water hole to Zambia. Now, if anyone comes over queer, I've emergency supplies of tranquillisers in my handbag. This is the first time you've faced the public for many years and you may be shocked at their deterioration. But I would ask you that, if you feel hysteria mounting, please mention it to Fliss or myself before you make an exhibition of yourself.

Rummage sale opera. After the opera the **Women** *take their places behind their own area of table.* **Gwenda** *looks at her watch and stands by the door as if to open it on the stroke of two.*

The opera:

All One pound, two pounds, three pounds, four pounds, do you think maybe I could ask for more? It's just that this one's ten p, that one's twenty-five and this one's torn so fifteen's plenty.

Fliss *Beano, Dandy* come in handy
When you're in regression.

Bell-Bell Plastic flowers last for hours
Cheery for depression

Katrina Sequins, spangles, furs and bangles
Pretty compensation

Margaret (*playing with toys*) Dolly, teddy, getting ready
For a conversation

Gwenda Cardigans and panties
Dressing-gowns and hankies
Underskirts and trousers
Overalls and blouses

Fliss *Kevin Keegan's Life* and
How to be a Wife and
Ten of Enid Blyton
Kids have used to write in

Bell-Bell Candlesticks and toastrack

Gwenda Buttons off this old mac

Margaret Action Man keeps falling
He's on his knees and crawling
Supposed to be a hero
His sex appeal is zero

Gwenda Denim jeans and shirts
Dirty mini-skirts
Stained and smelly knickers

Margaret They must be the vicar's

Fliss Murder Mysteries, Katy Did
Little Sister, A to Z
Barbara Cartland's here to see
If there's honey left for tea

Margaret Rabbits, doggies, gollywoggles
Rubik Kubes and Kermit Froggies
Hula-Hoops and plastic crap
Made in Taiwan by a Jap

All Knives and forks and coloured chalks
Caps and coats and broken boats
To be offered to the poor
Pray they'll pour in through the door

Gwenda Guard the saucers with your life
Bell-Bell careful with that knife

Margaret take it seriously

Katrina Gwenda, I'm sure I've caught a flea.

Fliss (*looking at a statue*) What a priceless piece of kitsch.

Margaret It's horrible you stupid bitch.

There is knock on the door.

Company

Door!
Oh!
No!
Help!

Gwenda *throws open the doors.*

Act Two

It is just getting dark outside. The rummage sale is over. Not much has been sold. The standard lamp is still there. The Elvis mirror and two of **Katrina**'s *dresses have gone. Only one of* **Derek**'s *suits is left. The toy gun is still there, together with the majority of the shoes, clothes, books and bric-à-brac.*

Gwenda *is mopping the floor and sprinkling disinfectant around. She has an expression of revulsion on her face.* **Bell-Bell** *is standing at the open door looking out.* **Katrina** *is sitting reading* Woman. **Margaret** *is retching (off) and* **Fliss** *is making soothing, comforting noises (off).*

Katrina Close the door, Bell-Bell, you're letting the smell of the streets in.

Gwenda Leave it open, Bell-Bell. If there's one thing I can't stand it's the smell of vomit from a neurotic stomach.

Bell-Bell Do you think any more customers will come now, Gwenda?

Gwenda You know, Margaret ought to be doing this. (*She swabs the floor furiously.*)

Katrina Nobody will come now, not now it's dark.

Gwenda (*getting angrier*) I ought to make *her* clean it up.

Bell-Bell Shall I make her some tea? She'll have a nasty taste in her mouth.

Gwenda She ought to have more control over her stomach.

Katrina (*to* **Gwenda**) It's her nerves. (*To* **Bell-Bell**.) Milky and three sugars please.

Katrina *shivers, gets up and closes the door.*

Gwenda There's nobody more highly-strung than I am. I'm a veritable Stradivarius, but I don't give into it. (*To* **Bell-Bell**) Strong and no sugar.

Bell-Bell *goes out to the kitchen.*

Katrina You have nervous rashes instead, don't you, Gwenda?

Gwenda I have discreet nervous rashes, **Katrina**. (*Pause.*)

Margaret Gittings won't come to another of my public functions, she was shouting and bawling as if she were a continental stall-holder on Petticoat Lane.

Katrina People seemed to like her though, didn't they?

Gwenda Well, there are people and people, aren't there? It was hardly the Marks and Spencer set, was it? Tattooed grandfathers, single parents, Alsatians, delinquents and maladjusted children. Hardly a discriminating public was it? Nothing of any taste was sold. (*She strokes the standard lamp.*)

Katrina That big coloured boy asked Bell-Bell if he could put a deposit on Derek's binoculars and pay her so much a week.

Gwenda We call them blacks now, Katrina. You must get up to date with your terminology. You could cause offence.

Katrina Why have blacks got white palms, Gwenda?

Gwenda It's something to do with the sunlight not getting to them in Africa. Though heaven knows, they have them outstretched enough over here. She didn't agree to his crooked suggestion, did she?

Bell-Bell *enters.*

Bell-Bell No, I gave them to him.

Gwenda Genuine Ox-hide binoculars, and you gave them away?

Bell-Bell I wanted to. Can I have my gloves please?

Gwenda He's probably scanning the streets of Acton looking for somebody to mug.

Bell-Bell He won't see far, not in the dark. (*She goes out.*)

Katrina I can't stand her, can you?

Margaret *and* **Fliss** *enter,* **Margaret** *wiping her mouth on a tissue.*

Fliss Now sit down and take it easy, you've been running around like a Trot in a Labour constituency.

Margaret It's not being used to people what does it. I enjoyed it, don't get me wrong. But it's after it gets me.

Fliss It was noble of you to clean up, Gwenda.

Margaret (*to* **Gwenda**) You should have left it. I'd have done it.

Gwenda (*martyred*) It's too late now isn't it? It's all done now, isn't it? We couldn't paddle around in a lake of vomit, could we?

Margaret Christ! It were only a few fucking Rice Krispies! (*Pause.*) Anyway that disinfectant smells worse than my puke.

Gwenda I'm surprised you know what disinfectant smells like, Margaret. I didn't know it was a commodity you were in the habit of purchasing.

Margaret (*offended*) Oh that's nice, innit? Choice that is!

Fliss Calm down, Gwenda, c'mon, give me the mop. You can take it easy now that the rush is off.

Fliss *tries to take the mop but* **Gwenda** *resists.*

Gwenda Rush! Twenty-five people and two Alsatians. I don't call that a rush. The working classes are getting so apathetic that they can't even stir themselves to come out to a rummage sale.

Margaret You're just pissed off 'cos no one wanted your poxy old lamp.

Gwenda (*still wrestling with the mop*) That was my father's lamp! He was sitting under that lamp when our Lord took him.

Margaret Pity he didn't take the bleedin' lamp, an' all then.

Gwenda (*throwing the mop*) I can take anything you throw at me, Margaret. But when you drag Daddy into the argument . . . a dear sweet old man . . .

She rushes out into the loo. Everyone watches her. She re-enters.

Has anyone got a tissue?

Katrina I have. How long will you be crying?

Gwenda About five minutes.

Katrina You better have a few then.

She hands over some tissues.

Gwenda Thank you, I shall always have you, shan't I?

Gwenda *goes out with tissues covering her face.*

Katrina I can't stand her, can you?

Margaret Bleedin' good riddance. The best thing she can do is piss off home.

Bell-Bell (*off*) Tea up!

Bell-Bell *enters carrying a tray with a teapot, milk jug, sugar bowl and five cups and saucers.*

Margaret Give it 'ere, Bell. I'll be mother, you can do the sugar.

Bell-Bell Gwenda's in the lavatory making a funny noise. Is she ill?

Margaret Not ill so much as off her bleedin' head.

Fliss The only thing we can do for her is to keep her tea warm.

Margaret How long's her old man been dead then, not recent is it?

Fliss *pours the tea,* **Bell-Bell** *polishes the spoons and passes the sugar.*

Katrina Not really, he died watching football in 1966.

Margaret Fulham supporter, was he?

Katrina No, he was watching the World Cup on television and he had heart failure during the last four minutes. Gwenda blames Geoff Hurst for her father's death.

Margaret Remember that, Fliss? Nobby running round with his gums all bare, half the country pissed as newts. (*She is on her feet.*) England! (*Clap, clap, clap.*) England! (*Clap, clap, clap.*)

World Cup Song.

Fliss Actually I didn't see the match, my father loathed football so he wouldn't have it on. The smug pig sat out in the garden listening to *Down Our Way.* Mummy and I went shopping in Reading. It was like a ghost town. I felt quite peculiar, not of the common herd.

Margaret Yeah, you can tell you were brought up proper, Fliss. You use nice words and say 'em in the right order.

Fliss An accident of birth. Merely the coupling of a middle-middle-class sperm and a lower-middle-class ova. Result: Felicity Sarah Markington's birth is announced in the *Daily Telegraph.*

Katrina Just think, you could have been Margaret Gittings.

Margaret I ain't always been a Gittings. I changed into one. I took 'is name to stop the bleedin' neighbours talking.

Fliss Who's name?

Margaret Darren's father.

Katrina I didn't know he had a father.

Margaret Well he weren't off Tesco's meat counter; he *had* a father. Our Darren took after the evil little git an' all. Got that same weasel face.

Katrina What a thing to say about your own little boy.

Margaret He ain't never been a little boy. He only come out of my womb to see what he could nick. Robbin' little bastard.

Fliss Does Darren ever see his dad?

Margaret He'd 'ave a job. He's dead.

Bell-Bell What did he die of?

Margaret He was digging a trench and it fell in on him.

Fliss That's a bit heavy.

Margaret Not as heavy as it was for him.

Pause. **Margaret** *has shocked herself.* **Bell-Bell** *starts to laugh.*

Katrina Oh you're really awful!

They all laugh.

Margaret Who's going to see how Gwenda is? Her tea's getting cold.

There is a pause as all the **Women** *wait for someone else to volunteer.*

Margaret It's no good me going, she hates *me*.

Bell-Bell I'm sure she doesn't *hate* you, Margaret.

Margaret Oh I don't mind, I have that effect on everybody. I could never keep a friend.

Bell-Bell Don't say that, Margaret.

Margaret Just letting you know, Bell.

There is a pause as the two **Women** *glance at each other. Everyone drops their voice.*

Katrina Gwenda's always crying, she has trouble with her hormones.

Margaret Well she wants to have 'em out then, don't she?

Fliss You can't have them *taken out*. They circulate in the bloodstream . . .

Margaret Well *drained out* then.

Fliss What does she find to cry about?

Katrina It's mostly how wicked the world is, that and her vacuum cleaner breaking down.

Margaret I reckon she's the one that's breaking down, only it'll take more than new suction hose to get her right.

Katrina She's having treatment for it.

Fliss Don't tell me she's on the happy pills.

Katrina No, she's having the electric shock. EEC.

Margaret EEC? Ain't that the Common Market?

Katrina No, it's a machine that they plug you into. It does something to your brain.

Margaret What?

Katrina I don't know. I'm not an electrician am I?

Fliss It's ECT and no one knows how it works. Poor Gwenda, how often does she light up?

Katrina Once a week on Wednesday afternoons.

Fliss I saw her last Wednesday, she said she'd been in convulsions, but I thought she meant a bloody good laugh.

Margaret Poor bleeder. She kept that quiet.

Katrina I was sworn to secrecy. She said if it ever got out, she'd be ruined in voluntary social work. She said they're a vicious, spiteful lot in charity work. She said she'd be thrown off all the committees. She's on a lot of committees you know. She does a lot for the British Limbless Ex-Servicemen.

Fliss What does she do?

Katrina She takes them to the limb-fitting centre in her car. But they have to make their own way home. She believes that people should stand on their own two feet.

Bell-Bell, Fliss and **Margaret** *laugh.*

Katrina (*straight-faced*) I don't see what's funny about it.

Margaret Just 'aving an 'armless joke, Kat. (*She waggles a bent arm about, laughs, and chokes on her tea. She has her back patted.*)

Katrina You shouldn't laugh at Gwenda. She's worked very hard getting the rummage sale organised. All the arrangements, the posters, collecting the rummage, queuing up in the bank for the small money for the float.

Fliss Actually Gwenda didn't do any of those things. I did.

Margaret How d'you mean?

Fliss Gwenda didn't want us to have a rummage sale at all. She rang the caretaker last week and cancelled our booking. I had a lot of hassle getting the room back from the Acton Morris Men. They practise in here on Saturdays.

Margaret Do you know what? I reckon she don't want us to get better. I reckon she wants to keep us in. She likes having us at home.

Bell-Bell Ah, your mouth's running away with you again, Margaret.

Margaret She does! The poor cow wants to keep us to herself!

There is a pause. Then **Gwenda** *enters, red-eyed, snuffling and blowing her nose.*

Gwenda Is that my tea? Oh dear, it's got a cold look about it. Now I don't want any fuss made of me, carry on as if nothing had happened. Oh, I meant to say before Margaret's outburst, we must be out by six o'clock.

She notices the **Women**'*s faces which are registering shock and surprise as each* **Woman** *realises the truth of* **Margaret**'*s last sentence.*

Goodness gracious me, what in heaven's name is wrong?

Fliss Nothing, I think we're all a bit tired.

Gwenda You look like conspirators. (*She gives a little laugh.*) What have you been plotting? (*Pause.*) Katrina, my pet, would you count our takings? Put the ten-pence pieces in piles of ten and collect the paper money together with this paperclip . . .

Fliss She won't need a paperclip. We only took one five-pound note.

Katrina Can't somebody else do it? I'm not used to money, Maurice does all that for me. I don't even use a purse any more.

Margaret She's like bleedin' royalty our Katrina is.

Bell-Bell Shall I count the money? I'd like to know how much we've taken.

Gwenda Well actually, Bell-Bell, I'd already got a little job for you. A nice easy little job cutting buttons off the shirts.

Fliss What do you want shirt buttons for?

Gwenda I'm making a collage of St Paul's Cathedral, I need the buttons for the clouds.

Margaret You count the money if you want to, Bell-Bell.

Gwenda *cuts buttons off the shirts.*

Fliss Katrina, you can help me, you've hardly moved all afternoon.

Katrina I'm not used to moving. That's why!

Margaret Well it's time you bleedin' well did then, you lazy cow!

Katrina I'm not lazy. I hardly have time to draw breath.

Fliss What on earth do you do all day?

Katrina Starting from when?

Fliss From when you wake up.

Katrina Well at eight o'clock Maurice brings me my breakfast on a tray. I have half a grapefruit, a soft-boiled egg, toast soldiers, a cup of tea and a five-milligram Librium. Then when he's gone to work I listen to Terry Wogan. He sometimes plays one of Barry's records but he can never pronounce his name properly, he calls him Harry Banilow. Sometimes I think Terry

does it on purpose. Then what do I do? Yes, so I get up and
have a Sainsbury's bubble bath. Then I get out, cream my knees
and elbows, Immac under my arms, put all my make-up on and
do my hair. Then of course I have to choose what to wear. Well
time's getting on so I go downstairs, he's done all the housework
but I have to water the plants. Then I sit and listen to Barry
until Maurice comes home.

Margaret Bleedin' hell!

Fliss Shush!

Katrina He's home at one o'clock. He has tomato soup and two
slices of bread and I have a doughnut, a cup of coffee and a five-
milligram Librium. No sooner that's done than he goes back to
work and I have to have a sleep until he comes back at teatime.
Then, while we eat our digestives Maurice tells me all the news;
all about the riots and the muggings and the rapes and the old
people being murdered (*More emotionally.*) and the blacks
kidnapping white women and all the little kiddies that's
molested by perverts and the animals that's tortured by
teenagers and the multiple crashes on the motorways and how
people have been trapped inside their cars and been burnt alive.
(*She continues more normally.*) Well, when he's told me all the latest,
I have a ten-milligram Librium and he cooks the dinner. (*Pause.*)
Meat, two veg, gravy, tin of fruit and Dream Topping, let's say.
Then Gwenda comes round and Maurice and her talk about
how the country's going down the drain. Then it's cocoa, two
Cadbury's Fingers, Mogadon and bed.

There is a long pause during which time a siren is heard.

Margaret Your Maurice is a fucking maniac!

Gwenda Maurice is *not* a maniac!

Katrina And he's not a fucking one, not any more.

Fliss Katrina, Maurice has been telling you lies.

Katrina No, I know it's true. He cuts bits out of the newspapers
and puts them in his scrapbooks. You've seen his scrapbooks,
haven't you, Gwenda?

Gwenda Yes, they're meticulously kept.

Katrina It must be true. If it's in the papers, it must be true.

Margaret I wouldn't wipe my arse on the papers.

Katrina East west, home's best. Nothing can happen to you if you're inside, can it?

Fliss Katrina, you're more likely to die choking on a digestive biscuit than being burnt to death in a motorway pile-up.

Gwenda How ridiculous! You're just trying to frighten her.

Katrina Is it true that if you stop breathing for long, you die?

Fliss Yes.

Katrina Awful isn't it? Sometimes I wake up in the middle of the night just to make sure I'm not dead.

Margaret You might as well be dead. You're already livin' in a coffin and Maurice is diggin' your bleedin' grave.

Fliss And we all know who the undertaker is, don't we? (*To* **Gwenda**) How could you have allowed this to go on?

Gwenda What to go on?

Fliss Why have you let Maurice terrify Katrina into staying at home?

Gwenda She's happier at home. (*To the group.*) You all are. The streets aren't safe for women.

Margaret I wouldn't mind finding out for myself though. I ain't been out there on my own since Darren was born.

Bell-Bell How old is he now?

Margaret He'll be fifteen in June.

Pause.

Bell-Bell (*in a panic*) I've got to get out soon. I don't want to be in for fifteen years.

Fliss Well don't look to Gwenda for any help 'cause she's already said you're better off at home.

Gwenda You lying filthy Red! You Socialist lefty-pinko-liberal-beatnik-Bennite! I knew you had militant tendencies! I spotted i the first time I saw you. Do Social Services know you're a Communist?

Katrina I've never seen a Communist before, not in the flesh.

Fliss (*to* **Katrina**) I'm not a Communist, I'm apolitical.

Gwenda (*shouting*) A political what? Come on, out with it!

Katrina Must you shout, Gwenda? I've got a headache due in five minutes.

Gwenda I've given the best years of my pre-menopausal life to these women. I visit daily –

Margaret (*cutting in; to* **Bell-Bell**) She always comes in the middle of *Crossroads*. I missed the fire because of her.

Gwenda Without me, Margaret, you would starve to death. Who is it brings your groceries every day?

Margaret I don't ask you to. My Darren could get 'em.

Gwenda Your Darren is a kleptomaniac and is banned from every grocery store within a two-mile radius of Acton High Street!

Margaret Yeah well, the walk'll do 'im good, won't it?

Gwenda What about you, Bell-Bell? Do you still want me to get your household cleaners from the cash and carry?

Bell-Bell I've got enough Harpic to clean up the River Ganges, Gwenda.

Gwenda Kat?

Katrina You can still come round to my house if you like, I never listen to what you say anyway, so you don't bother me.

Fliss (*kindly*) You've got too involved, Gwenda. It's the cardinal sin of social work. It's almost the first thing you learn on the training course.

Gwenda (*more to herself*) The Communists at Social Services stopped me doing any training. I told them straight at all my interviews. I said what this country needs is more men like Daddy. Capital punishment in schools. Teenagers in the army, fathers working and mummies at home. I was a naughty girl too once but thankfully I had a daddy who wasn't afraid to use discipline. They were against me from the start. I distinctly saw one bearded revolutionary sniggering at my interview hat.

(*Pause. Then she continues more emotionally, getting hysterical.*) It's you and your kind who have made this country what it is today. A country where no decent God-fearing woman can walk the streets without being molested. (*She cries and hangs onto the lamp.*)

Bell-Bell She shouldn't have brought that lamp here, it reminds her of her father.

Margaret Tall and thin and wore a flowered hat, did he?

Bell-Bell *laughs.*

Gwenda I can see I'm surplus to requirements here, so if you'll excuse me I'll make my way home. (*She puts her coat on with jerky movements.*)

Katrina What about me?

Gwenda What about you?

Katrina You can't leave me here.

Gwenda It's quite clear where your affections lie now, Katrina. I've been tossed aside like a withered lettuce leaf, all that I ask is that you allow me to go with dignity. (*She falls over the mop.*) Goodbye!

Fliss Don't be so bloody melodramatic, you can't leave us here with all this rummage.

Gwenda You've staged a successful *coup d'état*, Felicity, and now like all revolutionaries you are left with the problems of who is going to attend to the drains.

Gwenda *leaves. The group quietly panics.*

Margaret What bleedin' drains?

Fliss She was speaking metaphorically.

Margaret What?

Fliss She was using a metaphor to illustrate a point.

There is a pause.

Margaret Well I ain't cleaning no bleedin' drains.

Katrina (*to* **Fliss**) Are you in charge of us now?

Fliss No.

Bell-Bell Who is then?

Fliss You're in charge of yourselves.

Margaret How are we getting home?

Fliss I don't know how you'll be getting home.

Margaret You're ditching us are you? A fine bleedin' social worker you've turned out to be.

Fliss I'm not here as a social worker. I'm here as a student to see how a self-help group functions. I'm merely an observer.

Margaret If we'd known that we'd of had a whip-round and bought the bastard binoculars for you.

Bell-Bell Somebody must be in charge of us.

Katrina We can't get home on our own.

Margaret And we can't stay here, the caretaker's locking up at six.

Katrina I could phone Maurice, is there a telephone near here?

Fliss (*irritably*) I don't know. Go outside and look for one.

Margaret What are you being horrible for, Fliss? What have we done wrong?

Fliss You've done nothing wrong, Marg. But I'm not getting saddled with running your lives, I haven't got the time.

Bell-Bell Just help us to get home.

Fliss It won't stop there, will it? It'll be Fliss, fetch my family allowance, or Fliss, pick up my prescription, or Fliss, pay my rent. I can't do it. Look, you wouldn't let yourselves bloody starve, would you? If you *had* to, you'd get to the shops.

Margaret Are you saying pull yourselves together?

Fliss No, social workers are not allowed to say that. But you've got to face up to it sooner or later.

Bell-Bell Face up to what?

Fliss Whatever it is that's keeping you in.

Katrina We know what it is, it's agoraphobia.

Fliss That came second, what came first?

A con brio choir sings offstage. Music. There is a long pause as each **Woman** *finds something to do.* **Bell-Bell** *starts to count money,* **Katrina** *starts to repack books into boxes,* **Margaret** *starts to fold clothes.*

Fliss Margaret!

Margaret I don't know any more. I can't remember anything.

Bell-Bell She's been on Librium for fourteen years.

Margaret Fifteen.

Katrina I've only been on it for four and a half years.

Bell-Bell I'm not on it at all.

Katrina You're brave!

The **women** *start dismantling the tables and packing the rummage.*

Bell-Bell I'm on Valium instead.

Katrina Valium and Librium. Go together nicely, don't they?

Margaret Like Dandelion and Burdock.

Katrina 'Cept you don't get money back on the bottles. (*She laughs.*)

Margaret Wish you did. I'd be a fucking millionairess. (*She laughs.*)

Fliss What would you spend the money on?

Margaret I'd go round the world.

Katrina Oh I wouldn't. I'd go somewhere nice.

Fliss How can you go round the world if you can't go the end of your street?

Margaret (*in a raised voice*) You seen my street?

Fliss Why don't you move?

Margaret (*shouting*) Because, Felicity Sarah Markington from Reading, I ain't got no money and the council won't give me a transfer and I'm shit scared every time I put my nose out of doors.

Fliss So you don't like where you live?

Margaret Who would? It's a shit hole.

Fliss It's urban decay.

Margaret What's that?

Fliss That's what you live in.

Margaret Sounds like a tooth disease.

Fliss Well it's not, it's a building disease. But most people at least function in it. In as much as they can go from A to B.

Margaret (*shouting*) What are you talking about?

Fliss I'm trying to find out why you're scared.

Margaret (*shouting*) I don't know why!

Fliss Don't shout. Why are you always shouting?

Margaret (*shouting*) Because no bleeder takes no notice of me unless I do!

Fliss I'm trying to empathise with you. (*She shouts.*)

Margaret (*shouting*) I don't know what you're talking about!

Fliss I give up.

Margaret (*quietly*) That's better, I understood that.

There is a pause.

Fliss Don't you want to get better?

Margaret I don't know where to begin.

Fliss Open the door and take two steps outside.

Margaret You know I can't do it.

Katrina Not in the dark!

Fliss Darkness is a scientific phenomena, Katrina. It is not a veil of evil dropped on half the world. Go on, two steps, two measly little steps. Then you can come back inside.

Margaret Will you leave the door open?

Fliss Yes.

Margaret *goes to the door, opens it and looks out. The others watch her. After a pause* **Margaret** *hurries back into the room and sits in a far corner.*

Margaret I ain't dressed right for going out at night am I?

Fliss For Christ's sake, Margaret, you're just procrastinating.

Margaret No I'm not. I'm putting it off until I'm dressed right.

Fliss You're only going a yard away.

Katrina Shall I get you dressed to go out?

Margaret (*evasively*) No, it's all right, don't bother.

Katrina Oh let me! I know all about dressing up. What did you used to wear when you went out at nights?

Margaret Well, I'd put me best coat on.

Katrina What about dancing or nightclubs?

Margaret What about 'em?

Katrina What did you wear?

Margaret Nothing.

Katrina Nothing?

Margaret No, I never went to places like that.

Katrina So you've never had lamé next to the skin?

Margaret No.

Katrina Never had a frou-frou underskirt on and wobbled when you walked?

Margaret (*scornfully*) Piss off.

Katrina *fetches a glamorous dress.*

Katrina Oh Margaret, now's your chance. Oh I've always wanted to do this, just like they do in *Woman*. It's only clothes, make-up and hairdos, Margaret. Even *I'm* quite ordinary when I'm bare and naked. Try 'My Way' on.

Margaret What's 'My Way'.

Katrina This! I used to change into it for my big number. I had flowers thrown on the stage at the Leicester Boot and Shoe, that was a night to remember. It was in the Hawaiian Lounge and they had this fountain spurting water and a real plastic palm tree with real plastic pineapples on it. I got a standing ovation. Then somebody fell in the fountain and a fight broke out. All my dresses had names. Go on, put 'My Way' on.

Margaret No, I'll look pissin' stupid in it, won't I?

Katrina No, you won't.

Margaret I will here won't I? It ain't exactly Las Vegas, is it?

Fliss Go on, Marg. It'll please Katrina.

Margaret *starts to undress self-consciously.*

Margaret (*laughing at* **Fliss**) It's you who needs doing over, look at the state you're in! You look like a bag of shit tied in the middle.

Female screams come from outside. The **Women** *stand quite still, terrified. They turn and look at* **Fliss** *who rushes to the door leaving it open.* **Bell-Bell** *rushes to the door and slams it shut. The* **Women** *watch the door. The screams turn into high-pitched, shrieking laughter. The* **Women** *relax a little.* **Fliss** *comes back in, puffing.*

Fliss Only kids playing about on the gravestones.

Margaret I thought some bleeder's throat was being cut.

All the **Women** *laugh and relax.*

Fliss Come on then, Marg.

Margaret *undresses.*

Katrina I'm going to Las Vagas one day. It's my ambition. I've got the talent, Maurice says. He's making me some really amazing dresses. I haven't seen them yet. He keeps them at the Kabin but he says they're amazing, really amazing.

Fliss I bet.

Margaret Don't look at my bra – it's got a safety pin in it. Where do all these bits and pieces go?

Katrina Come here! I'll do you up. (*She fiddles with the zips.*)

Margaret What do I look like, Fliss?

Margaret *stands in the dress and clumpy shoes.*

Fliss You need shoes. What size do you take?

Margaret Four and a half, or fives.

Fliss *rummages around in the shoe pile.*

Katrina Sit down, I'll do something with your hair. It looks like a Brillo pad that's been left in soak.

Margaret *sits down and* **Katrina** *fusses with her hair, taking pins out of her own.*

Bell-Bell, pass my make-up bag out of my handbag.

Margaret I don't want that shit on my face.

Katrina Margaret, your pores are crying out for something. Be quiet, I know what I'm doing.

Bell-Bell *passes her the make-up bag.*

Now, carry on backcombing, Bell-Bell.

Fliss *finds a pair of old stilletos and puts them on* **Margaret**. **Katrina** *makes up her face.*

Margaret I feel like a bleedin' human sacrifice.

Katrina Keep still. Stop wriggling around.

Bell-Bell You're coming on nicely, Margaret.

Fliss You're very clever with feminine artefacts, Katrina. Did you have any training in transformation?

Katrina No, it just came naturally to me. I've never climbed a tree in my life.

Margaret How much longer?

Katrina Open your mouth, I'm putting your mascara on.

Katrina *opens her mouth.*

Margaret 'Ere careful! You nearly 'ad my eyeball on the end of that stick.

Katrina (*indignantly*) Stick! It's called a wand!

Margaret Is that why I'm feeling like a fucking fairy?

Katrina You've got good long eyelashes, Margaret, do you do anything with them?

Margaret Open an' shut 'em, that's all.

Katrina What a waste! I've had to wear falsies since I was sixteen. Maurice said my eyelashes had no impact over the footlights. Right, now for the pulse points.

Katrina *sprays perfume on* **Margaret.**

Margaret Leave it out, Katrina! I smell like a one-woman knocking shop!

Katrina (*shocked*) This is Chanel Number Five. You won't find this on any old pulse points. They're very fussy who they sell it to. You have to know somebody.

Margaret Have you finished?

Katrina Yes, you can stand up now.

Margaret *stands, wobbling on the high-heels, round-shouldered and self-conscious.*

Bell-Bell I don't know you, Margaret.

Katrina Margaret, stand up straight, push your knobs out.

Margaret *attempts to.*

Katrina Like this.

She assumes a showbiz pose.

Margaret I can't do it, I ain't built like you.

Katrina Of course you can. Now walk round like this.

Katrina *makes a showbiz entrance.*

Margaret What for?

Katrina You're going to make a big entrance in front of the public soon. Bell-Bell play us some music, do you know 'My Day'?

Bell-Bell *sits at the piano and plays 'My Day'.* **Katrina** *and* **Margaret** *sing.* **Margaret** *gets a kick out of floucing about in the dress.*

At the end of the song **Fliss** *opens the door, points to* **Margaret**, *then points to the door.* **Margaret** *walks to the door, hesitates, then walks out looking to left and right. She takes two steps forward, then walks backwards into the hall. The* **Women** *cheer and shout.*

Margaret It were only two bleedin' steps.

Margaret *sits down looking pleased with herself.* **Katrina** *passes* **Margaret** *a tissue.*

Get us me fags, Kat.

Fliss Well done, Marg. Did you have a good time out there?

Margaret Don't know – I had me eyes shut.

Katrina You've got me to thank for that. I improved your self-image.

Margaret Bleedin' hell, Kat.

Bell-Bell You did awful well, Margaret.

Margaret I know, I'm doing it again tomorrow.

Pause. **Margaret** *lights a fag.*

Bell-Bell We made nine pounds thirty-seven and a half pence.

Katrina Freddie *will* be pleased.

Bell-Bell Freddie who?

Katrina Freddie Laker. Gwenda's sending him our rummage sale money. Didn't she tell you?

Fliss I'd sooner throw it down the bloody drain.

Bell-Bell What shall I do with the money, Fliss?

Fliss Give it to the caretaker and tell him Gwenda owes him sixty-two and a half pence for the hire of the room. We made a loss.

Margaret Ten pounds for this poxy hole? It ain't worth that to buy it.

Katrina We've still got things to sell. The rummage isn't over yet. I've not bought anything yet.

Fliss You haven't got any money on you, have you?

Katrina (*thinking*) Oh no. Margaret, do you want to buy 'My Way'?

Margaret How much is it?

Katrina Sixty-two and a half pence.

Margaret It don't fit properly does it?

Katrina I could always get Maurice to alter it. He's very good with awkward figures.

Margaret I had a good figure before Darren was born.

Bell-Bell Was he a big baby?

Margaret No, he was a little runt like his dad. But he damaged me somehow. I ain't been the same person since I had him.

Fliss Did you want him?

There is a pause. A long siren sounds.

Margaret No! And I didn't want his dad neither. I had 'em both forced on me.

Katrina You could have said no. I do.

Margaret I did say no.

Bell-Bell Oh dear.

Bell-Bell *moves away.*

Fliss How old were you?

Margaret Eighteen and three days. I'd never seen a man's cock before. Hard to believe ain't it? So when it come poking out of his trousers I thought he'd got a banana in his hand. Then I twigged and tried to get to the door but he stood with his back to it.

Bell-Bell I don't want to hear any more.

Bell-Bell *gets up and goes to the door.*

Katrina I do. I like anything like this.

Fliss Shut up! Go on, Margaret.

Margaret He said, 'Lie down and take your drawers off.' He was only a little runt. I could have floored him, smashed his face in, but I didn't. He knew I was scared, see. So I laid down on the bathroom floor and he fiddled around with me and grunted like a pig and when it hurt me, he put his hand over my mouth. I could hear my old lady downstairs whipping a Yorkshire pudding. I could hear the chink of the spoon in the bowl.

Bell-Bell (*upset*) She should have used a wooden spoon for Yorkshire pudding.

Katrina Did he go all the way?

Margaret No, he stopped when he got to my bleedin' backbone!

Bell-Bell Don't joke about it, Margaret.

Margaret Sorry, Bell. I could hear the kids playing and screaming outside in the street an' I thought, this isn't happening. Then he got off me, did his buttons up, took some change out of his pocket and threw half a crown on my belly. Then he went out. I heard him shout 'Tara!' to our mum. She shouted, 'Dinner'll be on the table at two o'clock sharp, Norman.' Then the front door slammed. I waited until his footsteps had died away and then I got up and looked in the bathroom mirror.

Fliss What were you looking for?

Margaret A sign that would tell everybody what had happened. Then our mum called me down to peel the sprouts, so I went down after I'd washed. Our mum was like she always was Sunday dinnertime. Pissed off 'cos the men were in the pub and she was stuck at home with the fuckin' dinner.

Fliss You didn't tell her?

Margaret No, our mum thought the sun shone out of his scrawny ass.

Fliss Who was it?

Margaret It was somebody it shouldn't have been. I'll never tell who, never.

Fliss And Darren was his baby?

Margaret Copped out first time. First and only. I didn't know see? So when I started putting weight on, I thought nothing of it. Then one of the girls says, 'You in the pudding club, Marg?' I says, 'Don't be daft, Vera, I'm Acton's last living virgin.' Because inside me I still was. I must have been five months gone by then. I gave up my job and told our mum I'd got the sack for nicking the laundry. She believed me 'cos every towel we had was stamped with the laundry's name. I stayed in bed most of the day after that. I was like an invalid, like a frozen invalid. Six weeks later I had him. I was reading the Sunday paper in bed. I had backache, then I had a pain so bad that my eyes turned inside out and he was there.

Fliss What did you do?

Margaret I wrapped him in the *News of the World* and put him under the bed.

Bell-Bell Wasn't he crying?

Margaret Him and me. I daren't look at him properly, I thought he'd be a monster like it says in the Bible. Then our mum shouts upstairs, Margaret, have you got that paper?' She comes up, pulls the paper out from under the bed and ages ten years in one second.

Fliss Christ, Margaret. The *News of the World*!

Margaret He'll end up that way an' all, the rate he's going.

Bell-Bell Why did you keep him?

Margaret You've had kids, Bell. You know what it's like.

Bell-Bell My circumstances were very different, Margaret. We always did things properly, how they should be done.

Margaret It didn't do you no good in the end though, did it, Bell? You ain't got a bloke now, same as me.

Bell-Bell I don't want another man. (*Pause.*) I only wanted Derek.

Fliss How did Derek die, Bell, was he ill?

Bell-Bell *busies herself stacking teacups.*

Bell-Bell He didn't die, he was made redundant. It was such a waste.

She turns her back.

Margaret (*going to* **Bell-Bell**) Bell, you're wasting yourself staying in. You're a good woman, you should share yourself out.

Bell-Bell I've got nothing to share. I only know how to keep a nice house. I give it a good clean through every day, windows, walls, floors, doors, furniture, carpets.

Fliss What do you do when you've finished your housework?

Bell-Bell (*agitated*) There's no time for anything else. As soon as I've cleaned one surface, another one is dirty.

Fliss (*suspiciously*) What happens if you are interrupted, say if the telephone rings or somebody comes to the door?

Bell-Bell Oh if that happened I have to start all over again.

Fliss From scratch?

Margaret *holds* **Bell-Bell**'s hand.

Bell-Bell Yes. I have to start off in the box-room, and I have to finish in the porch. It's just my way of doing things.

Fliss Did you do this when Derek was alive?

Bell-Bell Yes, he was very good, he changed before he came into the house and kept his feet on the newspapers.

Margaret What bleedin' newspapers?

Bell-Bell The newspapers on the lounge carpet. (*Pause.*) I know it's not normal.

Margaret What happened when he was made redundant? Where did he sit all day – while you were cleaning?

Bell-Bell He didn't tell me he'd been made redundant. (*Pause.*) He didn't tell me. I didn't know until I saw his boss at the funeral.

Fliss How long was that?

Bell-Bell Three months. He killed himself when his redundancy money ran out. He was very thoughtful, he did it in the bath so there wouldn't be much mess.

Katrina That was nice of him.

Bell-Bell Liquid Gumption is very good on bloodstains.

Margaret (*holding* **Bell-Bell**) Bell, we're a pair of headcases ain't we? But it don't mean we have to stay in all the time, does it?

Fliss (*trying to comfort*) You're not mad, Bell, you're just a bit neurotic.

Margaret You trying to cheer her up or what?

Fliss It's normal to be a bit neurotic, nearly everybody's scared of something.

Katrina Maurice doesn't like spiders.

Margaret And you can't get our Darren into a lift for love or money.

Katrina What's Bell scared of then?

Bell-Bell Germs!

Margaret Well you can't spend the rest of your life at home killing the bleeders.

Fliss She won't have to – you're going out at least once a week from now on.

Katrina Where are we going?

Fliss Christ knows, I'll find somewhere.

Bell-Bell Are you going to give us treatment?

Fliss I'm not. I'm not qualified and anyway I'm as neurotic as the next.

Margaret Why, what are you scared of?

Fliss I break into a cold sweat whenever I see a semi-detached house.

Margaret So where do you live?

Fliss Tower Hamlets.

*The **women** start the final packing away.*

Margaret You can have treatment the same time as us.

Fliss No thanks. The thought of being able to see my parents again . . . ugh! (*She shudders.*) And that shrine of a house, those flowerbeds! Spring is a nightmare. Daffodils grow in clumps of six, no more, no less. The privet hedge is only allowed to flourish six inches above the fence. My God, the brutal way my father treats that privet, hacking at the leaves as if they are a battalion of Japanese. He doesn't garden, he controls. He spends so long in his greenhouse I expect him to take root in a bag of John Innes. Poor Mummy!

Margaret What's your old lady like?

Fliss (*trying to think*) I don't know, there was nothing there, nothing tangible. She sort of wandered around with a J Cloth in her hand desperately trying to anticipate my father's moods.

Margaret Do you go and see your mum and dad?

Fliss No the suburbs are out of bounds for me. The sound of a lawnmower starts me off.

Katrina What do you start doing?

Fliss Sweating.

Margaret Palms of your hands?

Fliss Yes. And a sort of buzzing . . .

Katrina In your ears?

Fliss Yes. Then I feel my legs going . . .

Bell-Bell All weak and wobbly?

Fliss Yes! And I think to myself, come on, Fliss pull . . .

Katrina Yourself together! But you can't, can you?

Fliss No. And I feel sure I'm going to faint . . .

Margaret Right there in the street and that some bastard's going to look up your skirt and see your drawers?

Fliss Well no, not exactly, Margaret.

Margaret You think you're going to spew up?

Fliss Yes.

Katrina What about the shops, can you go into shops?

Fliss Woolworth's is okay. Harrod's is out.

Agoraphobia song – 'Panic Attack'. There is a terrible panic-stricken banging on the door.

Margaret It's the caretaker come for his bleedin' money.

Fliss *opens the door. A* **Woman Police Constable** *rushes in in a panic, then sees the* **Women** *and becomes officious.*

Woman Police Constable I saw the light on.

Fliss Is it against the law?

Woman Police Constable Well it could be at time of war.

Bell-Bell We've been having a bazaar and rummage.

Woman Police Constable Oh, is that what the smell is? I couldn't place it.

Margaret It's old clothes.

Woman Police Constable Is everything all right then?

Fliss Yes, we're going soon.

Woman Police Constable Could I stay for a moment?

The **Woman Police Constable** *slumps.*

Fliss Aren't you well?

Bell-Bell Would you like a drink of water?

Woman Police Constable No thank you, I've just had a cup of tea at the station.

There is a long, uncomfortable pause.

Margaret (*breaking it*) Have you got the time?

Woman Police Constable It's five fifty-seven and thirteen seconds, Madam. (*She is near to tears.*) It's a long while since anybody asked me the time.

Fliss Do you mind if we get on?

Woman Police Constable No, don't let me interfere in the course of your duties. I know how annoying that can be.

The **Woman Police Constable** *sits down heavily. The* **Women** *start to pack away, looking every now and then at the* **Woman Police Constable** *who sits slumped in the chair. There are loud whispers, the* **Woman Police Constable** *is an intruder.*

Margaret (*to* **Fliss**) What are we going to do with all this bleedin' rummage?

The trestle tables and chairs are put away.

Katrina Shush, Margaret! You'll get us done for obscene language. (*She looks at the* **Woman Police Constable**.)

Fliss We're taking it with us.

Margaret Where are we going?

Fliss Out!

The **Woman Police Constable** *sits with her head in her hands.*

Bell-Bell What's wrong with her?

They all look at the **Woman Police Constable**.

Margaret I ain't seen her before, I thought I knew 'em all round here. Our Darren brings 'em home with him.

Katrina *nervously approaches the* **Woman Police Constable.**

Katrina *(smiles)* Excuse me. *(She is trying to charm the* **Woman Police Constable**.)

Woman Police Constable *(jerking)* Yes, Madam?

Katrina Could you give me a lift home please? I'm an agoraphobic.

Woman Police Constable Frightened of cupboards are you?

Katrina No. The public. I was once pelted with plastic pineapples during my big finale.

Margaret Is that what they did to you, Kat?

Katrina Yes, one hit me in the eye. I had an awful bruise.

Margaret The bastards!

Woman Police Constable I agree with you, Madam, the public are bastards, lying, thieving, undisciplined bastards.

Fliss Are you sure you're in the right job?

Woman Police Constable I was all right in my panda car, but they took it off me for sleeping on the hard shoulder. I was thrown on to the streets – community policing. But I only clocked on at five. *(She cries.)*

Margaret If she's scared, there's no bleedin' hope for us, is there?

Katrina The public can be terrible once they turn.

Fliss But we're the public, aren't we? For Christ's sake we're half the population. Why should we be forced to stay at bloody home? Come on, we're going out. Grab a bag and a box each.

Katrina I can't, Fliss.

Bell-Bell Hold on to me, Katrina.

Margaret I'm shit scared, Fliss.

Fliss We'll keep together. We'll be all right if we keep together.

Woman Police Constable I joined because I wanted to help.

Margaret Come on then, Mrs Dixon, grab hold of this. (*She gives her a basket of shoes, then puts a box of toys and bric-à-brac on top.*) You look like a big, strong girl. Here!

Bell-Bell You all right, Kat?

Katrina Yes. (*She laughs.*)

Fliss Walk them down the path. Go on. (*She shuts the piano lid with a bang. The* **Woman Police Constable** *grabs the water pistol.*) You won't be needing that. Go on!

The **Woman Police Constable** *crosses to the* **Women** *at the door. They take a deep breath. They are still terrified of the outside world. They are not cured of their agoraphobia. They are leaving because they have no other choice.*

The **Women** *move together in an untidy, chaotic group holding bags and boxes. They turn and look into the hall. Then they leave.* **Katrina** *closes her eyes against the darkness outside.* **Fliss** *picks up a bag and box, looks around the room, crosses to the crucifix and looks at it for a moment.*

Cheer up!

She crosses to the door, puts the lights out, goes out and slams it shut.

Blackout.

Groping for Words

Groping for Words was first presented at the Croydon Warehouse Theatre on 10 March 1983, with the following cast:

Kevin	Andrew Paul
Joyce	Jan Davies
Thelma	Sarah Kenyon
George	Denys Graham

Directed by Sue Pomeroy
Designed by Kate Burnett
Sound by Carl Sutton
Lighting by Wiard Sterk

Act One

Scene One

A small classroom in a Victorian school is furnished with tiny chairs and tables, a square of carpet, floor cushions, the usual crèche teaching aids: beans in jars, a goldfish nature table, blackboard, wendy house, bricks, little library and jars of paint. On the walls are real children's paintings, (3 to 5 years old). There is one door and a large stock cupboard facing the audience.

*Voices are heard and keys rattle at the door. The door opens. **Kevin**, the caretaker, opens the door with some ceremony. He switches on the lights. He is wearing a short brown caretaker's coat, badges decorate the lapels. Underneath he wears a baggy 'Damned' T-shirt, blue jeans, big studded belt and training shoes. A copy of the* Sun *newspaper is sticking out of one pocket, a plastic container of darts is in his top pocket. His hair is slicked back 1950s American style. He is wearing one long dangling earring. His right hand is bandaged.*

Kevin (*as he puts the lights on*) Here we go.

Joyce *enters the room. She is middle-class, expensively and conventionally dressed, and is carrying an 'organiser' handbag.*

Kevin (*indicates the room*) This do you?

Joyce What is it?

Kevin It's the crèche.

Joyce So why are you showing it to me?

Kevin It's your room.

Joyce I'm teaching adults and I expect them to be the usual average height. (*She picks up a tiny chair with one finger.*) Could I see a proper classroom please?

She turns to leave.

Kevin There ain't one.

Joyce There is one. I booked it. I spoke to the caretaker last week.

Kevin Who, Horace?

Joyce A Mr Fillingham.

Kevin Bloke with a cleft palate?

Joyce He did sound rather indistinct over the phone.

Kevin Yeah, that's Horace. The Head Caretaker.

Joyce Where is he?

Kevin At home takin' care of himself for a change.

Joyce Why isn't he here doing his job? It's the first night of term.

Kevin He's been suspended for nickin' the cleanin' stuff.

Joyce So who's in charge?

Kevin Me. I'm Acting Head Caretaker until Horace has his court martial. He's bound to get done though. County Hall did a dawn swoop on his house. His box room was choc-a-block wiv dusters and bottles of bleach. (*Pause.*) His bleedin' house is filthy an' all.

Joyce I haven't time to listen to sordid little anecdotes, would you please show me to an adult-size classroom?

Kevin I keep tellin' you, there ain't one left. 'Livin' Wiv the Bomb' had the last one.

Joyce But there must be a room somewhere, this place is Victorian. The Victorians were extremely generous when it came to rooms.

Kevin An' it's full of people improving themselves. We've had a run on rooms. Look I'll have to go, I've got things to do.

Joyce *closes the door and stands in front of it.*

Joyce Oh no you don't, my lad.

Kevin Look the only empty room I've got is the boiler house an' it gets a bit hot in there.

Joyce Where's your allocation book?

Kevin I ain't got one, I carry it in me head.

Joyce Huh! That explains a great deal.

Kevin Whatja mean?

Joyce Well your outside appearance is extremely

unprepossessing isn't it? I shudder to think what the *inside* of your head is like.

Kevin Let me out, I've got a ballcock to fix.

Joyce Not until you've given me your name and works number.

Joyce *takes a pad and pencil from her bag.*

Kevin What for?

Joyce Reference.

Kevin Can't. (*He holds up his bandaged hand.*) I'm an injured soldier. (*Pause.*) A ferret took a bit out of my wrist.

Joyce In Clapham?

Kevin Straight up! I was cleaning its stinking cage out an' all. Ungrateful little bleeder! You do a dumb animal a good turn and where does it get you?

Joyce What's your name?

Kevin Kevin Muldoon.

Joyce (*writes*) And your works number?

Kevin Well Horace is number one in the hierarchy so I must be number two.

Joyce *writes.*

Kevin *is rebandaging his wrist.*

Joyce You're making an awful mess of doing that. (*Pause.*) Have you had it looked at?

Kevin I look at it now an' again. It's alright apart from the gangrene.

Joyce Gangrene?

Kevin (*laughs*) I wouldn't mind losing the odd finger, less weight to carry round ain't it?

Joyce I don't suppose you had a tetanus jab did you?

Kevin No I didn't. I'd sooner die of tetanus than have a needle stuck up me bum.

Joyce You're a very silly boy. And you're extremely lucky that you didn't get lockjaw. I have some medical knowledge and I've seen the consequences of neglect.

She is by now bandaging his wrist.

Kevin (*admiringly*) The consequences of neglect – (*Pause.*) You weren't here last term were you?

Joyce No, tonight's my first night.

Kevin Oh, you ain't 'Coming to Terms With Death' are you?

Joyce No I'm not. I hardly give it a thought.

Kevin Good job. Right miserable sods've registered for that. All got one foot in the grave.

Joyce You really are a mess aren't you? You should take a pride in your appearance.

Kevin So should you.

Joyce Don't be so rude! I do. I'm neat and tidy.

Kevin Bit boring though. If you hadn't spoke, I wouldn't have noticed you. An' I was looking your way.

Joyce Yes, well. Unlike you I don't wish to thrust myself into the foreground. I'm quite happy melting into the distance.

Joyce *touches* **Kevin**'s *earring.*

Joyce I'll never get used to seeing men wearing earrings. In my day one was suspicious of any man wearing suede shoes. Boys would follow them in the street, shouting 'Hello Oscar'.

Kevin Oscar who?

Joyce Oscar Wilde.

Kevin Who's he?

Joyce He's a very famous writer! He's a household name!

Kevin Not in our house he ain't.

Joyce *completes pinning the bandage.*

Kevin (*starts to remove his earring*) Wanna try it on?

Joyce No thank you. I can't wear cheap jewellery.

Kevin It ain't cheap! I paid two quid for this. Me mate makes 'em out of melted down bean tins. You pay for the labour, see. Go on, try it on.

Joyce Don't be so silly. My students will be arriving soon.

Kevin What you teachin'?

Joyce Literacy.

Kevin Books an' stuff? Well you'll be alright in here then, won't you? You can read books anywhere. My Grandma used to sit on the toilet to read her *Woman's Realm*.

Joyce You're mixing books up with magazines.

Kevin It's all writin' in it?'

Joyce *sighs and looks despondent.*

Kevin Tell you what. I'll swap you and the Buddhists over next week. They ain't into furniture.

Joyce Thank you.

Kevin Try it on. I wanna see what it looks like on you. I'm thinking of buying a pair for my auntie.

Joyce *inclines her head,* **Kevin** *brushes her hair away from her neck and ears.*

Kevin You got a nice neck for your age.

Joyce Thank you.

Kevin It's lovely an' soft. Clean an' all.

Joyce *stiffens.*

Kevin (*starts to insert earring*) You had a bath before you come out didn't you?

Joyce (*weakly*) Yes.

Kevin You got a big gob of talcum here. Shall I rub in in for you?

Joyce No don't bother.

Kevin S'all right.

Kevin *rubs the back of her neck.*

Kevin Lovely smell. Expensive I bet.

Joyce Sainsbury's, 76 pence family size.

Kevin *adjusts her collar, pushes her hair behind her ears and gives the earring a final tweak.*

Kevin You deserve better than that. (*Pause.*) It takes ten years off you. You look (*Pause.*) forty-five.

Joyce I *am* forty-five.

Kevin All right thirty-five then. You gonna let me go now?

Pause, he smiles.

Joyce Yes, all right. If anybody enquires for Adult Literacy could you let them know that that's me and where I am?

Kevin Can't you just stick a notice up?

Joyce No, my students can't read. That's why they're coming.

Kevin (*shocked*) Oh that's Literacy! (*Recovers.*) Poor sods, hard to credit it in this day an' age ain't it?

Joyce Yes it's very sad so please, be polite to them. They'll be awfully nervous.

Kevin It's the age we're livin' in, ain't it?

Kevin *exits.*

Joyce *takes a deep breath. She takes paper, pens, pencils and red exercise books out of her bag and arranges them on a little table. She takes her coat off, takes a mirror out of her bag and combs her hair. She looks at earring, grimaces, tries to take it out and can't do it. She struggles. She looks at her watch, struggles again and panics. She takes her scarf out of her bag and ties it turban-like around her head and ears. She tucks the earring inside and looks in her hand mirror.*

Joyce My God! It's Hilda Ogden! And I so wanted it to be Germaine Greer tonight. Stupid cow!

Scene Two

The corridor and caretakers' office and store.

A notice board listing the courses is on one wall. There is a sign saying 'lavatories'. **Kevin** *is in his cubby hole, brooding over a box of papers and smoking a cigarette.* **George** *enters hesitantly, he is wearing an old suit,* *shirt and tie and carrying a cloth bag and a plastic Marks and Spencer carrier bag. His shoes are polished, he seems to have spent some time in a cubicle in a men's hostel trying to disguise his poverty. He has a red, blue and black pen in his jacket pocket.*

George Evenin'.

Kevin Evenin'.

George It's cold out there. (*He rubs his hands together.*)

Kevin It's winter. It's bound to be cold.

George But we've not done bad have we, considering?

Kevin Look, I 'ate talkin' about the bleedin' weather.

George Yes, it is somewhat restricted as a topic of conversation. There's not a lot you can say about it really is there? Rainy, hot, cold, misty, windy . . .

Kevin (*more to himself*) Barmy!

George Yes, balmy. (*Pause.*) And humid's not a bad word.

Kevin Do you mind, only I'm doin' me paperwork. (*He rattles the box.*)

George Sorry. (*Pause.*) Do you mind if I have a peruse?

Kevin Feel free, peruse away. (*He raises his eyes.*)

George *peers at the notice board,* **Kevin** *reads.*

Kevin Are you for 'Comin' to Terms With Death'?

George No, I'm only fifty-seven! (*Pause.*) I don't know what I'm here for. I'm a bit undecided. I can't quite make up me mind.

Kevin You sound like a natural for 'Positive Thinking', pity the tutor rang and cancelled.

George What else is there?

Kevin It's all up there. (*He points to notice board.*) Creative Wine Drinkin's full though. Had to turn 'em away. It ain't everyday you can get pissed on the rates though, is it?

George You ought to take the notice down, then. Folks'll be disappointed. I don't mind for myself. I'm a beer drinker, wine's not my cup of tea.

Kevin *comes out of his cubby hole.*

Kevin I'm into cocktails. Quite heavily into 'em.

George Bit expensive in't it, for a young lad like you?

Kevin I can afford it. I'm in full-time employment. I'm one of the few. I work so that three and a half million can be free.

George That's one way of looking at it.

Kevin It's the only way. Survival of the fittest in this world ain't it? Which one *says* Creative Wine Drinkin'? I've come out without me glasses.

George Sorry I can't help you there. I've got new contact lenses in and me eyes are swimmin'.

Kevin (*staring into* **George**'s *eyes*) I can't see no contact lenses.

George No, but then you wouldn't would you? Not if you've not got your glasses.

Awkward pause.

Kevin There's 'Know Your Engine'.

He points randomly at the notice.

You got a car?

George No, I'm a pedestrian. I prefer walking.

Kevin Gettaway! You're the first *I've* met!

Pause.

Kevin (*impatiently*) Well have a look at the notice and choose yourself something! I've got these forms to fill in.

George *moves off, then turns.*

George Is there ought about writing up there?

Kevin Creative Writing's down the corridor. Bit of a Shakespeare are you?

George Not so you'd notice.

Telephone rings inside cubicle.

Kevin (*answers phone*) 'ello, Kevin Muldoon, Head Caretaker 'ere.

Tiny pause.

Spoggy! How ya doin'?

Pause.

Fuck me, we only done one last night!

Pause.

Yeah all right. What's the address?

He sees **George** *listening and half shuts his door.*

George *takes an airmail envelope from out of his inside jacket pocket. He takes a letter out and looks at it. He moons over a photograph and kisses it.*

Thelma *enters.*

George *puts the letter back in his pocket and stares at* **Thelma**. **Thelma** *is wearing dance class gear underneath very unmodish winter clothing. She is a young twenty year old. She should convey a bizarre appearance.*

Thelma I'm looking for the lavatory, do you know where it is? The Ladies' lavatory, that is?

George No, I've had no call to know, being a man.

Thelma I shall *have* to find it.

She does a little cross-legged dance. **George** *looks anxiously up and down the corridor.*

George The Caretaker's in there, but he's on the telephone.

Thelma *bangs on the cubicle door.* **Kevin** *opens the door angrily.*

Kevin I'm on the phone. (*He speaks into phone.*) Hang on, Sproggy.

Thelma Where's the Ladies' lavatory?

Kevin (*to* **Thelma**) Hang on!

Thelma I can't hang on! (*She is near to tears.*)

Kevin (*into phone*) Right, I'll have to go. See you about half-past eleven at your place then.

Short pause.

(*Into phone*) Right. See you. (*He puts the phone down.*)

Thelma (*to George*) It's because I'm nervous. I know it's all in my head but . . .

Kevin *comes out of the cubicle.*

Kevin Yeah, well keep it there. I only done this floor an hour ago. Down that corridor, second on the left.

Thelma *checks her left and right, then rushes off leaving her tote bag on the floor.*

Kevin (*indicating the lavatory sign*) I dunno, you go to the trouble to make bleedin' signs out, but do people bother to read 'em? Do they buggery!

George She's left her bag.

Kevin She'll be back for it. You know what women are like about their bleedin' handbags. (*He picks the bag up and puts it in the cubicle.*)

George (*plucking up his courage*) Have you got ought like a reading room here?

Kevin Yeah. But it has to be locked up at night. Some of these self-improvers are right tea leaves. Mind you half the bleedin' books are collectors' items. Been here since the building was opened.

Kevin *brings his tool box.*

George Can you manage with that hand?

Kevin Yeah, I got used to the pain, in fact I think it's made me a better 'uman bein'.

George How did you do it?

Kevin I slipped and fell on a cocktail stick. Went in one side. (*He holds his bandaged hand up.*) And came out the other. I 'ad to go down casualty and have the cherry removed.

George *walks back to look at the notice board.*

George (*quietly to himself*) Silly bugger!

Thelma *rushes in anxiously.*

Thelma Where's my bag?

Kevin It's in 'ere. Keep your hair on. (*He picks up the bag.*)

Thelma You shouldn't touch other people's property! Especially mine!

Kevin Why? What you got in here? A bomb? Dirty books? It's heavy ain't it? Let's 'ave a look!

He unzips the bag.

Thelma (*shrieks*) Don't! (*She snatches the bag from* **Kevin**)

Kevin All right! All right! Keep the noise down. You'll disturb the Buddhists.

Thelma I'd like to report that there's a man in the Ladies' toilet. He's in the last cubicle.

Kevin How do you know?

Thelma Because I could see his feet underneath the door.

Kevin Yeah, well the Ladies is bisexual tonight on account of flooding trouble in the Gents.

Thelma You might have warned me. I wasn't prepared for it.

Kevin There's a notice on the door ain't there?

Thelma No. There's a piece of toilet paper with rude drawings of a lady and a man.

Kevin They ain't rude! They're international symbols. Even an Eskimo would understand what they meant.

Thelma Well I'm not as Eskimo, am I?

Kevin *scrutinises* **Thelma.**

Kevin Dunno, you could be, it's hard to tell what you are under all that gear.

Thelma I'm Miss Thelma Churchill, (*Automatically.*) no relation. I registered over the phone. I don't trust the post.

Kevin It weren't me you spoke to.

Thelma Well whoever it was he said he'd put my name in the book.

Kevin What book?

Thelma I don't know! I was on the other end of the phone wasn't I? I was in Kensington.

Pause. **Kevin** *is sorting through papers in a box.*

Thelma And there's no toilet paper in the toilet either. (*Pause.*) You ought to have a system.

Kevin *waves a piece of paper about.*

Kevin Here it is. Miss Thelma Churchill. Room eleven and you'd better hurry, they're about to break the pain barrier.

Thelma *fiddles around in her bag.*

Kevin Right. I'm off on an errand of mercy. (*He picks up a double pack of toilet paper.*) Before they start wiping their bums on *The Standard* and clogging my 'S' bends.

Kevin *exits.*

Thelma Are you in a position of authority?

George No I'm just looking.

Thelma Oh. I thought you might be a teacher.

George (*pleased*) Did you? I expect it's because I'm wearing a tie, there's not many bother now-a-days.

Thelma No it's the pens. I like to see a pen in a man's pocket. It imparts an air of learning. My father had a very impressive array.

They stare at each other, then drop eye contact and shuffle.

Thelma Do you know where room eleven is?

George No. I'm a stranger here myself.

Thelma *looks around anxiously.*

George (*indicating notice board*) Can you see ought up there about reading and writing? I've come out without me glasses.

Thelma It's no good asking me. I've got a disease, it stops me reading properly.

George Oh I *am* sorry, is it painful?

Thelma No it's nothing like that. It's a brain problem.

George Oh dear. Are you under the hospital?

Thelma (*contemptuously*) Them! They don't know what they're on about, do they? It's a waste of time going down there. My mother took me to a private brain consultant. She said, 'My Thelma's got dyslexia.' He said, 'Who says?' My mum said, 'I say.' She'd been reading up on it, but he wouldn't have it! He wouldn't listen! He said that I was over-anxious! And he tried to give me and my mother something for our nerves! We were that disgusted we walked out! We thought about reporting him, but what's the point? They all stick up for each other don't they?

George Yes they're bound by their hypocritical oath.

Thelma Do you know what time it is? I've got to register at half-past seven.

George (*bringing out alarm clock*) It's a quarter to eight! I'm late. Me first lesson and I'm late! (*He panics and stuffs his gear into his bag.*)

Thelma A quarter to eight! Oh no! I shall be told off!

Joyce *enters, still wearing the scarf. She goes to the cubicle and sees* **Kevin** *isn't there.*

Joyce (*to* **Thelma**) Excuse me. Have you see the caretaker?

Thelma The scruffy one?

Joyce Yes.

Thelma Sorry, you're not his mother are you?

Joyce Certainly not!

George He's gone off replenishing supplies.

Joyce Oh dear . . . (*to* **Thelma**) Look, I know this is perfectly absurd, but could you help me with this wretched earring? (*She has taken her scarf off.*) I can't get it out on my own. I've been struggling for . . . (*She gives a feeble laugh.*)

Thelma I've never seen one like that before. I wouldn't know where to begin. And anyway I'm supposed to be in my night-class, do you know where room eleven is?

Joyce Upstairs, next to the big hall.

Thelma *rushes off.*

George Do you want me to have a go?

Joyce It's very kind of you . . . but I don't want to detain you. You look as if you're on your way somewhere.

George No. No. I'm just . . . here.

Joyce Well perhaps we could go into my room. This is very embarrassing. I wouldn't wear anything like this normally . . .

George *is peering at the earring.*

George You just fancied a change did you? Well why not?

Joyce But I'm expecting students and first impressions are so important aren't they?

George Yes. They colour everything. Once seen never forgotten . . . Well if you'll just sort of bend your head.

Joyce *bends,* **George** *twists and turns trying to avoid body contact while he unfastens the earring.*

Scene Three

In the crèche.

George You're an infant teacher are you? (*He puts his bag down.*)

Joyce No, I teach adults. At least I'm hoping to, nobody seems to have turned up yet.

George If you could sit down sort of . . .

Joyce *sits on a little chair.* **George** *squats at her side.*

George I don't know how to tackle it. It's in a right old mess.

Joyce If I put my head to one side like this . . . (*She turns her head away from* **George**.)

George That's better. Now the dog can see the rabbit.

Scene Four

Back outside **Kevin**'s *cubicle.* **Thelma** *is waiting.* **Kevin** *enters.*

Thelma You sent me to the wrong place! I don't want to go to Jane Fonda's robotics classes.

Kevin How did I know? You look like a robot. You're dressed like a robot. You even sound like one.

Thelma Well I'm not. I put my name down for the reading lessons. It's in the book.

Kevin What readin'? We got Shakespeare Can Be Fun . . . Clapham Playwrights' Circle . . .

Thelma This is *just* reading. From the beginning, starting from scratch.

Kevin Literacy is the word you're looking for.

Thelma No it isn't! I don't know what it means so how can I be looking for it?

Kevin Adult Literacy. Room six.

Thelma Where's that?

Kevin Bleedin' 'ell! It's up there in black and white! Can't you do numbers either?

Thelma No, not when I'm upset.

Kevin Come on!

They leave for **Joyce**'s *room.*

Scene Five

Joyce's *room.*

Joyce (*loud scream*) Ah! That hurt!

George I'm sorry. Shall I desist?

Joyce No just get it out will you?

George Just one more pull. (*He tugs.*)

Joyce *screams.*

George Shall I proceed?

Joyce Yes I'm sorry, it's just that I've got a very low pain threshold.

George I don't like hurting you.

Joyce No please go on, hurt me.

George Right. One, two, three ready?

Joyce nods, **George** *tugs,* **Joyce** *screams louder and falls over,* **George** *falls on top of her.* **Kevin** *runs in, jumps astride* **George**'s *chest and pins his arms down.* **Thelma** *enters.*

Kevin You dirty bleeder! (*He turns to* **Thelma***.*) Ring 999 and tell 'em I've got the Wandsworth Wanker.

Thelma *moves towards the door.*

Joyce Don't you dare!

Kevin (*to* **Joyce**) He didn't touch you did he?

Kevin *threatens* **George** *with a head butt.*

Thelma I thought he had funny eyes!

Thelma *is helping* **Joyce** *up.*

Kevin Yes I had him marked down as a deviant, they all wear pens in their top pockets. It's a well-known fact that is.

Joyce (*to* **Kevin**) Get off him! Get off! You're hurting him.

Joyce (*to* **George**) I'm terribly sorry.

Thelma Shall I fetch the police?

Kevin Yeah.

Joyce (*shouting to* **Kevin**) Get off! Get off!

She pushes **Kevin***, then turns to* **George**.

Are you all right?

George No, I'm having a few difficulties breathing.

Thelma What is it, 999?

Kevin Yeah, go on! Just wait 'til they get you down the nick, pervert. They'll knock the breath out of you permanent. You'll be lucky if you come out there with your balls intact.

Thelma They ought to castrate them.

Kevin (*to* **Thelma**) What you waiting for?

Thelma Have you got five p?

Joyce *is pushing* **Kevin**, *she is grunting with the effort.*

George (*to* **Kevin**) I was very careful to avoid any erotic contact. I kept strictly away from any danger zones.

Kevin Not far enough! She's a decent woman. She's got Marks and Spencer labels all over her!

Joyce (*bellows*) Leave him alone! He was doing me a favour!

She punches **Kevin** *repeatedly.*

Thelma I shall have to go. All this violence is unsettling me.

Joyce (*to* **George**) Don't just lie there man! Help me!

George *wrestles* **Kevin** *backwards.* **Kevin** *lies on the floor panting.*

George That's the last time I help a stranger out of a dilemma situation.

Joyce *and* **George** *kneel together, mutually supporting each other, dishevelled and breathing heavily.*

Joyce (*to* **George**) I'm awfully sorry. (*to* **Kevin**.) This gentleman was removing your odious earring. You owe him a grovelling apology.

Thelma (*to* **Kevin**) You must have a mind like a sewer, in fact a cess pit.

Kevin I thought he was the Wandsworth Wanker. I have to be careful, you get a lot of nutters coming to night classes. They've got the time for it.

George It was a case of mistaken identity was it? (*Worried.*) Do I look like this Wandsworth . . . (*Gags at saying wanker.*) . . . ladies present.

Kevin Nobody's seen his face, he wears a pair of 'Y' fronts over his head. So you could have been him see?

George Yes I quite understand. Here. (*He hands* **Kevin** *the earring.*)

Kevin It's a funny shape for an earring.

Joyce Yes, it's made out of a baked bean tin.

Thelma Crosse and Blackwell or Heinz?

Kevin It's symbolic.

Joyce Of what?

Kevin Society and how it screws you up. (*He offers it to* **Joyce**.) Do you wanna keep it?

Joyce No thank you. I don't wish to be regarded as one of society's victims.

George (*dusting himself off*) Well I'd better depart. (*He starts repacking his belongings.*)

Kevin (*indicates* **Thelma**) I found you a student.

Joyce Oh, I'll be with you in a moment, dear. Hello.

Thelma Hello.

Kevin Anybody else turn up yet?

Joyce No, not yet.

Kevin You should try teaching someting a bit more popular. Cocktail Shakin', somethin' like that. Adult Literacy! Don't reach out and grab you, do it?

George You teach Adult Literacy do you? That must be very interesting.

Joyce Yes. I'm sure it is. Perhaps one day I'll find out.

Kevin Can't imagine not readin' or writing' can you?

Joyce You'll be surprised how many there are.

George Two million they reckon. It was on Radio Four. Jill Archer told Walter Gabriel.

Thelma Your ear's bleeding. Do you want a plaster on it?

Joyce Yes please. My husband warned me about coming into Clapham at night, he said I'd return home bloodstained. I'd hate to give him the satisfaction of being right.

Thelma There's a washbasin in the bisexual lavatory. I've got some cotton wool in my bag. I could see to it for you. I know what I'm doing. I was in the St John's Ambulance once.

Joyce Thank you.

Joyce *and* **Thelma** *exit.*

George So she's the teacher is she? I didn't expect a woman somehow.

Kevin You don't want to go to her class. You heard her, she's for the dumbo's what can't read.

George All the same I think I'll have a word with her. I've got a friend who's a bit rusty on his reading. She might be able to help him.

George *sits down.*

Kevin Hey! How's Joe Grundy doing? I ain't heard it since my Grandma died.

George (*pleased*) He's cheered up a lot since Clarrie's happy event.

Kevin Eddie still giving him bovver is he?

George Yes, that's one lad who'll never change.

Kevin It's hard to change yourself though, ain't it? Least, that's what I've found.

George It's making the first move that's the hardest.

Kevin See you around. Sorry about the bit of bovver.

George Oh I'm getting used to it now I'm domiciled in London. It's part of my daily existence.

Kevin *exits.* **George** *picks up the text books, looks through them, decides that the contents are beyond him and loses his nerve. He picks up his belongings and exits into the corridor.*

Scene Six

The corridor and **Kevin***'s cubby hole. Follow on from last scene.* **George** *passes* **Kevin** *who is throwing darts savagely into the notice board.*

Kevin You ain't staying for a chat then?

George What?

Kevin About your friend's reading?

George No. He's decided not to bother.

Kevin You're in telepathic communication are you?

George No, he's not on the phone.

George *exits.*

Scene Seven

In the classroom. Follow on from last scene. **Thelma** *and* **Joyce** *enter.*
Joyce *is holding a piece of cotton wool to her ear.*

Thelma (*gushing*) It's a lovely little room isn't it? I didn't have
time to notice it before, and you've even got a goldfish! He's got
a lovely little face.

Pause.

(*She turns to the fish*) What's your name then?

Joyce Joyce Chalmers.

Thelma That's a funny name for a fish.

Joyce The fish's name is written on the bowl.

Thelma *turns her back on* **Joyce.**

Thelma (*in a totally different grown-up voice*) I've just told you I
can't read, so it's no good telling me that is it?

Joyce (*crossing to the bowl*) I'm sorry. It says 'DARREN'.

Thelma Darren? How do they know it's a boy? Hello Darren. I
love all living creatures, don't you?

Joyce Not quite all.

Joyce *finds a plaster and a pair of children's blunt scissors, she gives them
to* **Thelma.**

Joyce Would you mind? Then we can get down to some work
can't we?

Thelma Oh aren't they sweet! Just think about all the chubby
little fingers that have held these scissors.

Joyce *sits down on a tiny chair,* **Thelma** *stands over her. She pulls*
Joyce'*s head around and prepares to place the plaster.*

Thelma I shall have to take my things off first. I can't move my arms.

She removes her scarf and coat and leaves her hat on. She is now looking distinctly odd. She is wearing a neon body stocking, leg warmers, a P.E. skirt, granny boots and a hideous shrunken cardigan which says 'Thelma' on the back. Her cardigan has a 'T' brooch hanging loosely from it. She is also wearing a chain necklace with a 'T' pendant.

Thelma I promised Mum that I'd wrap up warm when I came down to London. I've got a chest – and bad ears.

Joyce Have you lived in London long?

Thelma No. I've only been here for three weeks. But I know it really well already.

Joyce I hardly know it at all and I've lived here all my life.

Thelma You ought to go on a double-decker tour of the tourist spots. It's the only way to see it properly. It gets a bit blowy so make sure you wear something over your ears.

Thelma *puts the plaster on.*

There!

Joyce Thank you. Right, now if you'll give me a moment to get myself sorted out.

Thelma You're going grey, did you know?

Joyce (*with gritted teeth*) I've known for some years.

Thelma I only pointed it out in case you wanted to do something about it.

There is a knock at the door.

Joyce Excuse me.

She opens the door, **George** *is standing there.*

George Sorry for disturbing the peace. I'm Mr Bishop. I know we've been in contact, but we haven't met.

They shake hands solemnly.

Joyce Come in. (*She ushers him in.*) I'm Mrs Chalmers. Joyce.

George Can I have a word with you? Well more than one to be exact. A few words. (*He sees* **Thelma** *and drops his head.*) In private so to speak.

He wipes his face with his hands.

Joyce (*to* **Thelma**) I don't know your name do I?

Thelma Thelma Churchill, no relation.

Joyce Thelma would you mind if I spoke to Mr Bishop privately? Alone?

Thelma Do you mean you want me to go into another room?

George Sorry to put you out. Inconvenience you.

Thelma I've only just got here myself!

Thelma *goes into the wendy house and sits down.* **Joyce** *and* **George** *stand awkwardly looking at the wendy house.*

Joyce (*in a loud whisper to* **George**) Is this private enough?

George (*to* **Thelma**) Would you mind closing the door?

Thelma *bangs the wendy house door shut and pulls the curtains. Pause.*

George Well, it's took me a long while to get here and now I'm here I can't seem to . . . say what I came here to say.

Joyce Shall we sit down? (**Joyce** *sits down on a tiny chair.*)

George I'm used to standing. I'm a pedestrian. (*He remains standing.*)

Joyce (*after a pause*) Is it connected with reading?

George Yes.

Joyce And writing?

George Yes. I've got a friend who's a bit rusty.

Joyce And your friend needs help with his reading and writing?

George He can't read and he can't write. He's illiterate so to speak. But he's made up his mind to do something about it. He's getting on a bit. As a matter of fact he's the same age as me or thereabouts. Give or take a week. But he says he's had enough of guessin' and tellin' lies. He's fed up with it. He's had enough. He's not too old is he?

Joyce No.

Long pause.

Joyce When does your friend want to start?

George As soon as possible.

Joyce Does he live in London?

George Yes he's down here looking for work. He's not having much luck. There's a lot of avenues closed to him.

Joyce Shall I give you a few details?

George *sits down on a tiny chair.*

George Details, yes that's what he wants.

Joyce We meet on Wednesdays from half seven to half nine. It will cost your friend fourteen pounds a term . . .

George Oh, he thought it was free.

Joyce No, unfortunately we have to pay for the room.

George *looks round.*

Joyce We won't be in here every week. Don't worry. (*Pause.*) Tell your friend not to worry. (*Pause.*) Will the money be a problem to your friend?

George He's out of work you see. He hasn't got fourteen pounds. Not on him.

Long pause.

Joyce You could pay me so much a week. Would that be convenient?

George Yes. (*He lowers his head, ashamed of lying.*) When can I start?

Joyce Tonight.

George Right, that's all right then. (*He smiles.*)

Joyce And your full name is?

George (*very drawn out*) George Arthur Bishop.

Joyce *writes.*

Joyce And where are you living, Mr Bishop?

George In London.

Joyce Whereabouts?

George (*evasively*) Not far from here.

Joyce I have to register you with the Education Authority. So I'll need your full address.

George Care of the Rowton Ho . . . Hotel, Wandsworth Road.

Joyce Can I reach you on the telephone there?

George Oh no. I'm incommunicado in that respect. (*Slight pause.*) And they're not too keen on their guests having visitors either, that's the rules.

Joyce (*slight laugh*) It doesn't sound a very hospitable hotel. Who's it run by, the War Office?

George It's sort of run on military lines.

Joyce Oh a sort of ex-serviceman's club! I see.

Thelma *draws the curtains and sticks her head out of the window.*

Thelma Can I come out now? Only, the walls are closing in on me.

George *gets up and opens the door,* **Thelma** *shuffles out on her hands and knees.* **George** *helps her to her feet.*

Thelma Are you learning as well?

George Yes, why are you?

Thelma I was here first. (*To* **Joyce**.) Are you sure you can manage two? I saw a programme on telly and this man had a teacher to himself. He got on ever so well. He was reading the *Sun* within weeks.

Joyce The *Sun*! My dear girl we're going to set our sights a little higher than that.

George *sits down and wipes his face.*

Joyce Miss Churchill, Mr Bishop . . .

George Very nice to . . . (*He stands up and the chair comes with him. They shake hands.*)

Joyce I'll need your address, Thelma.

Thelma Do you want to know where I live now, or where I really live? Because I really live in Northampton. I'm only here in London because of my job. It takes too long to travel to Northampton every day. I don't know how those computers manage it, going backwards and forwards.

Joyce Your London address is fine.

Thelma 10, Gladstone Mansions, Kensington.

Joyce *writes it down.*

Joyce Why have you come all the way to Clapham?

Thelma I don't want Mrs Eirenstone to find out. She thinks I can read. ·

Joyce Mrs Eirenstone is your employer, is she?

Thelma Yes. I look after her children. She's one of those working mothers who couldn't do without me. And I don't want her to do without me. I love London. It's got a bit more life than Northampton. There's more to do at night. Mrs Eirenstone's out every night, she's ever so popular. You should see her clothes! I've known her pay twenty pounds for a scarf! Hard to believe isn't it? But it's true. Twenty pounds!

George She sounds a wonderful woman, a bit extravagant perhaps but vibrant. Is she having a night in tonight then?

Thelma Yes. She's having a row with Mr Eirenstone. (*Pause.*) Mrs Eirenstone has asked me to teach Davina, that's her little girl, to read.

Joyce Oh I see.

Thelma She's got her into a very expensive school, you see, and Davina will feel left out if she doesn't know how to read.

Joyce How old is Davina?

Thelma She was three at Christmas. Mrs Eirenstone has sent away for the early reading books. In fact they've already come. But Mrs Eirenstone doesn't know yet.

George You intercepted the postman did you?

Thelma No, I took the parcel and shoved it in the back of my wardrobe. I have to take it out with me if I go out. I've been carrying it around all week. (*She pulls the parcel out of her bag and puts it on the table.*) So if you can teach me to read these I'd be ever so grateful.

Joyce *thumbs through the early reading books.*

Joyce (*disapprovingly*) But these books were written in the 1940s and they're far too simple.

Thelma Well I'm simple myself. Least that's what they said at school. (*Little laugh.*) I was bottom of the class. 31 out of 31.

Joyce But Thelma, my approach is going to be quite different. These books are written for very small children. I'd like you to leave me in a few years being able to read everything.

Thelma A few years! But I haven't got that long! Mrs Eirenstone's already talking about complaining to the Post Office about the late delivery.

George I can't wait a few years either. I've got a daughter in Australia! It's not the reading I'm so bothered about, it's the writing. I want to learn to write so I can reply to her letters.

He pulls an air mail letter out of his pocket.

Look! (*He passes it to* **Joyce**.) She's a lovely writer isn't she? She won a prize at school. She got *Uncle Tom's Cabin* for neatness of handwriting.

Joyce Yes. (*She hands it back.*) Very nice.

George Would you like to see her photograph?

He passes a photograph.

Joyce What a pretty girl!

Thelma Can I have a look? (*She looks.*) She's lovely looking isn't she? She's not a bit like you. What's that funny shape in the background?

George That's her husband, Malcolm.

Thelma No the *big* funny shape?

Joyce *looks.*

Joyce It's the Sydney Opera House. My husband was there last year.

George Has he got kith and kin in the antipodes?

Joyce No, he was there on holiday. He's a Grand Opera lover. At least he was until he saw the Sydney Opera House.

Thelma And he didn't take you? That's not very fair is it?

Joyce (*this still rankles*) No it wasn't, was it? I mentioned it to him at the time.

George (*gazing at photo*) She'd do anything for anybody. You could warm your hands on her heart. (*His face crumples.*)

Joyce *stands and pats him on the back.*

Joyce (*kindly*) It won't be long before you can reply. I'll help you, that's what I'm here for, isn't it?

George But I can't even read it. I don't know how she is or ought.

Joyce But somebody would have read it to you.

George Who?

Joyce Anybody.

George I didn't want *anybody* reading her letter.

Joyce Haven't you got a family?

George In Australia. My wife, her new husband and my girl and her husband. They're all out there to grasp the opportunities. They're carving out better futures.

Joyce Friends at work?

George I haven't got any work. Not anymore.

Joyce I see. Perhaps when you know me better . . . I'd be pleased to.

George You can read it now! (*He holds the letter out.*)

Joyce But we really ought to get on. I need to find out what you can both do.

George Can't do more like. (**George** *moons over the letter.*)

Thelma (*to* **George**) And I'm in a hurry. It's not fair on me if she starts reading your letters.

Joyce (*to* **George**) How many pages are there?

George Just the one.

Joyce (*to* **Thelma**) Do you know what tracing is?

Thelma Of course I do! I'm not that stupid! Honestly!

Joyce I have to ask, don't I?

Thelma I know what most words *mean*. It's the writing and reading stage I'm stuck on.

Joyce Can you write your name?

Thelma I can do Thelma.

Joyce But not your surname, not Churchill?

Thelma No, I was away when we did surnames.

Joyce I'm going to write 'Churchill'. (*She writes Churchill in very large print on a flash card.*)

Thelma That's too big! I'd never write it that big would I?

Joyce It's to get you used to the shape of the letters.

Thelma It seems stupid to me! It's a waste of time.

Joyce Look, I know what I'm doing.

George She's trained for years to be a teacher. Haven't you Mrs Chalmers?

Joyce Not years.

George Well a year then.

Joyce Not a year, no.

George Some months then?

Joyce Six weeks.

George Six weeks is a long time. (*Pause.*) Quite long.

Thelma So you're not a proper teacher?

Joyce I'm trained to teach literacy.

Thelma I thought I'd be in the hands of an expert. I need expert attention. I'm very slow.

Joyce Who said?

Thelma The school. They said I was backward.

Joyce You're not backward, Thelma.

Thelma Oh yes I am! Cleverer people than you have told me I am!

Joyce Mr Bishop, would you mind stepping out a moment?

George (*holding up the letter*) What about . . .

Joyce Two minutes.

George *exits into corridor.*

Joyce I'm going to tell you something, Thelma. (*Dramatic pause, her intention is to galvanise* **Thelma**.) I'm a very clever woman. I'm cleverer than any of your teachers at school. I could have been a professor of English if I'd wanted, but I thought it might be more fun to get married and live in Streatham, so I did, and it wasn't. (*Small pause.*) But! I carried on studying and reading and I got cleverer and cleverer. I wouldn't be surprised if I'm not some sort of genius by now, actually. Then I thought what shall I do with all this cleverness? (**Thelma** *is wrapped up in the story.*) I know! I said. I'll be a literacy tutor. I'll share my genius. So you see Thelma, just by coming into contact with me, *your* brain power is automatically increased. You *will* learn to read and write, because *I* Joyce Chalmers, am teaching you.

Thelma Oh I see, that's a different complexion isn't it?

Joyce Yes, so trace over my letters will you?

Thelma *picks up a pencil.*

Joyce Hold the pencil a bit further down.

Joyce *adjusts the pencil for* **Thelma**. **Thelma** *traces very carefully over the letters. Her tongue is out, she is tense and anxious.*

Scene Eight

George *is in the corridor talking to* **Kevin** *in his cubicle.*

Kevin Your friend change his mind did he?

George I thought I might as well ask for him as I was in the vicinity.

Kevin You been having a long chat, ain't you?

George You know how it is, one word leads to another and before you know it you're having a conversation. (*Pause.*) Finding you've got things in common.

Kevin What have you and that dumbo teacher got in common then?

George (*pause*) Well we're both interested in . . . Rolf Harris.

Kevin Rolf Harris! What's interesting about Rolf Harris?

George How he gets away with it, I suppose.

Kevin Here, do you reckon if I wobbled a bit of cardboard and threw a bit of paint on the wall, I'd end up living in a mansion with peacocks on the lawn?

George He lives in a mansion does he?

Kevin Yes, with round-the-clock alsatians.

George How do you know?

Kevin I don't do I? I just make it up, it keeps me brain active. I might be needing it one day.

George In what capacity?

Kevin Well I might go in for an education.

George Yes, it's just as well to have something to fall back on.

Kevin Bloke I know murdered his next-door neighbour. Got ten years in Gartree, does six, comes out with a degree in English literature.

George That's wonderful! (*Slight pause.*) Bit hard on the next-door neighbour though.

Kevin He should have turned his stereo down when he was asked.

George Mind if I sit down? (*He sits on the floor.*)

Kevin No. You *look* knackered.

George I am, I didn't get any sleep last night. We had a little unpleasantness at the . . . er . . . hotel. One of the guests went a little berserk and stabbed a social worker. It caused a bit of a rumpus. Fortunately the injuries were superficial.

Kevin Yeah, I heard about that, only it wasn't a hotel it was a hostel.

George Yes, yes that's right a hostel. I keep getting it wrong.

Kevin Bleeding horrible place that is. You don't want to stay there, you'll catch something.

George And the residents are quite troublesome. If they're not drunk they're stealing off you. I had an overcoat once.

Kevin So where are you kipping tonight then?

George I don't know. Me Post Office book is down to seventeen pence. I'm in the hands of fate so to speak.

Joyce (*off*) Mr Bishop.

George I've got to go.

Kevin Yeah. Lucky you. She ain't bad for an old bird is she?

Scene Nine

George *enters the classroom.*

George Miss Churchill looks busy. What are you doing?

Thelma Don't! You'll make me go wrong.

Joyce Over here Mr Bishop, I'll read your letter.

They settle down.

Joyce 'Dear Dad, Well we got here after a safe journey. Malcolm didn't like the plane but I thought it was fantastic. I'm sitting writing to you in shorts and a halter neck on account of how hot it is here. Malcolm got sunburned and had to have the doctor. But he is all right now.

George He's very fair skinned.

Joyce (*reading*) 'Malcolm has gone to see his Auntie Kath, that's why I have a few moments to spare. Gordon . . .

George Gordon's my wife's husband.

Joyce (*reading*) is still getting on my nerves. I'll never take to him, Dad. Still, me and Malcolm will soon have our own place with a bit of luck. We are still in the hostel as yet. It isn't bad but it's noisy at night. Anyway Dad, God bless and take care of yourself. Your loving daughter Jennifer.' And there's a P.S.

Kevin enters jangling keys.

Kevin Don't mind me. Oh 'ello, still here Wandsworth? You *are* havin' a long chat about your friend ain't you?

George My name's George.

Kevin (*to* **Thelma**) Christ gel. You'd never get on the list of the world's best dressed women.

Thelma You can talk, I've seen scarecrows better dressed than you.

Joyce What are you doing in here? We're in the middle of something important. We've been allocated this highly unsuitable room, now the least you can do is to leave us in peace in it.

Kevin I've got to come in here. It's where I keep the harmful chemicals.

He unlocks the store cupboard.

Joyce In the crèche?

Kevin Don't blame me! It's Horace's doing. I've inherited his system.

He takes a bottle of Harpic powder and a gallon container of bleach out of the cupboard.

Joyce Do you realise how dangerous that stuff is? If any child got hold of these containers . . .

Kevin I keep it locked don't I? I ain't a fool. Just 'cos I'm doing a menial job it don't mean I ain't got it up here. You shouldn't underestimate the workers Mrs Chalmers. It could land you and your sort in a lot of bother.

Joyce What do you mean by 'my sort'?

Kevin Well it's the opposite of my sort ain't it?

Joyce You're talking about the great class divide are you?

Kevin Yeah, that and other things.

Thelma My mum says that we're all working class now, even the Queen has to work, opening power stations and things.

Kevin (*mock forgetfulness, hand to forehead*) Course, I keep forgettin' the old working class ain't workin' anymore is it? All you educated people have got the jobs. Course, there's a few of us left to mess around with ballcocks.

Thelma Do you have to swear? It's not nice is it Mrs Chalmers?

Joyce He wasn't swearing Thelma. A ballcock is a technical term, it's part of a cistern.

Thelma I don't care what system it's part of. I don't like language.

Kevin That's 'cos you're bleedin' ignorant of what language is!

George Well we're all here for that reason aren't we? Can we get on?

Kevin You ain't got long, I'm locking up in twenty minutes!

He goes to exit.

Joyce That's a lethal mixture of chemicals. I hope you've read the instructions on those containers.

Kevin (*scornful laugh*) It ain't exactly bedside reading is it? (*Mocks.*) Oh what shall I read tonight? Yes, I'll take a bottle of Harpic up with me and snuggle down for a good read. (*Contemptuous laugh.*) Can't stand here chatting, I've got a filthy bog to clean out. One of your posh creative wine tasters has just spewed his guts up. Rather an 'amusing' little vintage. Goodnight, dumbos!

He slams the door and exits. **Joyce** *is furious, trembling.*

Joyce Try not to let him bother you.

There is lots of displacement activity.

Joyce My God! It's no wonder the country's on its knees! I've always thought of myself as a humanitarian but just lately compulsory euthanasia for teenagers looks an attractive proposition. Don't you agree?

George (*baffled*) Yes.

Thelma I didn't understand anything you said.

George I got the drift, so to speak. Can we carry on with the letter?

Joyce Yes. As I was saying (*She is trying to calm down.*) there's a P.S. (*Reading.*) 'I know you hate writing Dad, but please let me know how you're getting on in London. By the way, Mum doesn't know I am writing to you. It's easier that way.'

Joyce *folds up the letter.*

George So she's all right. (*Pause.*) Thank you. Very nicely read.

Joyce So your daughter doesn't know about your difficulties?

George No, her mother did all the writing that there was to be done. It made things very awkward for me when my wife remarried . . . Awkward in every which way.

Joyce How long have you had the letter?

George It's coming up for eight weeks. She'll be getting worried. I haven't been able to reply.

Thelma (*to* **Joyce**) He could have sent a telegram. Dictated it. That would have been the sensible thing to do.

George Not a telegram! She'd think I'd passed on!

Thelma She'd know that you hadn't when she opened it!

George But it's the first shock. No, not a telegram.

Joyce A postcard wouldn't overtax her would it? You could write something like, Everything OK. Love Dad.

Thelma (*scornfully*) Everthing OK. Love Dad! It's not much of a message to send thousands of miles.

Joyce It's better than nothing.

George Yes, it says everything I want to say.

Thelma But he can't write can he?

George That's the stumbling block.

Joyce I can. I could write it for you.

Thelma But she'll know it's not his handwriting.

George I haven't got any handwriting! (*Pause.*) But it's deceitful isn't?

Joyce It'll stop her worrying.

Thelma And they do say . . . (*Small pause.*) What the something doesn't know, the something doesn't grieve over.

George (*not convinced*) Yes.

Joyce I've got a postcard somewhere, (*She hunts in her bag.*) and a stamp.

Thelma That's an organiser bag isn't it?

Joyce Yes, and I can never find a thing in it.

She finds the postcard and produces it.

George It's very colourful. Go on then, yes she'd like that.

Thelma Ugh, it's modern art. My mother says that chimpanzees could do better.

Joyce Your mother knows what she likes, does she Thelma?

Pause.

The address Mr Bishop.

She copies the address from the letter.

Thelma Yes, she's got firm opinions on most things, she's a bit set in her ways. It's because she's old. She had me late, I was an afterbirth. (*Pause.*) She's one of the oldest women in Britain to give birth, she's famous for it in Northampton. I used to fetch her pension on my way home from school. Her home help gets it now.

Joyce There you are, Mr Bishop.

George Well, that's most kind, and very neat. If I had a copy of

Uncle Tom's Cabin I'd present you with it. (*Admiring the postcard.*)
The bloke who painted this knew his stuff.

Joyce Picasso.

George Yes. I've heard of him. (*He puts the card away.*)

Joyce *gets up and walks about the room.*

Joyce I want to talk to you for a moment about the learning
process. You see, although you both *think* you're illiterate –
(*Speaks quickly.*) Ugly word, like illegitimate. You can probably
read a lot more than you think. Street names, shop names, brand
names like Kelloggs, Persil, Bisto and so on. So we'll start with
these very familiar words and then progress to more formal
exercises. I want to get away from the formality of the classroom,
after all, the classroom failed you once so . . .

George*'s hand is in the air.*

What is it Mr Bishop?

George Could I be excused, please Miss?

Joyce Mr Bishop, there's no need to . . . Yes of course.

George *gets up and exits.*

Joyce How are you doing? (*She looks.*) Very good! Well done!

Thelma Can you read the first page of this for me now? (*She
picks up the* Janet and John Work Book.) Just teach me the first
word.

Joyce But what use is a word like Janet going to be to you? You
need to know useful words like 'Stop', 'On', 'Off', Etcetera!

Thelma Etcetera! That's a word I'd never use.

Joyce We'll do a deal. You do half a lesson for Davina. All right?

Thelma All right.

Joyce (*with book*) This word says Janet. What does it say?

Thelma Janet! You've just told me!

Joyce Now do the same as you did when you traced your surname.
This letter says 'J' pronounced 'Juh'. Do you know the alphabet?

Thelma Of course I do!

Joyce Say it for me would you?

Thelma *sings the alphabet song. She gets as far as 'N', when she is interrupted by a loud battering on the door.*

Thelma It's Mrs Eirenstone. She's found me! She thinks I'm here to do Robotics! Quick, teach me a few steps. Pretend to be my Robotics teacher, please! Please!

She's in complete panic.

Joyce All right! Calm down!

Joyce *opens the door,* **George** *falls in with a semi-conscious* **Kevin.**

Thelma Oh that's a relief!

George Help me to get him to the table!

Joyce *and* **George** *support* **Kevin.**

Joyce What have you done to him Mr Bishop?

George I've done nought to him. I found him with his head down the lavvy!

They lay **Kevin** *on his back on the table, his head overlapping the table facing the audience.*

Thelma Ugh!

George He's had a go at doing himself in!

Kevin I ain't!

George There's a horrible smell in there, like gas it is. It fair knocked me back.

Joyce Kevin, Kevin! Did you use Harpic and bleach in the same lavatory bowl?

Kevin I always do. Normally I chuck it in and run back out quick, but the bleedin' door jammed. Next thing I know is old Wandsworth here is leaning over me telling me I've got everything to live for.

Joyce You didn't read the instructions did you?

Kevin No.

Joyce You can't read can you?

Kevin No. Not a fucking word.

After a long pause.

Kevin 'As anybody got a fag?

Thelma You mustn't smoke! Your lungs will explode!

Joyce You need some fresh air and then you must go home and rest.

Kevin No, I've gotta ring the bell for home time.

George I can do that, I'm a dab hand at bells.

Kevin No, I've gotta lock up.

George I can do that an' all! There's nought I like better than having a bunch of keys in my hand.

Joyce Let Mr Bishop help, Kevin, you ought to rest.

Kevin *sits slumped on the table, he unclips the keys from his waist.*

Kevin Look if the Education find out that I'm . . . that . . .

Thelma You're illiterate.

Kevin (*shouting*) All right! That I'm illiterate, I'll lose my job.

Joyce None of us will say anything will we?

She turns to **George** *and* **Thelma**.

George I won't.

George *exits and rings the bell.*

Joyce Thelma?

Thelma But he's dangerous isn't he? Who knows what could happen next? He's in charge of the gas and electricity and everything.

Long pause.

Joyce Thelma! You wouldn't tell anybody?

The bell rings.

Thelma I'm going home, I've got to give Rory his ten o'clock feed.

Thelma *puts her coat and hat on.*

Joyce Will you be coming next week?

Thelma I don't know, people like him shouldn't be in charge of things. It's not safe.

She exits.

Joyce (*comfortingly*) She won't say anything.

Kevin An' she ain't gonna write an anonymous letter is she?

Joyce No, but give me time. (*Pause.*) How have you been coping with the paperwork?

Kevin I ain't been coping. Since Horace went, I've been bunging it in a box.

Joyce And trying to forget about it?

Kevin Yeah, but it's the first thing I think about when I wake up in the morning. Well the second thing. (*He grins.*)

Joyce What sort of paperwork is it?

Kevin (*irritably*) I dunno, it's all black squiggles to me. (*Small pause.*) It's letters and forms and things. (*Pause.*) I ain't thick! I ain't a genius either, but I ain't thick!

Joyce (*resignedly*) I know that, go and fetch the papers.

Kevin What you gonna do with 'em?

Joyce Take them home and read them.

Kevin *exits.* **Joyce** *puts her coat on, packs her books, pencils and flashcards away in her bag. She picks a doll from the shelf, cuddles it for a moment, then tenderly lays it into a doll's cot and covers it over with a blanket. She switches the light off and exits.*

Scene Ten

The cubicle. **Kevin** *is wearing an old tweed coat. He stands at the cubicle door holding the box of papers.* **Joyce** *enters, he hands the box to* **Joyce**.

Joyce I'll ring you in the morning. You'll be here?

Kevin I'm always 'ere.

Joyce *starts to leave, she turns back.*

Joyce How old are you?

Kevin Nineteen.

Joyce *nods.*

Joyce Goodnight.

Kevin Night.

Joyce *exits.* **Kevin** *throws darts violently into the notice board.*

Kevin (*as first dart is thrown*) Interfering! (*As second dart is thrown.*) Stuck up! (*As third dart is thrown, shouts.*) Bitch!

George *enters hesitantly.*

George I've done upstairs.

Kevin Thanks. (*He holds his hands out for the keys.*) I'll do the rest. I've got me breath back now.

George I thought I'd retain possession of 'em for a bit just while I ask you something.

Kevin What?

George I've got nowhere to sleep tonight.

Kevin So?

George I wondered if you knew anywhere, so to speak.

Kevin Cheap?

George Not so expensive as cheap . . . Free.

Kevin No.

George *This* is a big place.

Kevin But it ain't a doss house.

Small pause.

Give me the keys.

George I'd be out early in the morning.

Kevin No! I'm in enough bleedin' trouble already, give me the keys, an' then piss off out.

George I could assist you in the morning . . . I'm a good worker, there's nothing I like better than good hard work. Me hands have gone soft now, but they'd soon harden up.

Kevin It ain't allowed. Go on, get out!

George (*desperate*) Don't make me threaten you Kevin. I want you to *ask* me to stay.

Kevin *You threaten me*! You daft old bugger! I could put you in Stoke Mandeville!

George I *don't* want to tell anybody.

Long pause.

Kevin Oh *that* kind of threat.

They stare at each other. **George** *breaks eye contact.*

George I'm sorry. I don't know what came over me. They'd have to tear me tongue out before I'd say ought.

He gives **Kevin** *the keys.*

Kevin Look, I've gotta be somewhere soon. So find yourself a room right?

George Right, thank you. It's very accommodating of you. Why don't *you* learn? Then you could dispense with your bandage.

Kevin Yeah, it makes liars of us all don't it?

Kevin (*starts to exit*) Don't forget the lights!

The main door slams.

Scene Eleven

George *enters the crèche, he puts the little chairs onto the tables. He opens the sides of the wendy house so that the interior is fully revealed. He gazes in, enraptured, then he crosses the room and switches the lights off.*

Act Two

Scene One

Three months later, early morning in the crèche, the wendy house is wide open displaying signs of George's occupation, filthy shirts are hanging on a wire coathanger. His alarm clock is on a small table next to a camp bed. His radio is on a little bookshelf, the 'Today' programme is on. George is painting at an easel. The painting depicts the exterior of an ironmonger's shop, George is concentrating hard, the sound of a key in the lock is heard.

Kevin enters carrying a video recorder box.

Kevin Mornin' Wandsworth!

George *(turning his head)* Morning Kevin. You're an early worm.

Kevin *(as he unlocks the store cupboard and puts the video on a shelf)* Yeah, couldn't sleep. I bin up all night.

George That's called something. Amnesia! No, I can't remember. Insomnia! That's it! You're an insomniac!

Kevin Yeah, some sort of maniac. Klepto probably.

George What's in the box?

Kevin A video recorder. I'm selling it for a friend.

George That's nice of you.

Kevin It ain't really. Between you and me I'm a bit of a bastard.

He crosses to look over George's shoulder at the painting.

Kevin That's nice.

George It's where I used to work. Hetheringtons the ironmongers. You don't know of any jobs going in ironmongery round here do you?

Kevin To tell you the truth, I ain't sure what ironmongery is.

George It's hardware. Nails, buckets, rawlplugs; you know.

Kevin Oh, like a DIY centre?

George Yes, but I want a job in a proper shop where you have a counter and somebody behind it. I used to be somebody when I was behind that counter. Lovely bit of mahogany it was.

Kevin You should've stayed there.

George I would have done if Mr Hetherington hadn't died. He understood my difficulties with reading and writing. He used to say, 'George so long as you can put your finger on the stock and manage the money I don't mind'. But his son! All systems and stock control and serve yourself. It were no good me staying on. I couldn't cope with it. It were humiliating, one day he said to me, 'What's up with you man, can't you read?' I said quietly like, 'No, I can't'. And I put me cap on and went home.

Kevin Still you're learnin' now, ain't you?

George Ay, forty years too late. But I can write me name and address now.

George *takes a piece of paper out of his pocket and gives it to* **Kevin**.

Kevin What's it say?

George Mister George Arthur Bishop. The Wendy House.

They laugh.

Kevin You'll have to be out soon, the kids'll be here at half eight.

George Yes I know, I'll clear up, then I'll be off.

Kevin Where you going?

George To the Barbican.

Kevin What's on.

George The central heating, I just go to keep warm. You don't get moved on there you see. It's a big place so you can get lost in it.

Pause.

Kevin You got your lesson tonight ain't you?

George Yes, so I've got something to look forward to. Right I'd better move. (*He stands.*) Oh me legs are stiff.

Kevin Here. (*He feels in his pocket for a coin.*) Go on the bus George, you look knackered.

George *looks at the fifty pence.*

George No, the walk'll do me good.

Kevin It's pissing down out there and you ain't got a coat. Go on, take it.

George No, I've always paid me own way.

Kevin You can't pay your own way if you ain't got the money can you?

George *packs his stuff away.*

Kevin *places the coin on the table in front of him.*

Kevin You'll have to start claiming the Social, Wandsworth. You can't live on nothin'. Even the invisible man had his bandages to support him.

George No. I'll find some employment soon. And I've still got a few things I can sell.

Kevin Like what?

George Me clock, and that's a good radio that is. I've had it for years.

Kevin You'd be lucky to get a quid for the two, an' how long's that gonna keep you goin'?

George *pins his picture on the wall.*

George Will I be able to impose on you again tonight?

Kevin Yeah, why not? Shall you be requiring the Wendy House Suite again Sir, or do you fancy a change? The boiler house is free since Mrs Onassis checked out last night.

George (*smiling*) No the Wendy House is all right. It's compact.

Kevin That's a nice one, 'compact'.

George Yes, I heard it on 'Talking About Antiques'. Arthur Negus used it in relation to an old tea caddy.

They exit. Blackout.

Scene Two

Later on the same night. The cubicle, **Kevin** *inside 'reading' the* Sun. **Joyce** *enters, she has a more dressy image.*

Joyce Evening Kevin. (*She lowers her voice.*) Anything for me to do?

Kevin (*loud voice looking around*) Evenin' Mrs Chalmers. (*He lowers his voice.*) Yeah.

He hands a stack of letters to **Joyce**. **Joyce** *passes envelopes to* **Kevin**.

Joyce (*shuffling through them*) They're mostly bookings, nothing urgent. Any problems with the replies?

Kevin No, but I've 'ad a few compliments on my written English. If I ain't careful, I'm gonna end up bein' promoted to Clerical Officer. You'll have to put a few spelling mistakes in or something.

Joyce Kevin I can't do your paperwork for ever you know.

Kevin I know that.

Joyce Well, when are you going to think about doing it yourself? It would solve so many of your problems if only you'd learn to read.

Kevin No thanks. I'd have to read about every other bleeder's problems then wouldn't I?

Joyce Then you'll have to look around for somebody else I'm afraid.

Kevin You ain't ditching me are you?

Joyce I'm not prepared to help somebody who won't help himself. So you'd better think about it. (*Pause.*) What are you doing with this?

She picks up the Sun.

Kevin I'm looking at the pictures.

Joyce Despicable Tory rag!

Kevin No it ain't. It's a Socialist paper. It's the paper for the workers. Everybody round our way reads it.

Joyce (*tersely*) Kevin, this newspaper supports the Conservative

Party. It also supports hanging, flogging, fox hunting, private medicine, cruise missiles, capitalism and Margaret Thatcher. If it dared it would advocate the abolition of the trade unions, the amputation of shoplifters' hands, the castration of homosexuals and the canonisation of Princess Diana. But you wouldn't know that would you? Because you only look at the bloody pictures, because *you can't read*!

Kevin (*shouting*) I don't wanna read about life. I wanna live it!

Joyce All right live it! But from now on you'll live it without my help.

Joyce exits angrily towards the crèche.
Kevin tears the *Sun* to pieces. He throws it all over the floor, then lights a fag and leans against the wall.

Scene Three

The crèche. **Joyce** *is taking off her coat,* **Thelma** *is wearing her dance gear.*

Joyce Thelma I can't waste valuable time on it! We only have two hours a week.

Thelma Just five minutes. Oh, go on! (*She sulks.*) I only want you to stand there and tell me if I'm going wrong.

Joyce Why don't you tell Mrs Eirenstone the truth, instead of all these lies?

Thelma I can't suddenly start telling the truth to people can I? Where would it all end? Please! I have to show her my dance steps when I get back. She says I've got a terrible technique, and she knows what she's talking about, she's started going to Covent Garden, she's talking of complaining to my Robotics teacher, and if she comes here and goes upstairs, I'll be found to be an illiterate liar.

Joyce Aerobics! How many more times? And you're not illiterate, you can read and write your own name now, you did last week.

Thelma Go on! *He's* not here yet. He's probably rooting around in litter bins.

Joyce That's cruel. The poor man's just down on his luck. All right, just until he comes.

Thelma *takes a tape cassette out of her bag and switches it on to play loud fast dance exercise music. She hands* **Joyce** *an exercise manual.*

Thelma (*shouting over row*) Look in the book and tell me if I'm doing it right.

Thelma *goes into clumsy unco-ordinated dance exercise routines.* **George** *enters unnoticed, he has walked a long way and is tired and hungry. Nobody sees* **George***, he sits down on a floor cushion.*

Joyce (*shouts*) Try to keep to the rhythm Thelma. (*She claps her hands to the beat.*) Like this.

Joyce *joins in the routine. She does quite well, and enjoys it.* **George** *taps his hand and foot to the beat.* **Kevin** *opens the door.*

Kevin (*shouting*) Turn it down!

They all turn to look at **Kevin***,* **Joyce** *hurries to turn the volume down.*

Kevin I've had a complaint from 'Positive Thinking'. They reckon they can't concentrate wiv that row goin' on.

Joyce Well kindly tell them that their constant chanting of 'I can' and 'I will' has filtered into our room more than once.

Kevin Oh I ain't getting involved, do what you like.

Kevin *exits and slams door.*

George Sorry I'm late, I got held up.

Thelma What, mugged, held up?

George No, detained, held up.

Joyce Did you manage to do your homework Mr Bishop?

George Yes.

He brings a sheath of papers out of a plastic carrier and hands them to **Joyce***.*

Joyce These are beautifully neat George, well done!

George I enjoyed it. It passed the time very constructively.

George *smiles.*

Joyce Did you manage to do yours Thelma?

Thelma Yes, but I couldn't bring it with me. Mrs Eirenstone pinned it up on the cork tiles in the nursery. She thinks Davina's done it. I could hardly tell her it was mine could I? (*Bitterly.*) So Davina's getting all *my* credit. Mr Eirenstone took her to see *Peter Pan* on account of it. But it was me who was up all night with her. If she wasn't screaming about the crocodile, she was in hysterics over Captain Luck.

Joyce Hook! 'aitch', huh!

She writes it on a piece of card.

George (*to* **Thelma**) It looks like a ladder wi' one rung.

Thelma Mrs Chalmers is the teacher, not you.

Thelma *looks at* **George**'s *homework.*

Thelma He's doing much better than me. He's making rapid progress.

George Well you've got those kiddies to look after. They can be very consuming of time.

Thelma Davina's had a smack from me, she's getting out of hand. Mrs Eirenstone blames me for it, but how can it be my fault? She's not my flesh and blood is she? She won't sit down and do her letters practice. I say to her, 'Davina you won't go to that nice school that your Mummy's found if you don't learn your letters'. She says some horrible things back to me. Swear words you know. She hears it from Mr Eirenstone.

Joyce (*trying to interrupt the flow*) You mustn't pressure Davina! Thelma, she's only a little child.

Thelma It's me that's under pressure! It's me that does all the housework and looks after Davina, and the baby, and now Mr and Mrs Eirenstone are both on at me to write down telephone messages. (*Tearful.*) I can't remember who's who. They should answer their own phone instead of lying in bed all day!

George So you're not happy in your work?

Thelma I was employed to look after the children, but I've ended up washing Mr Eirenstone's silk underpants by hand! In fact I have to do all the washing by hand.

Joyce Surely they've got a washing machine?

Thelma Yes, but I can't work it. Mrs Eirenstone gave me the instruction book and left me to get on with it. It's the same with the freezer, I don't know what the labels say. I have to defrost everything to see what it is then freeze it up again. Oh I wish I lived a hundred years ago, you didn't need to read then. You could just live your life in peace.

Joyce In ignorance.

Thelma It's the same thing.

George Oh no it isn't. When you're ignorant the clever people take advantage of you. They tell you what to do, and you have to do it. You don't know how to refuse, because you don't know the words.

Kevin *enters.*

Kevin Don't mind if I come in do you?

Joyce Kevin, these constant interruptions are very unsettling. What is it this time?

Kevin I just wanted somewhere to get out of the way. 'Paper Sculpture' are after me for chuckin' their poxy models in the bin.

He sits crossed-legged on the floor.

Joyce You didn't! Oh dear, there'll be a few tears shed under the duvet tonight!

Kevin How was I to know they wanted 'em saving? The hairy ponce of a tutor said he put a notice against 'em. 'Do not throw away'. He went bleedin't berserk when he found that in the bin.

Joyce But why come in here? Why don't you barge into someone else's class?

Kevin *starts to roll a fag.*

Kevin Nobody else would have me. Carry on, pretend I'm not here.

Thelma *looks resentfully at* **Kevin**, **George** *smiles at him.*

Joyce (*sighs*) We're going on with the game we played last week. I'm going to hold up a letter and you have to try and find a word that begins with it.

She sorts out 'D' and holds it up.

This is 'D' what sound does it make?

Kevin Duh! (*He laughs and holds his fingers to his head and adopts an idiot expression.*

Joyce Good, so I want a word beginning with Duh.

George Daughter.

Joyce Yes.

Thelma (*shouts*) Dog!

Joyce Good.

Thelma *is pleased and claps her hands together.*

George Down and out.

Joyce Yes, but that's three words. But 'Down' is good. Thelma?

Thelma (*triumphantly*) Davina!

George Well done!

Joyce George another one?

George Er . . . Dirt!

Joyce Yes.

Kevin Drip, drop, doom, day, damned.

Thelma You're not supposed to be playing.

George (*admiringly*) But he's got the hang of it.

Joyce Any more Kevin?

Kevin *stands and wanders around.*

Kevin Doughnut, drawers, doors, detention.

George Disgrace.

Thelma Dot.

Joyce Go on. Whenever you think of one.

George Dosser, dirty . . .

Thelma You said dirty before!

George I said dirt before. Dirty is different . . .

Thelma (*triumphantly*) Different!

Joyce Very good! Now another letter.

She sorts out 'F' looks at **Kevin**, *puts it away and takes out 'B'.*

George 'B' pronounced Buh!

Joyce Yes, go on, a word.

George Busby, Barclay.

Thelma Ball!

George Barbican!

Kevin Bugger, bollocks, bleedin' bastard.

Thelma *covers her ears.*

Joyce (*shouting angrily*) Stop it!

Thelma You shouldn't let him play!

Kevin I got it right didn't I?

George You mustn't swear in front of the ladies.

Thelma Tell him to get out.

Joyce He *did* get them right, they weren't words that I would
have chosen, but . . .

Kevin Barrel, barometer, butter, bacon, beans, bread.

George Better!

Kevin Beano.

Joyce We'll have another letter now.

She sorts another letter out.

Kevin Bottle, beer, brewery.

Joyce Thank you, we'll have another letter now.

Kevin *walks around the room.*

Kevin Beautiful, barmy, barnacle, barn, bastard.

Thelma You've had that one!

Kevin Which one?

Thelma The last one you said.

Kevin Book, bag, bouncer, bounce.

Joyce Thank you Kevin.

Kevin Banana, bullet (*Proudly.*) *Barrage balloon.*

George *and* **Joyce** *applaud,* **Thelma** *is jealous.*

Joyce Excellent.

Kevin Do I get a gold star?

Joyce (*pleased*) Yes, why not? There are bound to be some around here somewhere.

Joyce *searches.*

George You're a clever lad. How come you've heard of barrage balloons? I'd have though the generation gap would have intervened so to speak.

Kevin Me Grandma used to talk for hours about the war. How happy they were queuing for their bits of bacon.

Thelma You mean unhappy?

Kevin No I mean happy. Still what else happened in her life? Her next highlight was havin' her veins done in hospital.

Joyce *finds a tin of gold stars.*

Joyce (*taking one out*) Where do you want it?

Kevin (*mock dramatic*) Stick it here. (*Indicates his forehead.*) That way everybody can see it, and know that Kevin Muldoon is a gold star winner.

Joyce *sticks it on his forehead.*

Thelma Don't I get one?

Joyce Of course, you've *all* done well.

Joyce *gives a gold star to* **Thelma. Thelma** *puts it into her purse.*

Joyce And you George.

George I'll have it on my homework please.

Joyce *sticks it on his homework book.*

George First time I've had one of these. The highest I got at school was a red. (*Pause.*) I got that for a drawing of a cut up frog.

Kevin I've never like the French either.

George I used to draw them when the others were writing.

Joyce I could never draw a straight line. I envy anyone with that skill.

George I wouldn't call it a skill, but I used to enjoy it. I had a very envious collection of coloured pencils. They came in tins with pictures of lakes on them. I used to lay them on my bed and gloat over 'em. I were like a miser with his money.

He gives a small laugh.

Kevin I collected foreign fag packets. My big sister knocked about with all sorts.

Pause.

She collected three kids, different colours though, so you couldn't call 'em a set.

Joyce What about you Thelma? What did you collect?

Thelma Pictures of dogs. I love all living things.

Kevin What about you Mrs Charmer?

Joyce Chalmers.

Kevin I know what I said, what filled your empty hours?

Joyce Oh, I've always been a great reader.

She realises the gaffe.

Kevin Go on, rub it in.

Joyce I collected books. (*Pause.*) Now it's time for some practical work.

Joyce *starts to sort out papers.*

Kevin You're a bit cagey ain't you Mrs Chalmers?

Joyce What do you mean?

Kevin You take it all in, but you don't give nothin' out do you? Where do you live?

Joyce In Clapham.

Kevin On the common? Big house? Five bedrooms?

Joyce Yes.

Kevin Servants?

Joyce Don't be silly.

Kevin Domestic help?

Joyce A cleaning lady. And somebody comes in to mow the lawn.

Kevin *Somebody*! You're married ain't you?

Joyce Yes.

Kevin Happy?

Joyce That's none of your business.

Kevin What's your old man do?

Joyce He's a GP.

Kevin A doctor eh? That must come in handy.

George He likes opera, we know that much.

Thelma Have you got any children of your own?

Joyce No.

Thelma Have you been trying for some?

Joyce No, not lately.

Thelma Is it you or him?

Joyce Me or him what?

Thelma That's sterile.

Joyce It's neither of us.

Thelma But if you can't have a baby it must be somebody's fault.

Joyce It's not a question of fault.

Thelma Has your husband done the tests on you?

Joyce He certainly has not!

Thelma Why not? Then you'd know who to blame. What about adoption? With your husband being a doctor you could have your pick of the orphanages. Why don't you put your name down? You wouldn't have to wait long.

George That's enough Thelma!

Joyce Yes, we're losing valuable time!

Kevin What are you doing this for?

Joyce I'm not doing it am I? You're preventing me from doing it.

Kevin All right I'll go.

Joyce You don't have to go! You know we'd like you to join the class.

Kevin No, this room gives me the creeps. I shit myself first day at school. I spent the whole of the morning stuck to one of them little chairs.

Thelma (*gets up quickly from her chair*) Ugh!

Kevin *exits.*

Joyce I'm sorry about that.

George It's just a phase he's going through.

He takes an air-mail letter out.

George I've had another letter, would you mind?

Thelma I'm sure you won't mind if *I* go out will you?

Joyce *takes the letter with an air of resignation, sits down and reads it.*

Joyce Dear Dad . . .

Blackout.

Scene Four

At the cubby hole. **Kevin** *is sweeping the torn papers up.* **Thelma** *enters.*

Kevin What you doing out of class?

Thelma She's reading one of his daughter's boring letters. She ignores me when he's around.

Kevin She's in love with him ain't she?

Thelma Of course not. She's married to a doctor.

Kevin Don't mean she can't have a bit on the side.

Thelma With that dirty old man!

Kevin Some women like dirty old men. It turns 'em on.

Thelma You're the most horrible person I've ever met.

Kevin You've had a sheltered life though, ain't you?

Thelma I was brought up properly, if that's what you mean. There was no dirty talk in our family.

Kevin What did you talk about apart from lovin' all livin' things?

Thelma The usual things that families talk about: television, illness, what to have for dinner.

Kevin You didn't discuss philosophy then?

Thelma I don't know what philosophy is and neither do you. You're like George Bishop, you are. You use words that you can't read and you can't write and try to make people think you're clever. Well it doesn't work with me.

Kevin What you goin' to do when you can read then?

Thelma Mrs Chalmers says my whole life will change.

Kevin You gonna carry on being a nanny?

Thelma Yes, for a few years until I've had my fling.

Kevin When you havin' that then?

Thelma I'm having it now. What do you think I'm in London for?

Kevin Then what?

Thelma Get married of course.

Kevin Who to?

Thelma *I* don't know. I'm not a fortune teller am I? But there's bound to be somebody out there waiting for me isn't there?

Kevin Yeah, the Wandsworth Wanker.

He laughs. **Thelma** *goes to rush off.*

Kevin Oi Thelma!

Thelma What?

Kevin You ever had a bloke?

Thelma What do you mean?

Kevin Ever had a boyfriend?

Thelma No, I'm saving myself.

Kevin What for?

Thelma The right man.

Kevin How will you know when you've found him?

Thelma Because I'll fall in love with him stupid! And he'll fall in love with me.

Kevin (*acting*) Thelma do you think you could love me?

Thelma No!

Kevin Thelma.

Thelma What?

Kevin I love you gel.

Thelma No you don't, you're a liar. A born liar.

Kevin No straight up. I've been trying to keep it to myself but I gotta tell you. Thelma. Come to Kevin. Come on.

Thelma *comes closer.*

Thelma What for?

Kevin Thelma. Luh is for love. Luh. Love.

He puts his arms around her, he pulls her towards him.

Kevin Kuh is for kiss. Kuh. Kiss.

He kisses her on the cheek.

Kevin Duh is for Darlin'. Duh. Darlin'. Buh is for Bosom.

Thelma What's that?

Kevin It's a fancy word for tits.

He grasps her breasts, **Thelma** *screams and pushes him off.*

Thelma To think that Jesus gave his life to save the likes of you!

Thelma *rushes off towards the lavatory.*

Scene Five

In the crèche. **Joyce** *is rocking* **George** *to and fro.* **George** *is holding the letter, he is upset.*

Joyce Children are always a worry aren't they?

George I can't bear to think of her so unhappy and so far away. It's not as if I can get on a bus is it? You can't, not to Australia. I'd kill that Malcolm if I got my hands on him.

Joyce There, there. If she's so unhappy with him, she may decide to come back.

George I wish she would. You've no idea how much I miss her, she's such a lovely girl. She'd do anything for anybody. You could warm your hands on her heart.

A long pause.

Joyce I had a son. He'll be nineteen on the fourteenth of December. His name was Robert.

George Nice.

Joyce A gentle name.

George It would have been shortened.

Joyce Yes.

George He went ahead and died did he?

Joyce He was a very singular baby. The nurses said that they had never quite seen anything like him before. I wasn't allowed to see him, but by all accounts he had arms and legs all over the place. (*Pause.*) My husband won't have his name mentioned. He'd be at university by now. (*Pause.*) I look at them in the streets.

George *cuddles* **Joyce** *and strokes her hair.*

George I wish we could be friends Mrs Chalmers.

Joyce We are friends Mr Bishop.

George No, we're friendly, but we're not friends.

Thelma *enters. She sees* **George** *and* **Joyce** *with their arms around each other.* **George** *and* **Joyce** *get to their feet.*

Thelma It's too late, I saw you!

Joyce Mr Bishop has had some upsetting news.

Thelma Well I'm upset. I've just been indecently assaulted, but nobody puts their arms around me do they?

George Who assaulted you? Not the Wandsworth . . .

Thelma No! That caretaker!

She cries. **Joyce** *puts her arms around her.*

Joyce He's gone too far this time. What did he do to you?

Thelma *looks at* **George.**

Thelma He touched me here. (*She indicates her breasts.*) He said he loved me, then he did it.

Joyce They always say they love you. It's their way.

Thelma But I don't want anybody to touch me there. Not until I'm married. He said you're in love with him. (*She looks at* **George.**) It's not true is it?

Joyce No, of course it's not true! He's a nasty malicious boy to say that.

Thelma You *looked* as if you were in love with him when I came in.

George *looks at* **Joyce,** *she looks at him.*

Joyce Mr Bishop and I are friends.

George Yes, we're friends. (*He looks pleased.*)

Thelma But you do a lot for him don't you?

Joyce I hope I give you both the same amount of time.

Thelma You do more for him.

Joyce That's not true.

Thelma That's why he's learning quicker than me.

Joyce He has more time for practice.

George I haven't got a job. I'm free in the day.

Thelma No, you like him better than me.

Joyce I like you both equally.

Thelma (*shouting*) Don't tell lies! You've never liked me!

Joyce Stop shouting.

Thelma (*louder*) I'll shout as loud as I like! Mrs Eirenstone does, so why shouldn't I? She throws things about. (*She throws flash cards on the floor.*) And nobody tells her to stop. You don't post my letters.

Joyce You don't write any.

Thelma You don't kiss me!

Joyce (*quielty*) I can do. (*She kisses her.*)

Joyce Do you want me to come and see Mrs Eirenstone?

Thelma What about?

Joyce You're not happy there are you? She's not treating you well.

Thelma I haven't had any wages for two weeks.

Joyce How much does she owe you?

Thelma Forty pounds.

Joyce So eighty pounds in all. (*Pause.*) That's not much for two weeks' work!

Thelma No, she owes me forty pounds for two weeks.

Joyce She can't be paying you twenty pounds a week!

Thelma And my board. Mrs Eirenstone says it's what everyone gets on Youth Opportunities.

George Doesn't sound like much of an opportunity to me.

Joyce She's lying to you. A trained nanny wouldn't warm a bottle for twenty pounds a week.

Thelma Well I'm not trained am I? So she can pay me what she likes.

George We're not at liberty to pick and choose Mrs Chalmers.

Joyce I know that, but you will be, you're learning.

George No we've never been able to choose, we've always done as we're told.

Thelma I could have him up for indecent assault couldn't I? What he's done is against the law. I'm going to report him to the police.

Joyce No, don't do anything hasty.

George You'd have to go to court.

Joyce It'd be in the papers. 'Literacy Student Assaulted by School Caretaker'.

George Mrs Eirenstone would find out.

Thelma He ought to be punished!

She puts her hat and coat on.

Joyce Where are you going?

Thelma Back to Kensington.

Joyce You haven't finished your lesson!

Thelma I don't care! I've had enough for tonight.

Joyce Are you coming next week?

Thelma I don't know. I might. I might not!

George Next Wednesday is bonfire night.

Joyce Is it? Oh dear, I'm meant to be hostessing at a bonfire party. It's our turn to have the black patch on the lawn.

George Does that mean there won't be a lesson next week?

Thelma She's just said she's going to a party instead of coming here.

Joyce My husband arranged it. You see it's my birthday as well. He'll be awfully cross if . . .

Thelma Will you be here or won't you?

Pause.

Joyce I'll be here.

Kevin *stands at the open door.* **Thelma** *exits, ignoring* **Kevin.**

George I'll walk her to the bus, she's too upset to be out there on her own.

George *exits, passing* **Kevin.**

George (*to* **Kevin**) You want to learn to keep yourself in check. I know your hormones are churning round, but young Thelma's a decent girl, and now Mrs Chalmers is upset.

Joyce *is slumped and depressed. The door opens quietly and* **Kevin** *enters.*

Kevin What's up Joyce? George says you're upset. Tell Kevin.

Joyce Please call me Mrs Chalmers from now on.

Kevin Mrs Charmer, I call you that 'cos you're charmin' ain't you?

Joyce No!

Kevin You are.

Joyce Go away Kevin. I'm not in the mood.

Kevin I'm always in the mood. I had a thing about Mrs Thatcher last year. I couldn't see a navy blue tailored suit without sitting down and crossing my legs.

Joyce Kevin. I won't allow you in here if you carry on talking like that.

Kevin I can't help it if I've got a crush on you. Can I?

Joyce (*drily*) It'll pass.

Kevin I know, but how long will it take, that's the 'fing?

Joyce So you find me attractive, do you?

Kevin Yeah. I go for older women. They've got better bodies. Softer you know. Younger birds is all knees and elbows.

Joyce How many older women have you had?

Kevin Well it's hard to say.

Joyce Twelve.

Kevin No, not twelve.

Joyce One?

Kevin Something in between.

Joyce And how many young girls?

Kevin Look I ain't going into detail.

Joyce Would you like to come home with me tonight Kevin?

Kevin What for?

Joyce Well, let's call it . . . coffee, shall we?

Kevin Won't your husband mind?

Joyce My husband's not there, he's gone to a conference on herpes. We could get to know each other intimately.

Kevin You dirty old bag!

Joyce You clean young virgin! You touch Thelma again and I'll bloody castrate you!

She holds up a pair of scissors.

Snip! Snip!

Kevin *runs from the room.* **Joyce** *laughs.*

Scene Six

The crèche, the following week. A model of a guy sits slumped over the table. It is a good facsimile of a human being. It is wearing **George***'s best clothes.*

After five seconds, the door is unlocked and **Kevin** *and* **George** *enter.*
George *is wearing his oldest outdoor clothes, and looks like a tramp. He is carrying a large thin greetings card box.* **Kevin** *is carrying a step ladder.*

Kevin We'll have to get a move on.

He sees the guy.

Bleedin' 'ell! That it?

George (*going to guy and picking it up*) I were up all night constructing him. What do you think?

Kevin He's better dressed than you are George.

George He's got my best clothes on that's why.

Kevin Where'd you get the money from for that card?

George I sold me wireless. It'll be the first time I've missed *The Archers* for I don't know how long. Now I shall never know how Phil got his muck spreader out of that ditch. (*Pause.*) Still it'll be worth it when she sees it. Big i'nt it?

He opens the box and looks at the card, the card says 'To my sweetheart'.

Kevin She's forty-six ain't she?

Kevin *puts the step ladder in the middle of the room.*

George Yes, but they didn't have one with forty-six on. They stop at twenty-one.

Kevin I hope she appreciates all this.

George Oh she will. She's an appeciative type of woman. In fact she's the nicest woman I've ever met. So to speak.

George *hands* **Kevin** *a hanging structure that is decorated with cut out Halloween shapes.*

As **Kevin** *hangs decorations:*

Kevin What about your wife?

George Oh I liked her but she got fed up with me. I didn't push myself forward enough with her. It's a general fault I've got. She said I was boring.

Kevin Never!

George Well you see she was always a lively sort of woman. Always laughing.

Kevin Bit of a goer eh?

George Yes, she was always on the go. She had a thirst for amusement. I thought she might slow down a bit when Jennifer was born, but she was worse than ever. Rumours started circulating, I took no notice. (*Pause.*) You see, looking after the baby wasn't enough for her, didn't satisfy her brain. She wanted to meet people and have them tell her she looked pretty. (*Pause.*) I told her. Twenty or more times a day, but it wasn't enough, so I brought up Jennifer. She was a daddy's girl. I got as much pleasure from seeing her clean after her bath as ever I got from watching Sheffield score at home.

Long pause.

Kevin George?

George Yes?

Kevin You don't half stink, me old flower.

George (*hanging his head*) I've let myself go a bit lately . . .

Kevin No offence.

George No, none taken.

Pause as they hang decorations.

George I heard a new word today.

Kevin Yeah?

George Serendipity. Lovely isn't it? (*Slowly.*) Serendipity.

Kevin What's it mean?

George I don't know. I just came across it.

Kevin looks at his watch.

Kevin I gotta unlock the front door for Thelma.

George How long will you be?

Kevin Five minutes.

He climbs down the stepladder and closes it up.

George (*anxiously*) You're going to apologise to her aren't you for last week?

Kevin Yeah, I'll think of something.

George Good.

Kevin *goes towards door with the stepladder.*

George Better lock me in. We don't want Joyce to come in before we're ready.

Kevin George.

George Yes?

Kevin If I were you I wouldn't get too fond of Mrs Charmer.

George It's her birthday!

Kevin Yeah. And it's bonfire night an'll but you ain't gonna light her fire George.

Kevin *exits and locks the door.*

George *takes his clothes off, revealing newspaper padding and tattered underwear. He takes water from the goldfish bowl with a jam jar, then using a corner of his towel he washes under his arms, his face and neck. He hears voices in the corridor outside, he freezes, then panics when he hears the key in the lock. He runs into the wendy house taking his clothes.*

Thelma *and* **Kevin** *enter,* **Kevin** *looks round for* **George. Thelma** *is carrying a cake in a tupperware box.*

Thelma (*looking around*) Ah look what the kiddies have done! What's wrong with *him*?

Kevin *lights the pumpkin lamps.*

Kevin Wandsworth (*Indicating guy.*) ain't at his best tonight. I told him to get his head down for a bit.

Thelma *Look* at him, he looks like a tramp. In fact he *is* a tramp.

Kevin Oh he ain't a bad guy.

He laughs.

Thelma (*suspicious*) What are you laughing for? You're not going to go funny again are you?

Kevin (*acting*) I explained all that Thelma. I wasn't myself last week.

Thelma You should have told me about your whole family dying in a plane crash last year. It must have been awful for you remembering. I would have made allowances. Where were they going?

Kevin Who?

Thelma Your family.

Kevin Oh er . . . South of France for the sunshine.

Thelma In November?

Kevin Look I can't talk about it no more, sorry.

Thelma (*anxiously*) I wish you'd told me last week. I wouldn't have been so mad.

Kevin It doesn't matter.

Thelma It does!

Thelma *takes the lid off the cake box.* **George** *exits from Wendy House, he is wearing a bow tie.* **Thelma** *sees him and screams.*

George Sorry, I couldn't come out before I weren't properly dressed.

Kevin *laughs.*

Thelma I don't think it's funny. People have nearly died of shocks like that. I could have ended up in intensive care with a tube up my nose.

Kevin Show George the cake you made Thelma. I gotta open up.

Thelma *brings* **George** *the cake,* **Kevin** *exits.*

George Yes, it's very nice but you've spelt happy wrong. Happy's spelt with two 'P's.

Thelma She won't mind.

George I think she will.

Thelma No she won't, she'll be grateful to me for standing in the kitchen all day while Davina's been under my feet having tantrums on the cushion floor.

George Put another P on Thelma, you've got enough silver balls.

Thelma No it'll ruin it and anyway it doesn't matter.

George It does matter! That's not how you spell happy. (*He sings.*) I'm H. A. P. P. Y. H. A. P. P. Y. Please Thelma, before she comes. I'll do it if you like.

He tries to hold the cake.

Thelma No it's my cake. Leave it alone . . . so long as it tastes all right . . .

George But she's not a cookery teacher, she teaches the English language. She won't care what it *tastes* like so long as it's spelt right.

Three knocks on the door.

It's Joyce, light the candle!

Thelma *lights the candle.* **George** *switches the main light off, the pumpkin glows in the dark, the single candle flame flares.*

Come in.

Joyce *and* **Kevin** *enter.* **Kevin, Thelma** *and* **George** *sing 'Happy Birthday to you'.* **Joyce** *stands overwhelmed. She is wearing an elegant dress, high heels and fur coat.*

Joyce How lovely! Thank you!

Thelma I made the cake. (*Bossily.*) Blow the candle out then!

Joyce *blows, they applaud,* **Kevin** *whistles.*

George And I made the guy.

George *picks it up and holds it.*

Kevin An' I got the decorations back from out the bin.

Joyce How kind of you all to remember.

Kevin George set it up. That's George on the right.

Joyce It's a splendid guy.

Thelma It should have a cloak and a pointed hat by rights.

Thelma *unpacks her handbag and takes out her 'Janet and John' exercise book.*

George We thought we'd have our lesson and then have a party. Only a bit of one. A piece of cake and then burn the guy. Kevin's got a sort of bonfire built in the playground.

Joyce Well of course that *would* have been lovely. But I have to leave earlier than usual, we've got people coming, I did say last week . . .

George (*disappointed*) Oh!

Kevin (*sarcastically*) Oh well, if you've got *people* comin' . . .

Joyce Perhaps if we have a *short* lesson . . .

Thelma But I need a *proper* lesson, I want you to teach me to read this. I've got to read it to Davina tomorrow.

She shows the book to **Joyce**.

Joyce Would you mind taking a back seat tonight Mr Bishop?

Kevin No, he don't mind, do you George. He's used to it ain't you?

George Yes, I can get on and do something by myself but I would like a confidential word during the duration.

Kevin See you in a bit then?

Kevin *exits.*

Joyce, Thelma and **George** *settle down at the table.* **George** *opens an exercise book and reads it to himself moving his lips.*

Joyce (*reading*) Mother must do this.

Thelma The washing up.

Joyce (*reading*) Then she may go out. (*Pause.*) Good God, that can't be right.

Thelma Yes it is, look. she's got her coat on.

Joyce (*reading*) The man must do this.

Thelma He's sitting at a desk.

Joyce (*angrily reading*) And then he will do this. It's outrageous!

Thelma He's sitting in a comfy chair reading the paper, what's wrong with that?

Joyce But don't you see Thelma? Mother *must* do this.

George (*looking at book*) The washing up.

Joyce And then, and only then, may she go out!

Thelma So? My mother always does the washing up before she goes out. And so will I when I get my own kitchen sink.

Joyce But *must* Thelma? *Must?*

Thelma Somebody has to wash up.

Joyce But why is it always bloody Mother?

Thelma Because bloody Daddy's at work! Look!

She jabs her finger on the illustration.

Joyce You mustn't let Davina near this, it's years out of date.

Thelma No it's not! Mrs Eirenstone bought it yesterday, so there!

George Daddies do wash up. I used to do all the housework. I got called a big Jessy for doing it an' all.

Joyce Who by?

George Other men. I got caught ironing once, a rumour went round Huddersfield that I was a poof.

Thelma (*to* **Joyce**) I'm in a bad mood now. (*Small pause.*) I don't want to do anymore. (*She pushes the book away.*)

Joyce Please yourself. Would you like to see if Kevin's available? We can start the party.

Thelma You mean get it over with don't you?

Thelma *exits.*

Joyce You wanted a word with me George?

George *gets up, goes into the wendy house and comes out with the card.*

George Happy Birthday!

He gives her the box.

Joyce (*opening it*) Mr Bishop! It's so big! (*Pause.*) Oh!

George What's up?

Joyce (*lying*) Nothing, it's lovely . . . satin . . . hearts and beautifully written. 'All my love from Mr Bishop.' (*Abstracted.*) There's an 'E' on the end of love by the way.

George You like it then?

Joyce (*lying*) Oh yes it's the biggest and best card I've ever had. (*Reluctantly.*) It's just that, I don't think my husband will be as delighted as I am.

George Oh *him*. It's nought to do with him is it?

Joyce It says 'Sweetheart', you see 'To my Sweetheart'. (*Indicating.*) He may not understand.

George Don't show it to him then. Keep it in a drawer.

Joyce It won't fit in a drawer.

There is an awkward pause.

George You *are* my sweetheart. (*Small pause.*) So to speak.

Joyce But I'm not, I'm your teacher. You must get it straight. I can see it's difficult for you.

Pause.

You've probably never had such a close non-sexual relationship with a woman before have you?

George No, all the relationships I've ever had have been with relations.

Joyce There you are then, you're transferring all your affection onto me because I'm here every week helping you and interested in you.

George So you are *interested* in me?

Joyce Of course, in a student-teacher sort of way.

George Nothing else?

Joyce No, anything else is quite out of the question.

George You're not happy with *him* are you?

Joyce I don't expect to be *happy* with him. We've been married for twenty-nine years.

George You're not seeing me at my best.

Joyce It's got nothing to do with how you look or speak.

George I said nought about speaking.

Joyce No.

George What's wrong with how I speak?

Joyce Nothing, a northern accent is delightful.

George Ar, up North but not down here.

Small pause.

I wish I'd said nought now. I don't know what's up wi' me carrying on, speaking my mind.

Joyce You're lonely, you should try to make some friends.

George I haven't got the knack.

Pause.

This transferring, does it wear off . . . evaporate?

Joyce (*eagerly*) Oh yes. It gets transferred to someone else.

Kevin *and* **Thelma** *are heard off.*

George Right, I'll not speak of it again.

Joyce No, best not to, it could make things very difficult.

Kevin *and* **Thelma** *enter.*

Thelma Kevin's been promoted!

Kevin *is excited. He brings a letter out of his pocket and waves it around.*

Kevin I only knew just now. A bloke came round from the Education. He gives me this and says, 'I 'spose you bin expecting this'.

Joyce What are you promoted to?

Kevin Head caretaker! There ain't nowhere else to go.

George Well I think that's grand, just grand.

Kevin Could be a job 'ere for you George, now I'm moving up. I'll put in a word for you.

George (*delighted*) Well! Thank you.

Joyce Congratulations Kevin.

Joyce *cuts the cake into pieces.*

George When do you start?

Kevin I ain't sure, 'ave a look Wandsworth.

George *takes the letter, peers at it, but can't read it.*

George I can't do long words yet.

He hands the letter back to **Kevin**.

Kevin (*to* **Joyce**) You wouldn't like to run your eyes over this an' tell me when me money goes up would you?

Joyce *takes the letter and reads it, she frowns then re-reads it.*

George How much more will you get?

Kevin 'Bout twenty quid a week.

Kevin *hands* **George** *and* **Thelma** *a slice of cake each.*

Thelma I hope your hands are clean.

Kevin Course they are, I've just had 'em in running water.

Thelma *bites the cake.*

Down a drain.

He laughs and gives a piece of cake to the guy.

Joyce Kevin.

Kevin Yeah?

Joyce Oh Kevin.

Kevin What's up?

Joyce They're not renewing your contract.

Kevin What's that mean?

Joyce You've got the sack! I'm so sorry.

Kevin All right, joke over.

Joyce I wouldn't joke about a thing like that.

Kevin (*snatching the letter*) Where's it say?

Joyce There.

She points to the relevant paragraph.

Kevin *What's it say?*

Joyce It says, 'Your work has been found to be unsatisfactory, therefore the Education Committee reluctantly inform you that your contract is not to be renewed'.

George Unsatisfactory! He's been here from morning till night. He's kept this place going.

Joyce I'm sorry.

Kevin (*in shock*) The fucking bastards! I was the only one in our house that had a job. Now it's the whole bleedin' family on the dole. We'll hire a mini bus and go down there together, it'll be cheaper than the bus fare.

Thelma He told me that his family were dead!

Joyce You've been given a fortnight's notice.

Kevin They can stuff that! I ain't working where I'm not wanted.

He takes the caretaker's coat off and throws it on the floor.

An' I ain't locking up tonight neither, nor going round with the Harpic.

Thelma You can't just leave the doors open. The public will take advantage.

Kevin I don't care, they can take what they like. It belongs to 'em. It comes out of the rates.

George I'm sorry for your news Kevin.

Kevin I'm sorry for myself. It wasn't much of a job, but it were better than nothing.

Thelma You brought it on yourself. You never cleaned behind the toilets properly and the wash basins were always filthy.

Kevin Fanks Thelma. (*Pause*.) I shall remember that when I'm standing in the queue waiting for some hatchet face to say, 'Put your cross here Mr Muldoon'.

Joyce If only you'd learn to read and write Kevin. It would help you get another job.

Kevin (*shouts*) There are three and a half million can't get jobs. They ain't all illiterate.

George But why don't you learn just for the sake of learning? There's some beautiful words in the language.

Kevin Yeah, like work and money.

Joyce But *why* don't you want to learn?

Kevin Look, I spent twelve years at school bein' taught. Seven of 'em with the same poxy book in front of me. I knew it off by heart. *Here we go*, it's called. There's these two kids: one's called Janet and one's called John. They're both healthy lookin' kids, lucky bleeders an' all. They lived in this big posh house an' they was always goin' for picnics an' swimmin' in the river. There's no parents around in this book, though I have heard tell that they come on the scene in the next, but then I didn't get past the first did I? They're always tellin' each other to 'Look up!' 'Look down!', 'Look at the kitten!' 'Look the bleedin' dog!' 'See my aeroplane!'. The most excitin' bit is when the dog runs off with the ball.

George What happens next?

Kevin Nothing! It takes it into its kennel.

Thelma We had Dick and Dora. They lived in a nice house as well. Their father carried a briefcase home every night. I put my hand up and asked the teacher what it was. She said 'It's a briefcase' in a horrible sort of way, but I hadn't seen one before. None of the men I knew carried them.

Kevin They don't want us to read! There ain't room for all of us is there?

Joyce That's absolute balls and you know it! The country needs a highly intelligent, literate workforce.

Kevin Why ain't it got one?

A long pause.

George She needs prior notice on that question.

Joyce I'm on your side Kevin. Don't talk to me as if I were the enemy. I can't help being middle class. None of us can help our backgrounds. I vote Labour! And I do my best for the community. I don't have to come here every Wednesday, you know. My husband doesn't like it, and my friends think it's rather a joke.

Kevin They'll be laughing on the other side of their faces one day.

Joyce Come the revolution?

Kevin Yeah, come the revolution.

Joyce How novel! You'll be the only revolutionary not to have read Marx.

Kevin I've been told I've got street validity. Apparently it counts for more these days.

Joyce So you'll be distributing leaflets that you can't read yourself will you?

Kevin Leaflets? Who's talkin' 'bout leaflets? I'll be passing out the ammunition.

Joyce Oh armed revolution?

Kevin Well we gotta have something. Your lot have got all the long words. And what have we got? This!

He pulls the 'gotcha' *edition of* The Sun *out of his pocket.*

Joyce That paper's years old.

Kevin I found it in the boiler house, I only kept it 'cos I can read the headline.

Thelma What does it say?

Kevin Gotcha! The only headline I've ever been able to read an' you know why? Because they use it in the pissin' *Beano*!

He lashes out at the guy and knocks it on the floor.

George Steady on! There's a lot of work gone into that.

Kevin You've been wasting your bleedin' time George. Didn't anybody tell you what happens to guys when they ain't needed anymore? They're put on a pile of rubbish and burnt!

He kicks it around the floor.

Joyce Stop it!

George A lot of work went into that!

Kevin Why don't you do the country a favour George? Go on! Chuck yourself on the bonfire.

Joyce No more! Stop it!

Joyce slaps Kevin's face. Kevin slaps her back.

George You mustn't hit a woman!

Kevin It's an equal opportunity.

Thelma He's gone mad, he wants certifying.

Kevin Do you want one an' all? Cos nothin' would give me more pleasure, you bleeding lackey.

Thelma I'm not a lackey, I'm a nanny. Mrs Eirenstone got me from *The Lady*.

Kevin You're cheap labour ain't you? Gels like you are ten a penny. Another few months and Mrs Eirenstone will turf you out an' get somebody who can read an' write an' pay 'em the same pathetic money.

Thelma flies at Kevin. Kevin gets his arm around her neck.

George That's enough now, you've said enough.

Kevin Tell 'em where you live George!

Joyce I don't want to know.

George There's need for that. You're rubbing salt in the wounds.

Kevin He lives in the Wendy House, don't you George? In the bleeding Wendy House.

George lunges at Kevin, pulls Kevin's arm from round Thelma's neck and wrestles him to the floor.

Joyce Don't hurt him George.

George He promised me he wouldn't say ought.

George *tightens his grip*.

Joyce George, please don't hurt him, he's only nineteen.

Thelma People like him need hurting. They shouldn't be allowed to go around telling the truth. It's upsetting for all concerned.

Kevin Let me up George.

George I'll let you up when you're calm.

Kevin Just tell me one thing Mrs Charmer. Say if everybody could read good papers and good books how long would people stay on the Council Estates eh? And how long would it be before the dole and the Social Security were burning?

Joyce Let him up George.

George *gets off* **Kevin.**

Thelma That floor's filthy, it's no wonder he . . .

Kevin *gets up*, **Joyce** *and* **George** *dust him down*.

George (*shouting*) Shut up Thelma, don't start him off again.

Kevin *runs out. Everyone is very shaken.*

Thelma What was he talking about burning for? Is he going to set fire to the place?

George It's just a young lad's talk. It's just hot air.

Joyce (*picking up the guy*) Such a shame, it was a lovely guy.

George Those posh papers you saved me helped a lot.

Joyce Could you follow the instructions in them?

George No but they make better stuffing, there's more to 'em.

The lights go out. **Thelma** *screams. The pumpkins are glowing in the dark.*

Joyce Where are you Thelma?

Thelma I'm here, I'm on my own.

George Now don't you ladies panic. Everything's all right. I'm going to the door.

Joyce It's only a fuse gone Thelma.

Thelma I can't be in the dark. She used to put me to bed in the dark, but it didn't do any good. If you can't read, then you can't read.

Joyce Open the door George.

George I can't, it's locked. That silly bugger's gone and locked it.

George *gropes to the table and sits down.*

Joyce Put your arms around me Thelma.

Thelma *puts her arms around* **Joyce**'*s neck.*

Thelma What's he doing it for?

Joyce He's very angry. The streets are full of them.

Thelma It's not my fault he's lost his job is it? He shouldn't have touched me there.

Pause.

George I don't know where I'm going to sleep tonight.

Pause.

Joyce If he was my son he'd be at university by now.

Sound of a key in the door.

George That's him.

George *gropes towards the table where the women are sitting.* **Kevin** *opens the door, he has a lit sparkler in his hand.*

Thelma (*screams*) He's going to burn us to death!

With the sparkler **Kevin** *spells out 'G'.*

George Guh.

Joyce G.

Kevin *spells out 'O'.*

George O.

Joyce O.

Kevin *spells out 'T'.*

Thelma Tuh.

Joyce T.

Kevin *spells out 'C'.*

Joyce C.

Quicker now, **Kevin** *spells out 'H'.*

George H.

Kevin *spells out 'A'.*

Thelma A.

Joyce Gotcha!

Kevin Teach me to read!

The Great Celestial Cow

The Great Celestial Cow was first presented by Joint Stock Theatre Group at the Leicester Haymarket Studio on 15 February 1984, and on tour, before opening at the Royal Court Theatre, London, on 30 March 1984, with the following cast:

Spirit of Kali **2nd Official** **Mother-in-law (Dadima)** **Muslim Girl**	Zohra Segal
Prem **Old Age Pensioner** **Rose** **Cow in Field** **Auctioneer**	Lou Wakefield
Princess **Rachel** **Lila** **Classical Indian Dancer** **Indira** **Ram** **Nurse**	Shreela Ghosh
Princess **Martin** **Harmonium Player** **Kishwar** **Asian Elder** **Mr Patel** **Cow in Field**	Bhasker
Sita	Souad Faress
Daheba **Stewardess** **1st Official** **Fat Auntie (Masi)** **Liberal** **Sarla**	Jamila Massey
Bibi **Stallholder** **Cow in Nativity** **Anita** **Dr Mistry**	Feroza Syal
Naal Player **Photographer** **New Owner** **Raj** **2nd Fat Auntie** **Harold**	Dev Sagoo

Directed by Carole Hayman
Designed by Amanda Fisk
Lighting Designer Geoff Mersereau
Choreographer Sue Lefton
Costumes by Pam Tait/Amanda Fisk
Musical Director Lizzie Kean

Note on the layout

A speech usually follows the one immediately before it but:

1) when one character starts speaking before the other has finished, the point of interruption is marked /

eg. **Mother-in-law** Sita's chappatis are too hard/for my teeth.
    Bibi   I like them.

2) a character sometimes continues speaking right through another's speech

eg. **Bibi**   All that petting and baby/talk? It would drive
                    me
    Mother-in-law Raj is too soft with her.
    Bibi   mad. Bugger off until the floor is dry.

3) sometimes a speech follows on from a speech earlier than the one immediately before it, and continuity is marked * or **

eg. **Bibi**   All that petting and baby/talk? It would drive
                    me
    Mother-in-law Raj is too soft with her.
    Bibi   mad. Bugger off until the floor is dry.**
    Fat Auntie   She wants to be head of the house, you know.*
    Prem   **No, I want to walk on it.
    Bibi   You dare.
    Mother-in-law *What would happen to us if she was?

where 'the floor is dry' is the cue to 'No, I want to walk', and 'head of the house, you know' is the cue to 'What would happen to us'.

Act One

Scene One

1975

Early morning in a village in India.
A **Little Boy** *dressed in white shorts and vest is dragging a pile of grass towards a rickety compound. Inside the compound a* **Cow** *raises its head. It makes an aggressive warning noise. The* **Little Boy** *backs off slightly.*

Prem Today is the last day you send my heart diving.

He unties the bundle, throws grass to the **Cow.**

Stupid cow! I don't like you. Bad luck for you eh? But you started it! Go on, eat!

The **Cow** *doesn't eat.*

I got up before I was awake to cut that grass. (*He shouts.*) Eat! Or choke on it! Do something! Stupid, idiot cow!

The **Cow** *repeats the warning noise. The* **Boy** *backs off.*

(*He shouts louder.*) I'm going to England and you're staying here! (*He laughs.*) When I am flying over the ocean and Buckingham Palace you will still be here! When I am looking at the queen and the Bay City Rollers you will be a million miles away! When I am sitting on the toilet in Leicester (*He laughs, shouting.*) you will be here standing in your own dirt!

A **Woman** *carrying a pail runs on, she is* **Sita,** *the* **Boy**'s *mother. She is angry.*

Sita Don't shout at her, you will ruin her milk! (*Stroking the* **Cow.**) There there, he is excited. He is only a little boy. His head is full of the aeroplane.

The **Cow** *eats.*

(*To* **Prem.**) Without her milk you and I and your sister would have starved, when Bapu's money didn't come.

Prem Is starve the same as hungry?

Sita No and I hope you never find out the difference for yourself.

Prem I am always hungry. In Leicester I will eat and eat and eat until my belly bursts open.

Sita *milks the* **Cow.**

Sita Yes and then I will have to stitch you up. More work for me. It is five-thirty, go and tell your sister to come. Tell her to look her best for the photograph. Tidy hair and a clean face.

Prem *dawdles off.*

Sita *sings a small snatch of a lament.*

A **Neighbour** *enters. She is carrying a bundle of clothes. She walks past* **Sita** *ignoring her.*

Sita Daheba!

Daheba *turns slowly, looks at* **Sita.**

Daheba After six months of silence you speak to me?

Sita Yes I am leaving here today.

Daheba I know, you are going to Leicester. My uncle's cousin is there.

Sita (*slightly put out*) So, you know, do you, which flight I am taking?

Daheba No but you are landing at Heathrow.

The **Women** *smile.*

Sita A silly quarrel. I can't remember what it was about.

Daheba I can, you said that my daughters would never marry.

Sita But it was meant as a compliment to you. You are a magnificent mother, who would want to leave you?

Daheba (*bows her head accepting the lie*) The cow is sold satisfactorily?

Sita Oh yes. I am satisfied with the price.

Daheba And the milking bucket?

Sita No, not the bucket.

Daheba You are perhaps taking it with you?

Sita A bucket on an aeroplane?

Daheba Ridiculous! So the bucket remains here, without an owner.

The **Women** *sigh.*

Sita Of course there is hand luggage.

Daheba True.

Sita But a bucket is heavy.

Daheba And noisy. Clank, clank, clank. It would draw attention to you. Make a bad impression. English people would say, 'Tuh! Here comes another dirty immigrant with her children and bucket.'

Sita English people would say that?

Daheba Oh yes. My uncle's cousin has been there for five years now.

Sita But I am not an immigrant. I am a British subject.

Daheba They call us all immigrants over there.

Sita Then I will tell them the truth.

Daheba You can speak English can you?

Sita No, but I will learn.

Then to the **Cow**.

Thank you, good girl.

Daheba So, the bucket.

Sita *finishes milking. She carries the bucket out of the compound.*

Sita Yes, this is a good bucket. No leaks. No rust. Comfortable to carry. Hard to leave behind.

Bibi *enters. She is eleven years old. She is dressed in her best clothes. She has ribbons in her hair.*

Bibi Do I look all right?

Sita Let me see you.

Sita *goes to* **Bibi** *and gives her a severe motherly inspection. She tightens the hair ribbons etc.*

Show me your teeth.

Bibi *bares her teeth.*

Good, good. Yes you are as pretty as you can be.

Daheba (*to* **Bibi**) How tall you are. I hope you will not continue to grow or you will be nudging the stars.

Sita She will outshine them if she does.

Daheba But so lanky for eleven!

Prem (*off*) He's here, he's here!

Prem *enters.*

Daheba Ah, here is the one to melt hearts.

Prem He's here, Ma.

A **Photographer** *enters on a bike. He is wearing a mixture of Indian and Western clothes. The* **Women** *draw their scarves over their heads.*

Photographer Your son has told me that you want the photograph taken here. Is that true?

He looks round in disgust.

Sita Yes.

Photographer It will be most difficult, the light . . .

He peers at the sky.

Sita There is not enough light or too much?

Prem *hovers around the bike.*

Daheba Shush! He is a professional you know. You have a studio don't you?

Photographer Yes. The light in my studio is perfect. It is from Germany. (*To* **Prem**.) Don't touch the spokes.

Prem The light is from Germany?

Photographer My lamps are from Germany.

Prem Is Germany near England?

Photographer Yes. Very near. That's why they are always fighting.

Prem England won both times.

He does fighting acting at his sister.

Bibi Don't.

Sita Prem! Don't! (**Prem** *stops.*)

Prem Who is to be in the photograph?

Daheba *looks eager.*

Sita My children and Princess.

Photographer (*to* **Daheba**) You are Princess?

The **Children** *and* **Sita** *laugh.*

Daheba (*angry*) You dare to call me a cow? My husband and father-in-law will come and smash up your German lamps. (*Scornfully.*) Studio! Ha! A white sheet hung on a wall and he calls it a studio. (*To* **Sita**.) Keep your old pail. I don't want it! (*She exits.*)

Photographer Are the people in this village mad? What did I say? (*Pause.*) Is her husband tall?

Bibi I don't know. He doesn't leave his bed.

Prem He's dying.

Photographer Oh good. I have decided I will photograph you all in your house. I cannot work in these conditions.

The **Children** *laugh.*

Is there some sickness in this village that makes you all laugh and get angry for nothing? If so tell me and I will go back to my bed in my own village.

Sita Princess is our cow. You cannot take her photograph in our house because she will not get through the door.

Photographer You have brought me here to take a *cow's* photograph?

Sita Yes. Our cow has been good to us. I want to take a small piece of her with me.

Bibi We are going to England.

Photographer Then cut off one of her ears and take that because I refuse to take a cow's photograph. You bring me here at this terrible hour . . . the sleep still in my eyes . . .

Sita I am going to pay you! And your trousers show that you need the money.

Photographer Let me see your money.

Sita *shows money.*

I'm not used to this third class situation. I am going to Delhi in two years' time you know.

He sets up his rickety tripod, fusses around with camera and film.

Prem Don't touch the spokes, Bibi.

Photographer A big studio on a fashionable thoroughfare.

Bibi I'm only looking, no harm.

Prem Don't waste your eyes. You won't ride a bike, but I will.

Sita (*instructing the* **Children**) Prem, don't crowd in front of Princess She is the most important. I won't see her again. Kneel down. Put your arms around each other. Smile. (*To the* **Photographer**.) Go ahead.

Photographer What about you. Don't you want your photograph taken?

Sita No, I am there with my children. Ready, steady.

Blackout.

Flash of the photograph.

Scene Two

The aeroplane. **Bibi**, **Prem** *and* **Sita**, *sitting. Jet noise. Lights dim to half light.*

A **Stewardess** *tucks blankets around the family.*

Stewardess Sleep well.

Prem Ma, I can't go to sleep.

Bibi Tell him to be quiet, Mama.

Sita Prem, close your eyes now.

Prem I want to see the stars.

Bibi Shush. If you are not quiet Kali will come.

Prem Which one's Kali?

Sita The wife of Shiva.

Prem He's the best god, isn't he?

Sita Yes.

Bibi Kali was better than him. When Shiva was sleeping she killed the demons, didn't she?

Sita Yes but Shiva was thinking, not sleeping like you two will be soon. So demons came and started eating the villagers.

Bibi So the villagers that were left went to the top of the mountain and tried to wake Shiva, but he wouldn't wake so Kali . . .

Prem Let Ma tell it, Bibi.

Sita Shush. So Kali looked at the death and destruction that the demons were causing and a strange thing happened.

Bibi Oh yes I know, she changed into a monster!

Sita With many arms and many legs and a garland made of skulls and a hideous face like this.

Prem *cuddles closer to* **Sita**.

. . . but terrible though she was and even using many swords she could not defeat the demons. They fought for many days and nights.

Bibi (*sleepily*) Nine.

Sita Each time she killed one demon many more would spring up in its place formed by the drops of blood.

Bibi The worst bit now.

Sita So Kali drank their blood.

Prem Ugh!

Sita And maddened and made terrible by it, *she* started to kill the villagers.

Prem I would have killed her easy.

Sita No. She became all-powerful.

Prem Not better than Shiva?

Bibi Don't interrupt Prem.

Sita The villagers woke Shiva somehow. He came down from his mountain and tried to stop his wife. But he couldn't, and Kali fought him down to the ground and was about to kill him with a big sword when Shiva said 'No don't, I'm your husband'. And Kali looked down at him from her great height and she said 'Husband, I will not take your life'.

Prem So it ended happily?

He snuggles down.

Sita I don't know. I suppose it does.

Bibi For the villagers.

Pause.

Prem I bet he beat her when he got her home.

Sita Yes. Now sleep, and when you wake up you will be in England.

The **Children** *get into sleeping attitudes.* **Sita** *stares straight ahead.*

Princess appears.

Goodbye Princess.

Princess's **New Owner** *appears.*

New Owner C'mon cow what are you doing lying down? On your feet! C'mon, on your feet you lazy cow, there is work to be done.

He whacks **Princess**. *She makes an anguished cow noise.*

Sita *screws her eyes shut unable to bear it.*

Scene Three

The arrival lounge at Heathrow airport. The family sit on the floor, they have been waiting for two hours. **Bibi** *has the bucket on her lap.*

An announcement from the loudspeaker.

Loudspeaker Would Mr Raj Prakash come to the enquiry desk where his family are waiting for him. Mr Raj Prakash. Please come to the enquiry desk.

A uniformed **Official** *approaches.*

1st Official (*London working-class accent*) Mrs Prakash? Would you mind moving on to one of the benches please. You're in the way here. (*Pause.*) No English?

Sita Leicester. (*She shows documentation, passports.*)

1st Official Yes. Leicester. Now if you wouldn't mind moving.

2nd Official *approaches.*

2nd Official She still here?

1st Official Her old man ain't turned up has he?

2nd Official He's probably changed his mind, got halfway down the M bloody 1 and threw a wobbler.

They laugh, the **Children** *look up and smile.*

1st Official You can't blame him can you. He's had five years of freedom over here, then his missus and kids and a bloody bucket turn up.

2nd Official They'll cramp his style a bit.

1st Official Not half.

2nd Official Mind you the Asians are good family people . . . Look after each other . . . You know, the old people . . . Bit like the Jews.

1st Official Yeah, how's *your* mum?

2nd Official (*evasively*) Oh all right, (*Small pause.*) I think. We don't get over as often as we'd like . . . but it's a nice place . . . for an institution like.

1st Official Still you couldn't have had her with you, could you, Mick?

2nd Official No, her wheelchair knocked every bit of paint off the skirting boards. An' Brenda and her never did get on . . .

1st Official Well don't you feel guilty about it . . . You got your own life to live ain't you? Your mum's had hers.

2nd Official That's the problem. You see she *ain't* really. She's lived, but she ain't had what I'd call a *life*.

1st Official Well they didn't in the old days did they? They was too busy livin' to have a life.

2nd Official Well my old woman's makin' up for it, I tell you, the way she's going . . . out every bloody night. Weight Watchers, nightschool, jewellery parties . . .

1st Official 'Bout time you started cracking down.

2nd Official An' she's got opinions about everything.

1st Official Opinions?

2nd Official Yeah. Bloody this, bloody that. She'll be standin' for the bloody GLC next.

1st Official An' I'd vote for her if she'd put a few white people at the top of the housing list for a change.

2nd Official I know, dis-bloody-gustin'.

1st Official (*to the family group*) Right come on now! Quicki quicki, move to benchi!

The **Officials** *go.*

Prem What is he saying Mama?

Sita How do I know?

Bibi He is telling us to move I think. We must move, Ma. Look, nobody else is sitting on the floor.

Sita Exactly, so your father will be sure to see us won't he?

Bibi What time is it, Ma?

Sita Milking time.

Bibi Morning or evening?

Sita Evening. (*She cries.*)

Two hippies, **Rachel** *and* **Martin**, *watch.*

Rachel Oh Martin look. Oh how *sad*.

Martin Yeah.

Rachel Do you think somebody's been, you know, *awful* to them?

Martin Could be.

They stand over the family group.

Rachel Ask them what's wrong. Go on, Martin you're good with kids.

Martin Er . . . er . . . (*He pats his chest*) 'Mitra'.

Prem Tell the nasty man to go away, Ma.

Rachel (*pats her chest*) 'Mitra'. Don't cry! Me and him we've come back from India. Bombay, Calcutta, Delhi, Madras. We love your country. (*She smiles.*)

Martin Yeah . . . 'Mitra'.

Bibi They are saying 'friend' in Gujerati I think.

Prem Mama! Tell him to go away.

Rachel What did he say?

Martin Dunno. (*He squats down.*) Hey. C'mon kids.

Rachel If only we could explain that we *know* India and its people. We *know* it.

Martin (*to* **Sita**) Spiritually . . .

Rachel *puts her hands together and bows to* **Sita**.

Rachel You are my sister.

Sita *nods, baffled.*

Martin C'mon Rachel. I gotta get to the bank.

Rachel Look what's more important Martin, helping this poor, ignorant family, or cashing your bloody traveller's cheques?

Martin Look, don't pull that moral superiority shit on me again, right? I've had six fucking months of it. It's my traveller's cheques that have paid for your spiritual awareness right?

Rachel I shouldn't have come back. I should have stayed. I belong there. They need my skills.

Martin Yeah, they're crying out for English Literature degrees right?

Rachel I could dig an Artesian well! I could advise on basic hygiene . . . and Swami Niranda invited me back.

Martin Yeah, and told you to bring five hundred fucking pounds.

Rachel He didn't!

Bibi What are the dirty people saying?

Martin He did!

Sita They are quarrelling.

Prem She doesn't like his smelly face.

The **Children** *laugh.*

Sita Shush. Remember your manners. Don't laugh at the misfortunes of others.

Rachel *and* **Martin** *go off, still arguing.*

Prem When's Bapu coming?

Bibi Soon, soon. Here eat this. Keep your mouth busy. (**Bibi** *gives* **Prem** *a chappati.*)

The noise of the arrival lounge; slow fade of lights.

Scene Four

The family is sleeping on a bench in the arrival lounge. **Raj Prakash** *and his elderly* **Mother** (**Dadima**) *and* **Aunt** (**Masi**) *approach.* **Raj** *looks down at his family. His* **Mother** *goes to wake the group.* **Raj** *restrains her.*

Raj No.

Mother-in-law So son, how do you feel at this moment?

Fat Auntie (*broken voiced*) His heart is full and so are his eyes. (*She takes out a handkerchief.*)

Mother-in-law No let me. (*She mops* **Raj***'s tears.*) My grandchildren! (*Pause.*) Your wife has lost her beauty son. (*She then wipes her own eyes with the handkerchief.*)

Fat Auntie Children drain beauty away, they put the lines on our foreheads and the white in our hair.

Raj I hardly know her.

Mother-in-law Tired, she is tired. A long flight, remember Masi.

Fat Auntie Ai, ai, ai. So long. My head was in the clouds for a week.

Raj But so different.

Fat Auntie In five years people change, a baby becomes a child and a young woman becomes an old woman. That's how it is.

Mother-in-law Wake them. I want to go back to Leicester. I don't like it here, I can't hear my thoughts.

A jet starts to take off. They mime their meeting.

Prem *is greeted first. Then* **Raj** *and* **Sita** *politely greet each other, but* **Prem** *comes between them.*

The plane noise stops.

Come on everybody. Pick up the luggage. (*To* **Prem**.) Not you little one. Come on Bibi. Masi, you help.

They collect the baggage and bundles, **Bibi** *picks up the bucket.*

Why are you carrying a bucket? Put it down.

Bibi It's mother's. I'm in charge of it.

Sita You remember Princess, Raj? It's her milking bucket.

Raj There are no cows in Leicester, Sita. I have written and told you many times about Leicester.

Mother-in-law No land. Only parks . . .

Fat Auntie They are owned by the council and you may not walk on the grass. In some parks you may but in others there is a sign.

Mother-in-law 'Keep off the grass.'

Raj And our house opens on to a street. And the street is busy with cars and buses and lorries.

Mother-in-law I already have a bucket, it is red and made of plastic.

Sita I would like to keep it, please.

Raj But how will it look? We have to pass many people before we reach the minibus. No, I refuse to be seen walking with a bucket.

Prem Ma wants to buy a cow, she told me on the plane.

Bibi You were naughty, she told you stories so that you would sit still. Bapu are you going to beat Prem?

Raj (*laughing*) No, why should I beat my beloved son? I haven't seen him for five years.

He picks up **Prem** *and hugs him.*

Bibi I wish somebody would. He pulls my hair.

Laughter.

Mother-in-law Come on, I want to go home. (*To* **Bibi**.) Pick it up child, it won't carry itself.

They exit carrying luggage and bundles. **Sita** *walks behind them. She has picked up the bucket and hidden it under a piece of cloth.*

Scene Five

Raj *and* **Sita** *alone in their room.* **Sita** *looks around,* **Raj** *sits on the bed.*

Raj So what do you think of it?

Sita Such a big room for two people. Do we sleep alone?

Raj We do tonight, come here.

Sita *approaches him.*

Raj Take off your sari, I want to look at you.

Sita And a window!

Raj Sita, let me look at you.

Sita There's no hurry, Raj.

Raj After five years there's no hurry? You are my wife. Take off your sari, Sita.

Sita In India you would wait a little. Kiss me. Use fine words to help me.

Raj Who can blame me for being impatient? Come here.

Sita *approaches shyly*. **Raj** *gets up and unfastens* **Sita's** *sari*.

Raj (*quietly*) I will unfasten you as I did on our wedding night, remember?

He unwinds the sari slowly.

You were so young, and very beautiful. The most beautiful girl in the village. But tired, too tired to move. I had to teach you everything, didn't I Sita? I hope I was (*Still unwinding the sari.*) patient with you. I didn't want to frighten you. You lay still in my arms for the first months but then you began to move and . . . (*Still unwinding the sari.*) . . . how much longer? Are women wearing so much cloth in India now? Help me Sita.

Sita *clutches her sari to her*.

Sita I am afraid for you to see my body.

Raj Why? Is it scarred or diseased in some way? (*He laughs.*)

Sita No, but I have not cared for it as *you* liked. There was no time. And I lost interest in how I looked and only took pride in what my body could do. There was always so much work.

Raj Your work will be easier here. There are machines for cooking and washing. Your hands and feet will soon lose their roughness.

Sita How will I fill my time?

Raj I have arranged a job for you. You start at Mr Lakhani's dress factory on Monday. It is easy work. You will like it there and earn £55 a week. I told Mr Lakhani that you are an excellent machinist.

Sita *remains still*.

Now come to bed and prove that you are also an excellent wife.

Sita Raj, I feel frozen.

Raj I will plug in the electric fire.

Sita No, I'm not cold, but I'm frozen.

Raj *takes* **Sita** *in his arms, kisses her neck. Music; Indian film dance drama.* **Raj** *does melodramatic seduction acting,* **Sita** *is impassive. Suddenly* **Raj** *grows impatient and pulls* **Sita's** *sari, twirling her round and round.* **Sita** *is revealed in her petticoat and under-blouse.*

Raj *is about to remove her blouse when* **Prem** *runs into the room in some distress.*

Prem I dreamed I was being eaten by a cow!

He clings to his father's legs.

Raj The cows in England are miles away in the country. You are quite safe, now go back to bed. Ma and Bapu want to be alone.

Prem No, I want to sleep with Ma. I always do don't I Ma?

Raj Not tonight. Now go to your own bed.

Prem No I won't! I want to sleep with Ma. (*Shouts.*) I want Ma! I want Ma!

Raj And I want Ma. She was mine before she was yours.

Prem But she's mine now. I don't want you to sleep in her bed.

Raj It is not her bed, it is mine. I bought it from the Co-op. (*To* **Sita**.) Leave the room Sita.

Sita Don't beat him, Raj.

Raj I won't. I have things to explain. Father to son.

Sita *exits.*

My son, there is no need for this panic. You will never leave your mother. You will grow up and marry and bring your wife to our house and your mother will train your wife and help to bring up your sons and daughters, just like Dadima does now.

When I am old and no longer the head of the house, then you will take my place, you will make the choices. You will decide how the money is spent. How much to give to the Temple, how much to allow the women. It is a big responsibility and your mother and your wife will depend on you for their happiness.

Prem So Ma will always be mine?

Raj Until the day she is taken from you by God.

Prem I won't let God take her!

Raj Good little man, we'll have another talk when you are older. Now go to bed. Sita! Sita!

Scene Six

*Leicester market. Three weeks later. A fruit stall, a cacophony of sounds as stallholders compete in attracting attention. A **Woman** stands behind her fruit stall. She is wearing a sheepskin coat and a fur hat. She blows on her hands, stamps her feet.*

Stallholder Guavas, melons, all your exotics! Come on ladies! Fresh in today! Lovely fruit. Take some home to your old man. Ba-na-nas. O-ran-ges, Coxes Pipp-ins.

*A **White Woman** approaches the stall. She is a middle-class liberal. She looks at the fruit critically.*

Liberal Have you any unripe bananas left?

Stallholder Dunno love, I'll have a look. Cold enough for you?

She sorts through bananas.

Liberal I don't know how you do it. You're awfully brave to stand out in all weathers.

Stallholder (*shouting*) Ba-na-nas. Jaffa Oranges, Cox-es Pippins.

*An **Old White Woman** comes to the stall.*

Old Woman Can I have a few of each? Only I've got me husband in the infirmary. He likes a bit of fruit but it gus off so quick, don't it. In the 'eat of an 'ospital?

Stallholder You could grow tomatoes in them wards couldn't you?

Liberal Yes, the heat actually makes one feel worse.

Stallholder I was in last year, I didn't wear me bedjacket once.

Sita enters and hovers around the stall.

Old Woman He's a bit fussy, couldn't I pick me own?

Stallholder Sorry duck. No handling the fruit, that's the rule. I'll pick some out for you though. Just give me a minute to serve this lady.

Old Woman Sorry. I didn't mean to butt in.

Liberal Oh, that's all right.

*Sita gesticulates towards the fruit after catching the **Stallholder**'s eye.*

Stallholder (*to the **White Women***) Here we go. Pantomime time! (*Slowly and loudly.*) This twenty pence a pound. (*Pointing.*) This ten pence each. These eighteen pence. Understand? No, of course you

don't bloody understand. I don't know, they come over here, push
to the front of the queue . . .

Old Woman The hospital's full of black faces.

Liberal Yes. I owe my life to a black midwife.

Old Woman No, these are in the beds. Stopping us white people
from having our operations.

Stallholder They're taking over. No doubt about that. There's one
born every thirty seconds.

Old Woman (*alarmed*) In Leicester?

Stallholder No, the world!

Old Woman (*dismissively*) Oh that.

The **Stallholder** *is about to weigh the bananas, when she sees* **Sita** *picking
up the fruit.*

Stallholder Eh! Get your dirty black hands off my fruit! People
have got to eat that! They won't want it if they see you mauling it
about will they?

Sita holds an apple, uncomprehending but frightened by the violent tone.

I said put it down! Down! This is Leicester, not Calcutta.

Liberal She doesn't understand.

The **Stallholder** *grabs the apple from* **Sita**.

Stallholder She understands all right. They want to stick to their
own shops in their own districts. Not come into town stinking the
bleddy place out. (*To* **Sita**.) Go away. Go on. Go away. (*To*
Liberal.) That's thirty-nine pence, all right for you?

Liberal No. I don't want them now. I don't think you should have
spoken to her like that. It was very unkind.

Stallholder It's the only way they understand.

Liberal I shan't come to this stall again.

Stallholder Well I shan't cut me wrists over that.

Liberal (*to* **Sita**) I'm awfully sorry. Look would you like a coffee? No
of course not, well nice to meet you.

She holds out her hand. **Sita** *looks at it. The* **Liberal** *picks up* **Sita**'s *right
hand and manufactures a handshake.*

We're not all like that. At least not in Clarendon Park.

She rushes off in confusion.

Sita (*to the* **Stallholder**) Sabhat karna sikho.

Sita *exits.*

Old Woman What's she say?

Stallholder Paki talk. (*Calling after* **Sita**.) Come back when you've learnt to talk proper, like what I do! (*To the* **Old Woman**.) See how they go on?

Old Woman It's no wonder these racialists and such don't like them is it? I'm not one myself.

Stallholder Nor me. But I can feel myself turning.

Scene Seven

1976

Leicester. Outside a junior school gate. **Kishwar**, *a Muslim woman, is waiting outside the gate. She has a box of Pampers disposable nappies under her arm. She is in full Purdah, her face is completely veiled. From the school comes the sound of junior school children singing 'Away in a Manger'.* **Sita** *joins her.*

Sita They *are* late coming out today. It's twenty-five to.

Kishwar They are practising for the Christmas concert.

Sita Oh yes, I'm going to see it, are you?

Kishwar No, I am too busy tomorrow. I would like to see it . . . My daughter is an angel . . . She talks of nothing but her silver paper wings . . . (*Small pause.*) But there is singing and dancing and as you know it is forbidden for me.

Sita The singing and dancing of children?

Kishwar Yes. My husband has become very devout since we moved to this country. I did not always have this cloth between me and the world.

The sound of large numbers of children set free from school. **Prem** *and a little* **Girl** *in Muslim headdress run out of school.*

Zhora (*showing a painting*) Look Umy I painted an angel.

Kishwar Oh yes, it's very nice. But what are those lumps sticking out of its back?

Zhora That's her wings.

Prem The concert's dead good, Ma. I'm a horse.

Zhora No, you're a donkey, Mrs Mortlake said.

Prem I'm a horse. Donkeys are stupid.

Zhora Well so are you. You're only on Red Book One. Stupid git.

Kishwar Now Zhora don't be cruel. Prem has only been in England one year.

Sita He'll soon catch up. Won't you Prem?

Prem I *am* a horse. You'll see tomorrow.

Kishwar *and* **Zhora** *start to go.*

Zhora Are you coming to see me in the concert Umy?

Kishwar I'll ask.

Prem Her wings are stupid. They keep falling off. Mrs Mortlake tries to mend them but they just fall off again. Mrs Mortlake is a stupid cow!

Sita *slaps* **Prem**. *He bawls, open mouthed.* **Sita** *drags him away.*

Sita No Smarties on the way home!

Scene Eight

The school concert.

Sita *and* **Kishwar** *sit on hard chairs watching the concert. A piano plays 'We Three Kings of Orient Are'.* **Rose** *enters.*

Rose Eh up, Sita, is that anyone's seat or are you saving it? Trust me to be late. Me bleddy washer overflowed. Look there's my Delroy. (*She waves.*) Oh he's dropped his Frankincense. (*She looks anxious.*) Pick it up Delroy!

Sita Your daughter is a beautiful angel.

Kishwar Thank you. Your son looks very handsome as a donkey.

Rose Can she see?

Sita Tum dekh sakti ho.

Kishwar Han usko kaho main dekh sakti hoon.

Sita Yes she can, she's used to it now.

Rose (*to* **Sita**) Can she take it off at home?

Sita Yes, unless strangers arrive.

Rose It'd drive me mad. I can't stand anything around my face. Who makes her wear it?

Sita Kaun pehenata hai.

Kishwar Koi nahin, hamare dharm men hai.

Sita She says she wears it because it's traditional in her culture.

Rose That can't be right. I mean you wouldn't wear it out of choice would you? Shame really, she's ever so nice underneath it. I knew her before she took the veil. She's got lovely eyes. (*To* **Kishwar**.) OK?

Kishwar OK.

Rose Bloody hell, he's tripped over his dressing-gown now. He's a clumsy little sod! (*She mimes pulling a dressing-gown up, to her son.*) Sorry for swearing.

The piano changes to 'Silent Night'.

Sita I don't mind.

Rose You're not allowed to swear are you? Don't you get your hands chopped off or something?

Sita Shush Rose!

Rose Whoops a daisy, there goes Jesus, fell out of the crib! It's the same every bloody year.

Sita Who is that boy wearing the beard?

Rose That's Joseph.

Sita Who is he?

Rose He's the bloke Mary's married to.

Sita He's the father of Jesus.

Rose Well . . . No . . . Jesus is a miracle. He's God's child.

Sita Does Joseph know this?

Rose Oh he *knows*. Mary told him. But to my mind the true miracle was that Joseph believed her. I should have told my ex-husband that Delroy was God's child instead of Winston Johnson's.

Kishwar (*to* **Sita**) Oh her wings have fallen off!

Rose (*to* **Sita**) Tell her not to worry, it is traditional in our culture.

A primary school cow enters on its way to the stage. It stands beside **Rose**.

Rose Christ what's that?

Sita (*excited*) It's a cow, oh and so pretty. Look Kishwar, I've got a cow. Her name is Princess.

The cow goes on to the stage.

Rose That cow's name is Tracy Wainwright. I'd know them feet anywhere.

Sita (*clapping*) Good cow. Very good.

Rose Eh shut up. You'll get us chucked out. You don't clap at a nativity play, it's holy.

Kishwar Holy?

Sita Like Delroy's socks.

Rose You cheeky bugger, Sita. Oh don't they show you up!

Scene Nine

December 1977

Four **Women** *leaving a factory. Their scarves have slipped down. They are laughing.*

Lila . . . And his big fat behind! . . . Waddle, waddle . . . like my auntie-in-law dancing at my wedding!

She does a waddling impression.

It is ten years since Lakhani saw his toes!

The **Women** *laugh.*

Sarla Lila you are wicked! If Mr Lakhani heard you . . .

Anita You would get the sack.

Lila I can say what I like when I get out of his factory. He may have bought my time, but my tongue is still my own.

Anita Do his voice again, Lila.

Sita Do the bit about the talking.

Lila *takes on Mr Lakhani's physical characteristics: fat, pompous.*

Lila (*Mr Lakhani's voice*) You women are talking too much. It is slowing down your work. Do you want to bankrupt me? Do you want me to have to sell my £60,000 house and my mercedes . . . and my volkswagen bus . . .

Anita He didn't say that! (*She laughs.*)

Lila (*Mr Lakhani's voice*) Do you want to take the gold from my wife's throat? Or send my children to state schools? I will sack every damned one of you unless you reach the quota.

Sarla He did say that, about the quota.

Anita He is a foolish man, nobody can reach the quota.

Sita Not even if he put sticky tape over our mouths.

Lila The next time he shouts and raves I will prick his belly with a pin and he will fly around the workshop like a balloon.

She does a balloon deflating action complete with the noise. The **Women** *shriek with laughter and clutch each other. An elderly* **Indian Man** *walks by. He looks at them disapprovingly.*

Lila (*rattling car keys*) C'mon girls. Time to go, that's it for today. Chappatis to make.

Sita Children to fetch from school.

Anita Grandfather to wash.

Sarla Mother-in-law to quarrel with.

Lila Cheer up, work tomorrow! The quota!

Women The quota!

The **Women** *go, laughing.*

Scene Ten

The Prakash living-room, the next evening.

Raj It has come to my ears that you were behaving in a shameful manner yesterday.

Sita Me?

Raj After work, laughing and shrieking in the street with low-caste women.

Sita Can't I laugh now?

Raj Not if your laughter is loud enough to cause talk in the community.

Sita Who is this outraged person you listen to?

Raj The father of my work colleague Dev. He told his wife and his wife told my mother and naturally enough she told me. This is a small community, you must be careful!. I don't want to stop you working in the factory . . .

Sita Raj you wouldn't.

Raj . . . but if I hear any more bad reports on you I will have to consider it. Perhaps arrange for you to work at home.

Sita I laughed at Lila, she's so *funny*. You would have laughed if you had been there.

Raj But it doesn't matter if *I* laugh in the street.

Sita Is that fair?

Raj It's how things are.

Sita Not in India in our village.

Raj Laughter is different in a village. Here there are walls and echoes to make a woman's laughter sound defiant and coarse, and I don't want you to associate with Lila. She is a divorced woman.

Sita (*shouting*) Her husband is a lunatic who tried to set fire to her. What was she to do? Continue living with him until she was a pile of ashes?

Raj I can see that you care enough for this Lila to raise your voice in anger against me, so I forbid you to speak to her outside your workplace.

Sita Lila is my friend. She helps me with my English.

Raj There is no need for you to speak English. Anyone you need to speak to speaks your own language.

Spot on an **Asian Elder**, *who gives a speech.*

An **Indian Dancer** *performs a graceful, contained dance.*

Asian Elder As I was walking to the temple to perform my duties I saw some of our women laughing in the street. I heard the words they used to each other. They were bad words, invisible rough weapons of disrespect to the parents that gave them birth and culture.

We elders must protect our women from the invasion of Western attitudes and habits. They must be watched and guarded and cherished. They must not be allowed the terrible freedom that has ruined the family life of Westerners. Already there have been incidents, young girls complaining of restrictions, some even phoning the police and accusing their families of cruelty. One girl from our community left her home and sold her body to strangers. When I heard of this I was so ashamed I wept. Our women must not allow their bodies to be used by any man except their husbands. Sex must not be brought downstairs.

Sometimes I wonder if we were right to come here. Is it worth losing our culture just so that we play with Western toys?

When I see the bold brazen behaviour of some of our girls I wish that I was dead. For it is better to drown in a flood or starve during a famine than to see centuries of tradition wear away.

Each grain of sand once belonged to a rock. I am saving with the Bank of India, when I have enough money I will take my family home.

Scene Eleven

1977.

The Prakash living-room.

Bibi *is washing the floor on hands and knees.* **Mother-in-law** *and* **Fat Auntie** *are making chappatis.*

Mother-in-law Sita's chappatis are too hard/for my teeth.*

Bibi I like them.

Fat Auntie *She uses too much flour. I've told her but she won't listen.

Mother-in-law Raj likes soft chappatis.

Prem *enters. He looks down at* **Bibi.** **Mother-in-law** *and* **Fat Auntie** *smile at him.*

Bibi Wait a minute. /It's not dry yet.*

Fat Auntie We shouldn't be doing the kitchen work.

Prem *What am I supposed to do? I can't float.

Bibi Really? I thought you were a god/

Mother-in-law How many times has she burnt the lentils?

Bibi since you came to Leicester.*

Fat Auntie Twice this month.

Prem *You're jealous 'cos they like me best.

Prem *looks at* **Mother-in-law** *and* **Fat Auntie.**

Bibi All that petting and baby/talk? It

Mother-in-law Raj is too soft with her.

Bibi would drive me mad. Bugger off until the floor is dry.**

Fat Auntie She wants to be head of the house you know.*

Prem **No, I want to walk on it.

Bibi You dare.

Mother-in-law *What would happen to us if she was?

Fat Auntie She would turn me out.

Prem *walks over the floor.*

Mother-in-law I wouldn't let/her.*

Bibi /You rotten little sod!

She swipes **Prem** *with the floorcloth.*

Fat Auntie *But she might turn *you* out!

Mother-in-law Put me into an old/

Prem Cow!

Mother-in-law people's home you mean? Hai hai hai.

Bibi Do you want some more?

Prem *falls to the floor and works up to a tantrum.*

Fat Auntie
Mother-in-law } *(together)* Prem! What's wrong with/the baby?

Bibi He walked on the floor!

Mother-in-law *and* **Fat Auntie** *cuddle* **Prem.**

Fat Auntie ⎫ (*together*) Such a little one. What else is he to
Mother-in-law ⎭ do?

Bibi ⎫ (*together*) I asked him not to.
Prem ⎭ She hit me with a dirty cloth!

Mother-in-law Go upstairs to/your

Prem There's germs on it! I'll get a disease.

Mother-in-law room.

Fat Auntie She takes after her mother.

Mother-in-law Headstrong. Do as I say.

Fat Auntie Do as she says.

Bibi (*going*) Why do I always get the blame? (*To* **Prem**.) Why bother, they've given the Academy Awards out this year.

Mother-in-law *takes* **Prem** *and talks to him in Hindi.* **Fat Auntie** *goes back to the chappatis.*

Sita *enters.*

Sita What's the matter with him now? I could hear him in the street.

Prem Bibi hit me with a dirty cloth!

Fat Auntie For nothing.

Sita For nothing, Prem?

Sita *looks at him long and hard.* **Prem** *drops eye contact.*

Sita ⎫ (*together*) For nothing?
Fat Auntie ⎭ Bibi has to learn respect.

Mother-in-law She must learn to control/herself.

Sita For this spoiled boy? Why do you always take his side?

Mother-in-law I have to. You know that.

Prem (*to* **Mother-in-law**) She's always going on at me, always.

Fat Auntie Never mind, we love you.

Sita I love him, but I don't like him much, not now.

Fat Auntie You don't like England either do you?

Sita Everything is so grey.

Mother-in-law If you want colour go and see a film. We are here to work and save and go back to our village important people.

Fat Auntie Why am I doing this? It is her job.

Mother-in-law And I'm not well, but I have to look after the house. You shouldn't be out working.

Sita Maji. (*She grabs her by the shoulders.*) Promise me that the next time you are unwell you will tell me and I will do your work for you.

Mother-in-law Why this sudden affection? What do you want?

Sita I want us all to share this house peacefully. I don't want you to keep this feeling of resentment against me.

Prem Masi and Dadima don't like you Ma.

Mother-in-law ⎱ (*together*) Shush.
Fat Auntie   ⎰   Hold your tongue.

Sita I know. It makes me sad.

Fat Auntie (*to Sita*) Here, you make the chappatis!

Mother-in-law Yes. We'll take this poor boy and dress him in his lovely clothes, eh. Who's going to the dance tonight?

Prem We've been practising the stick dance at school today. I'm dead good at it.

They go.

Fat Auntie And not so much flour!

Sita *makes chappatis.* **Bibi** *enters and kisses* **Sita.**

Sita Don't worry about Prem, Bibi. I'm sure he deserved it. (*Small pause.*) You ought to dress soon.

Bibi Ma.

Sita Yes?

Bibi A terrible thing has happened to me.

Sita (*panic*) What? Are you ill?

Bibi Yes, I am bleeding.

Sita Where?

Bibi From my legs. At the top, I have such pains. Will I die?

Sita No, you won't die. You have become a woman.

She hugs **Bibi.**

I can't call you my little girl now.

Bibi I'm not ready to be a woman. I don't want to be a woman.

Sita But it's a good thing, women are strong and brave. We are the mothers of the world.

Bibi I don't want to be a mother. I might have a girl and then everyone will be angry.

Sita Silly! Silly! Have you washed yourself?

Bibi Yes, but it keeps coming back. I don't like it. I don't want to go to school tomorrow.

Sita Don't let it interrupt your life. Start as you mean to go on. I'll show you what to use. You're lucky living here – when I started my period . . .

Mother-in-law *and* **Fat Auntie** *enter.*

Masi, Maji, Bibi has started her period.

Mother-in-law Get away from the food!

Fat Auntie Why didn't you tell her?

Fat Auntie *takes over the chappatis.*

Sita I don't agree with it.

Mother-in-law (*to* **Bibi**) When you have a period you are unclean, you must not enter the kitchen. If you happen to approach a vessel of wine it will sour.

Fat Auntie If you touch any corn it will wither. Sit you under a tree, the fruit will fall. The very bees in the hive die. Iron and steel take rust.

Sita Nonsense! Old superstition. English women don't stop cooking.

Mother-in-law English women are not clean.

Fat Auntie You cannot go to Navratri now either. You may watch, but not dance.

Bibi But I want to dance.

Mother-in-law You cannot worship our Goddess if you are unclean!

Sita Our Goddess never bled?

Mother-in-law No, that is why we women worship her.

Raj *enters carrying an open* Leicester Mercury.

Raj Is there never any peace in this house? What's wrong with you all now?

Sita Raj. Our daughter became a woman today.

Mother-in-law Go out Raj. (*She pushes him.*)

Fat Auntie Don't listen!

Sita She started her period.

Raj *starts to move to* **Bibi**.

Mother-in-law In front of a man to use such words. (*She covers her ears.*)

Fat Auntie No shame!

Fat Auntie *and* **Mother-in-law** *wail*.

Sita Your mother has told Bibi she may not dance at Navratri tonight.

Raj (to **Mother-in-law**) Why not?

Mother-in-law It's not allowed, Raj. It will dishonour our family. It will insult the Goddess. Tell Bibi she may not dance.

Sita I say she will dance. Bibi, go and put your pretty clothes on.

Bibi No I'm dirty! I'm going to have a bath.

Fat Auntie No you must not bathe.

Mother-in-law She must not bathe, tell her Raj.

Sita She *will* bathe, and then she will dance. She will show our community how beautiful she is, and she will honour the Goddess. And all the while she will be bleeding, but she will hold her head high. And she will not be made to feel unclean!

Fat Auntie But not in front of the Goddess Raj!

Raj She will *not* dance Sita.

Sita Raj!

Raj She will *not* dance.

Sita She is my daughter as well, and I say she will dance. Why must we all do as you say?

Mother-in-law Your husband has spoken. Isn't that enough? (*To*

Raj.) She will kill me. Every day she is questioning. You should never have left her alone in India for so long. She has developed a will of her own, she is trying to dominate you.

Sita (*quietly*) I don't want to dominate, I want to share. I want to be up there with him, not above or below, but *with* him.

Scene Twelve

Navratri music. A big hall. A shrine containing a **Goddess** *to one side. A* **Male Dancer** *enters and dances around the stage. He is joined by members of the family.* **Raj, Mother-in-law, Fat Auntie** *and* **Prem** *dance in a circle.* **Sita** *and* **Bibi** *enter.* **Sita** *is carrying the bucket.* **Bibi** *sits on a chair and watches.* **Raj** *pulls* **Sita** *into the dance.* **Raj** *drops out of the dance and takes an offering of money to the* **Goddess**. **Prem** *follows him and examines the other offerings. They rejoin the dance.*

Mother-in-law *and* **Fat Auntie** *give offerings to the* **Goddess***, then they rejoin the dance.* **Sita** *leaves the dance and joins* **Bibi***. She picks up the bucket and gives it to* **Bibi**. **Bibi** *pours milk from the bucket into a dish at the* **Goddess***'s feet. The* **Goddess** *drinks the milk, then steps down from the shrine. She joins hands with* **Sita** *and* **Bibi** *and dances with them. They dance faster and laugh.*

Act Two

Scene One

*The Prakash living-room. A **Bride** is sitting. She is veiled and still. She is surrounded by **Women** laughing and talking.*

Mother-in-law It won't be long before she knows what it is to be a wife eh?

Fat Auntie I hope he is gentle with her. My husband frightened me so much I didn't open my eyes for a month! Never mind my legs!

2nd Fat Auntie You couldn't believe what you were seeing eh?

Fat Auntie It was a new sight!

Mother-in-law But you got used to it eh?

Laughter.

Fat Auntie Oh yes, but it didn't last long.

She lapses into melancholy.

2nd Fat Auntie No, no, I won't let you tell us about your years as a barren widow. We have heard it a thousand times. Come on, get up and dance with me.

*She pulls **Fat Auntie** to her feet.*

Come on! Everybody dancing! Come on old women, show these young girls how to dance. They are as stiff as broom handles. Bend! Bend! Dip and bend.

*The **Women** dance in a circle, young and old. The **Bride** sits with downcast eyes.*

*At the end of the dance **Prem** is led in.*

2nd Fat Auntie I hope you are prepared for this ordeal.

Prem *stands. The **Women** sit.*

Fat Auntie He eats with his mouth wide open!

Mother-in-law And sleeps with it open too, his snores rattle the windows! His poor bride will get no peace!

*The **Women** giggle and nudge each other.*

Fat Auntie But then look at the size of his big fat nose!

2nd Fat Auntie You know what they say. Big nose, big sou sou.

The **Women** *laugh.*

Mother-in-law No, that's not right! Don't you remember when we would dry him after his bath? His sou sou was so small, what did we need to find it? A magnifying glass!

Fat Auntie And have you heard that there is more hair on his hands than on his chest?

Bibi He will be bald by the time he's thirty. Look, his hair's falling out.

Prem Where? (*He looks at his shoulder.*)

Bibi It's all the whisky he drinks!

Mother-in-law That's why his eyes are pink like a rat's.

Prem I'm not here to be insulted.

Bibi That's exactly what you are here for, cretin.

Prem *fingers his nose.*

Sita Oh Prem, I thought you liked the traditions. It's traditional to respond with good humour.

Prem It's stupid!

Bibi He can't think of anything to say.

Fat Auntie He is dull witted!

Mother-in-law He was nine years of age before he could tie his shoelaces!

Prem I was eight!

The **Women** *laugh.*

Fat Auntie Is that the best you can do?

Mother-in-law Is it true he has no savings?

Fat Auntie Oh yes, it is true!

A loud whisper.

That's why he is marrying this girl.

2nd Fat Auntie (*loud whisper*) I hear she brings a cash dowry with her.

Sita (*quietly*) The insults are only for Prem. She is not here to be insulted.

Fat Auntie It is no insult to have a good dowry. It shows she comes from a provident family.

Prem Have you finished?

Fat Auntie No we have not! Come on, you young women, you are leaving us to think up insults. It is the only chance you ever get so don't waste it.

Bibi I can think of a few good ones, but Prem looks as if he's going to cry, so I won't. And look, she's crying. I don't blame her. I would if I had to marry him.

Prem You wait Bibi.

Mother-in-law Good Bibi, carry on.

Bibi If I carried on speaking the truth about Prem, this girl would get up and run from the room. So I will keep silent.

*The **Bride** wipes her eyes with the corner of her veil. **Sita** comforts her.*

Mother-in-law Sita, don't give her comfort. You will have kitchen trouble if you are too friendly.

Sita I'm not going to make an enemy of a seventeen year-old girl who is leaving her family to live amongst strangers.

Fat Auntie Prem is not a stranger. She has met him four times!

Prem They always cry the night before.

Sita (*to **Indira**, the **Bride***) Do you want to marry my son?

*Shock from everyone except **Bibi**.*

Look at him!

Indira *glances briefly at **Prem** then looks away.*

Indira It is all arranged.

Sita It can all be disarranged.

Mother-in-law No it cannot! The food is ordered! The hall is booked!

Fat Auntie People are coming from the M6 and the M1!

2nd Fat Auntie She will be disgraced if the wedding is called off. Then she will never marry.

Bibi There's love marriage. Lots of the girls at school had them.

Mother-in-law A love marriage is a step into darkness hoping that you will not fall too far. But Indira's and Prem's marriage has been gone into carefully, they are well matched.

Bibi I think they are very badly matched. Indira is a nice girl but Prem is a lying sneaky bastard.

Mother-in-law That's enough Bibi.

Prem I've had enough of this. Can I go?

Mother-in-law Yes. Go.

Prem *leaves the room without a backward glance.*

Fat Auntie Come on now! Come on, start the music up, Bibi. You know how to work that machine.

Scene Two

Rose's *living-room. Loud reggae music playing.*

Rose (*off*) Delroy! Delroy! Turn that bleddy music down! *Delroy*!!! I've gorra customer with me!

Sorry to keep you waiting – I'll be out in a bit – I'm just putting me face on. Ooh, it's like plastering a wall – Max Factor oughta present me with a long service medal.

Rose *rushes on.*

Right, this is me spring catalogue. We'll have a good look through it in a bit. But I can recommend it. If it weren't for this, me and Delroy'd be going round naked. I mean, who can afford to pay cash for new stuff nowadays? I never thought I'd gerrit going. When I seen the Indians moving in round here I thought, oh well, you can say goodbye to building yourself a round up, Rose. I were a bit suspicious of 'em at first. Well, when they first come, some of 'em looked at me like I were muck. I know I ain't much, but I ain't muck. You can get used to owt can't you? And some of them are really nice – not all, but some. Any road up, as it turned out, I've got myself a nice little round going in our street. I take me catalogue round of a Wednesday, collect the money, and after we've had a few drinks, I ask 'em if they want owt else. Sita's paying me one-fifty a week for some sheets she had last year. When she's finished paying, she's having a ottoman to put 'em in.

Bibi had her first pair of jeans from out my club – Christ, didn't that cause a stink! You'd have thought she'd had a G-string or sommat! Them two old bags, bleddy Dadima an' Masi wanted Sita to send 'em back, but Sita stuck to her guns.

O'course, that were a few year ago – she's having a bit of a wobbler now. I don't know what's up, but sommat is. She's not the same girl as come here eight year ago. To tell the truth, I don't know her now. She works too hard. She's out the house at eight, and don't get back till after six, and I know she don't sit down when she gets home. She's always up and doing – has to be busy. Now I've learnt the secret of relaxation? I take life gradual, have a few laughs. It's laughing's kept me going. An it's free, so I can recommend that and all! Anyway, what you going to have?

Scene Three

The next day.

Sita *alone looking in a blank mirror touching her body.*

Sita Sita, where are you? I don't know where you are. Come back to me. You've been away so long I'm afraid that I won't know you when you come back.

Raj *enters unnoticed. He watches* **Sita** *anxiously.*

Is this you? (*She pinches her arm.*) Is this your hair? (*She pulls her hair.*) Your belly? (*She punches her own belly. Shouts.*) No it is not you! (*She beats herself. Despairing.*) Sita! Sita! I want you, please come back!

Raj, *frightened and furious, walks up to* **Sita**, *turns her in front of the mirror, forces her head until she is staring into the mirror.*

Raj You *are* there you mad woman, you are there. You want proof?

He slaps her and knocks her to the floor.

If you feel pain then you are there. Now get to your feet. We have visitors soon.

Raj *exits.*

Sita *gets up calmly and tidies herself, applies lipstick in the mirror, turns to leave, goes back to the mirror.*

She exits.

Scene Four

Fat Auntie, **Mother-in-law** *and* **Raj** *in the living-room. The same day.*
Prem *enters smoking. He puts his cigarette in the corner of* **Fat Auntie**'s
mouth while she sleeps.

Prem Dead good impression *she's* going to make, look at her.

Looking at **Fat Auntie**.

Mother-in-law (*to* **Fat Auntie**) Don't go to sleep now! Take that
out of your mouth. They will be here soon. Look alert.

Prem How long they gonna be, Dad? I can't hang about, I've got a
meet set up. There's a guy after the Datsun.

Raj If they don't come soon I'll ring and tell them to cancel. They
are wasting my time.

He gets up and paces around the room.

Prem I should get three hundred quid, if he don't notice the filler.

Raj (*angry*) Two more minutes then I ring.

Prem Is this the one whose dad's got the video shops?

Raj Yes, four.

Mother-in-law Hear that sister? Video shops. We'll be all right for
films, eh?

Fat Auntie Let's hope she accepts this time.

Prem She reckons she don't want to get married.

Mother-in-law She is twenty years old, time is passing. People will
be thinking there is something wrong with her.

The bell rings.

Raj (*shouting*) Sita! They're here.

Sita (*off*) I know, I'm going.

Mother-in-law Everybody sit up! Look respectable.

Raj *goes to the door as two men enter. One is* **Mr Patel** *the other is his son*
Ram *who is wearing flared trousers.*

Mr Patel (*shaking hands with* **Raj**) I am most sorry to be so late.

Ram *looks shy, awkward.*

Raj Not at all, not at all, are you late? I didn't notice. This way.
My mother, my aunt and my son.

Prem (*giving his card to* **Mr Patel**) My card – Prakesh Motors.

Mr Patel Thank you. So you are in the car business?

Prem Purveyor of quality secondhand vehicles.

Mother-in-law Excuse me. I have kitchen work to do.

Mother-in-law *stares at* **Ram Patel** *before she leaves the room.*

Raj Please sit down.

They all sit. Long pause.

So how old is your son?

Mr Patel Twenty-one years.

Prem How many 'A' levels has he got?

Mr Patel Ram, show these people that you have a tongue.

Ram (*shy*) No 'A' levels, but three 'O' levels, English, maths and physics.

Mr Patel Good grades, nothing below a B.

Fat Auntie And have you had rickets?

Ram No.

An awkward silence.

Mr Patel He has passed his driving test.

Fat Auntie First time?

Mr Patel No third.

Prem Passed mine first time.

Fat Auntie What is his character like? I can see that he is shy.

Mr Patel Yes, he is a shy extrovert.

Fat Auntie What is that, extrovert?

Raj Always laughing.

Fat Auntie Heh! This one?

Mr Patel Speak up Ram. Talk about your hobbies.

Ram I like films and television and I write poetry.

Prem Poetry!?

Ram It is no good but . . .

Mr Patel Of course it is good. It is excellent poetry.

Fat Auntie And what are his vices?

Mr Patel He hasn't got any vices have you, Ram?

Ram I eat sweets. And my room is untidy sometimes.

Mr Patel The first is nothing. The second a wife will correct.

An awkward pause.

Raj Ah, the women with the food.

*The **Women** enter carrying tit-bits of food.*

My mother you've met, my wife. My daughter Bibi. Beautiful, isn't she?

Ram Hello.

Bibi Hello.

Mr Patel Bibi is how old?

Raj Eighteen.

Bibi (*corrects*) Twenty. I've got three 'A' levels.

Everyone takes a piece of food.

Raj Bibi cooked this herself, didn't you Bibi?

Bibi No Ma cooked it. I don't like cooking.

Mother-in-law (*alarm*) She likes to joke! She is a slave to the stove. We have to tear her away.

Mr Patel A sense of humour is a good thing – in moderation.

Raj Bibi is moderate in most things, aren't you Bibi?

Bibi No, I am considered extreme in most things.

Raj Again she jokes, she is so happy and cheerful!

Fat Auntie Stand up and show yourself girl.

Bibi *stands, does a twirl.*

Bibi I am twenty years old, Hindu. I am five feet six inches tall. My complexion is good, my skin tone light, my teeth (*She bares her gums.*) are perfect. I have two fillings, gold. I weigh nine stone when I am naked. My shoe size is five and a half, my pelvis is wide. Naturally I will have many sons. I speak English, Hindi, Gujerati, a little Punjabi, and French. I read two library books a week. I cook good chappatis and can make my own clothes. I have a light melodious singing voice, I dance gracefully and I am currently working in the gas offices where I earn £95 a week before tax.

She sits down to silence. A pause. She rises again.

And most important of all. I am a virgin.

Prem (*under his breath*) Fucking hell.

She sits down to horrified silence. She rises again.

Bibi Sorry. My dowry consists of blankets, sheets, an electric toaster, a fridge freezer, a portable colour television . . . a magi-mix with full accessories.

Mr Patel Come, Ram. The girl is laughing at us.

Mother-in-law She must be ill. She has never spoken like this before. Call for a doctor.

Sita She's not ill. She told the truth!

Raj Sita! (**Sita** *and* **Bibi** *stand together.*)

Sita She told them what they came to find out. Why waste everyone's time with fine words?

Mr Patel She is too Western. We want a traditional girl.

Mr Patel *and* **Ram** *back out of the room.*

Sita Go on then, go and look for your kitchen slave. My daughter will be an executive one day. She will have her own mortgage. She has money saved in the Leicester Building Society!

The **Patels** *exit.*

Mother-in-law Why doesn't she stick a knife in my heart and be done with it? (*To* **Sita**.) Go on, kill me now!

Fat Auntie It's her fault Bibi is so outspoken.

Raj (*to* **Bibi**) By tonight the whole of the community will have learnt of our shame.

Bibi Stop bringing them to the house, Pa.

Prem Four video shops and she blew it.

Bibi You think I'd marry a man wearing flared trousers?

Prem (*shouting*) For four fucking video shops *I'd* marry a man in flared trousers.

Sita She's going to buy land and a cow!

Bibi Ma I've only got thirty pounds saved.

Bibi *goes to leave the room.*

Raj Where are you going?

Bibi Out!

Bibi *exits.* **Raj** *sits with his head in his hands.*

From now on the rest of the family treat **Sita** *as though she were invisible.*

Mother-in-law Your wife is sick in the head. Cows! And land!

Fat Auntie Did you notice the strange look in her eye lately? I did.

Sita Who are you talking about? What strange look?

Mother-in-law Pressure takes different women different ways.

Raj But she's had no pressure.

Prem What about at work? She's a supervisor.

Sita You're talking about me?

Raj I should have stopped her years ago! I blame myself.

Sita Raj, I'm here look.

Mother-in-law You've got a soft heart, son. Sometimes it can be a curse.

Sita I'm here!

Fat Auntie It stops you doing your duty.

Sita Auntie!

Prem It's not as if she needs to work is it? Not now there's three of us bringing money home?

Sita Prem, can you see me?

Mother-in-law Yes, you must stop her working, Raj. Make her take a rest. We'll look after her won't we, sister?

Fat Auntie Yes. We'll take her to the doctor's.

Raj No, I'll take her. I'll make an appointment.

Sita I'm not sick!

Prem I reckon she started cracking up about the time of my wedding.

Mother-in-law The wedding that never was, poor boy.

Sita Ma Ge.

Prem It was all her fault it was called off.

Sita The girl didn't like you, she was brave enough to say no.

Mother-in-law People don't want madness in the family, who can blame them?

Sita (*shouting*) I'm standing here in front of you!

Fat Auntie Where is she?

Mother-in-law She'll be mooning over that stupid old bucket.

Fat Auntie You see? Only a mad person would do such a thing.

Raj I'll go and see.

Raj *crosses right in front of* **Sita** *and exits.*

Scene Five

The loo in the Palais. Midnight.

Bibi Well, I had a brilliant time tonight. Debauchery galore there was. I've been with every bloke in the Palais – must be 200. I came in at eight and it's Cinderella time now. So it's not bad going is it? It's my legs you see. One glimpse and the English blokes are sitting on their haunches panting for it and I'm so depraved and corrupted by the West that I let them have it. You see I've no morality of my own. No respect for my body. I've got three 'A' levels but no intelligence. I can't be trusted, after all I'm only twenty. Mum knows I come here. There's nothing I wouldn't tell her – well the odd thing. But Mum doesn't count for much in our family. When it's not at Sketchleys I keep me gear in a black plastic bag in Mum's wardrobe, next to her bucket. It's pathetic. Here I am an Asian girl caught in a culture clash. See these things each side of my head? Inverted commas. Now the English *are* lucky – they don't have family problems. No, they sit around in shafts of sunlight eating cornflakes, then get up and run around meadows in slow motion. One in four that is. The other three are undergoing divorce or family therapy. Yes we all jostle for space on the *Guardian* Women's Page. There's me, cheek by jowl with 'Shall I, a committed Socialist, send my Rupert to public school?' Now that *would* make you toss and turn at night. I'm educated. I'm healthy, and I'll make myself some sort

of life. But until then I'll change in the bog. Me mum's got enough
on her plate. (*Pause.*) If anyone asks, I've been babysitting.

Scene Six

Dr Mistry's *surgery. The next day.* **Raj** *and* **Sita**, *seated.* **Dr Mistry**
pacing about.

Dr Mistry So there are no problems in your family?

Raj No, no problems. My son is in business now, my daughter
passed her 'As' and will marry soon. We have a comfortable home.
No, no problems.

Dr Mistry Your wife is obsessed with cows you say?

Raj Obsessed?

Dr Mistry A medical term. It means morbidly interested.

Raj Yes, she is morbidly interested in cows.

Sita There is only one cow.

Dr Mistry Yes, naturally Mrs Prakesh. Of course there is only one
cow.

Sita Her name is Princess.

Raj You see?

Dr Mistry Charming. She is a pretty cow?

Sita Not particularly. Her eyes are nice but she was really nothing
special. She wasn't a film star.

Dr Mistry No, naturally.

Raj What will become of her? (*He weeps.*)

Dr Mistry I see many women like her.

Raj All morbidly interested in cows?

Dr Mistry No, your wife is lucky, at least this cow seems to give her
pleasure. (*To* **Sita**.) You like this cow don't you Mrs Prakesh?

Sita She is everything to me.

Raj Perhaps if she'd had more children. It is my fault! I will never
forgive myself.

Dr Mistry You have had your testicles tied?

Raj No, but I failed to impregnate her more than twice. Even her womb is stubborn.

Sita *laughs.*

Dr Mistry I will give you a prescription. You must make sure your wife takes the tablets I prescribe.

Raj Will she stop thinking about the cow?

Dr Mistry Oh yes. She will stop thinking altogether. Good morning.

Dr Mistry *stands.* **Raj** *and* **Sita** *exit.*

Scene Seven

Two months later.

Sita *is sitting in the ward of a mental hospital. She is perfectly composed, thinking.*

Nurse Visitors, Mrs Prakesh. (*Pause.*) Mrs Prakesh!

She shakes **Sita** *gently.*

Sita I want to go home. I'm not mad.

Nurse No, you are just here for a rest, aren't you?

Sita Not even that, I was not tired.

Raj, **Bibi**, **Prem**, **Mother-in-law**, **Fat Auntie** *enter.* **Bibi** *runs up to* **Sita** *and holds her tight.*

Mother-in-law To see her in such a place! I can't bear it, it will kill me. All these crazy people we passed.

Fat Auntie Did you do the right thing, Raj? She is looking perfectly calm now.

Raj I listened to the doctor's advice. I am not an expert in these affairs.

Bibi But you know your own wife.

Prem She was round the bend. You know she was. Cows! Cows! Cows!

Sita (*to* **Raj**) You put me in here. (*To* **Prem**.) And you.

Fat Auntie *and* **Mother-in-law** *fuss with the food looking for somewhere to put it.*

Prem Don't blame me!

Raj You were behaving so strangely, Sita.

Fat Auntie We have brought food for you, Sita. You must eat it all up and get well again.

Mother-in-law Will Raj put *me* in this place if I lose my keys again?

Fat Auntie No. Of course not. I won't let him. (*Pause.*) And what about me? I have been having strange thoughts lately.

Mother-in-law Thoughts?

Fat Auntie Yes. About so many things. Wrong things. Things I can't say aloud.

Mother-in-law Then don't say them aloud.

Fat Auntie But I can't stop my brain from thinking, sister.

Mother-in-law We are too old to start thinking.

Sita Bibi, the next time you come bring my bucket, will you?

Prem The hospital won't allow it, Mama.

Raj There are bound to be regulations, rules.

Bibi Yes, Mama I'll bring the bucket.

Mother-in-law Lila was asking for you, Sita. She sends her love and says work is now a dull place without you.

Raj Dull without Sita?

Mother-in-law Sita was the life and soul. That's what Lila said, the life and soul. I don't know what it means.

Prem It means Mama was good for a laugh, that can't be right.

Raj No, that *can't* be right.

Bibi That's what you think. We have a really good time don't we, Ma?

Sita When they let us.

Fat Auntie (*to* **Mother-in-law**) That is what I have been thinking! I have needed permission all my life. Permission. Father, husband, Raj, and if I live long enough, Prem. Permission, always permission.

Mother-in-law Sister keep your thoughts to yourself! You have stored them away in a jar like a good housewife for 40 years. Don't let them out to spoil in the air.

Bibi Masi, we'll sit up and talk tonight. And you Dadima don't go to bed at nine. Let's stay up late and keep each other company, eh?

Mother-in-law What will we talk about for so long?

Bibi We will open Auntie's jar and see what is inside eh?

Prem If you ask me you all belong in the loony bin.

Mother-in-law Nobody is asking you are they. So shut your ugly mouth.

Shock.

Oh I'm sorry, it is this place. It made me forget myself.

Prem *looks at his watch.*

Prem I've got to be somewhere in half an hour so when you're ready . . .

Mother-in-law Oh, we'd better go.

Bibi No, we've only just arrived.

Raj But Prem is driving so . . .

Bibi So I will phone for a taxi. We can be independent of Prem to get around –

Fat Auntie Yes, I never thought of a taxi. Simple isn't it?

Sita Don't look so unhappy, Prem. Go and keep your appointment. I can see that you don't like to be here. Take your father with you.

Raj But I'm not ready to go yet.

Prem Are you coming or do you wanna go home with the women?

Raj *and* **Prem** *exit.*

Scene Eight

The living-room. Later that day.

Prem *is sitting with the Princess photograph in his hand.* **Bibi** *enters. She hesitates before moving toward* **Prem**. **Prem** *doesn't notice* **Bibi** *until she pulls the photograph out of his hand.* **Bibi** *looks at the photo.*

Bibi I thought it was lost. I haven't seen it for years. God, I was skinny then!

Prem I had it in my wallet. I donno why I hated that cow.

Pause.

It just about cracked me up seeing her in there.

Bibi You were quick enough to take her in!

Prem I only drove the car. I didn't sign the papers! She hates me.

Bibi No, but she doesn't like what you've become and neither do I.

Prem The others like me.

Bibi You're their insurance policy, Prem. You'll be head of the house one day, you thick git!

Prem I didn't ask to be head of the house. I don't want them all on my back. I wanna live my own life.

Bibi Well, you've got a few years yet.

Prem What's gonna happen to Ma?

Bibi That's up to you.

Prem And you.

Bibi Since when did I have any influence over anything?

Prem Well I'm not doing it on me own. When I were driving back I kept thinking about in India. I donno how she did it. Bringing us up on us own. No money, just that cowin' cow.

Bibi She did it 'cos she's a bleddy wonderful woman.

Prem (*pause*) We should have stayed in India.

Bibi D'you reckon? I'm glad we came, I wouldn't have got three 'A' levels at the village school would I?

Prem You couldn't call it a school. It were a patch of ground under a tree.

Bibi And look how well you're doing with your garage.

Prem It's only a lock-up under a railway arch.

Bibi It's a start. You'd be a rich man in India.

Prem I wouldn't mind going back. Just to see it like.

Bibi Yeah.

Prem I'll go and see Ma tomorrow, on me own.

Bibi Take her the photo, she'd like that.

Prem No, I want the photo.

Scene Nine

One month later.

Sita *sitting in the mental hospital ward, her bucket at her feet. A* **Patient** *enters and stands to one side.* **Kishwar** *enters wearing a borqa.*

Sita Kishwar, is that you?

Kishwar Sita! Is that your voice?

Sita Yes, it's me. (*She takes* **Kishwar**'s *hands.*) Why are you here?

Kishwar I have lost my face. Why are you here?

Sita I want to buy a cow.

Kishwar Have you seen my face, Sita?

Sita No I have never seen your face. When did you see it last?

Kishwar I'm sure I had it last year. Perhaps I left it somewhere.

Sita Somewhere in the house?

Kishwar Yes, I have not left the house until this day so it is somewhere in the house. I have asked everyone. Have you seen my face? Where is my face? They say, Kishwar your face is still there. But it's not. It's not. It's gone.

Sita Let me see for myself.

Kishwar No.

Sita *raises* **Kishwar**'s *veil. There is nothing there.*

Sita You have not lost your face, Kishwar. It has been stolen.

The **Patient** *and* **Sita** *comfort* **Kishwar**.

Scene Ten

Mother-in-law, **Fat Auntie**, **Bibi** and **Lila** enter. The **Patient** exits.

Lila Sita!

She runs to **Sita**.

Sita Lila!

Lila They told me you were crazy! But look at you, you were pretending, eh? To get a rest!

Sita You're the one who should be in here. You were always a madwoman.

Lila When they told me you had gone crazy on cows, I said so what? If she wants a cow, buy her a cow.

Mother-in-law How are you Daughter?

Sita I am well. But I want to leave here now. This is a very sad place you know. It is depressing me.

Bibi I talked to the doctor.

Sita Him? He's mad. Don't listen to anything he says.

Bibi He says that you can come out for the day.

Sita Out? Do you mean home?

Bibi Yes, if you want to . . .

Lila Home! She doesn't want to go to boring home. I have the car. We will go out for a run. See the countryside.

Fat Auntie Oh yes! I mean whatever everyone else would like to do. Sita? It's your day.

Sita I can choose? What a gift!

Bibi Do you want to go to the country?

Sita Yes, could we walk on the grass?

Bibi You can take your clothes off and roll in the grass if you want to.

Mother-in-law No, that is going too far.

Fat Auntie But we have no food!

Lila There are cafés, shops, this is Leicestershire, not the foothills of the Himalayas. Well, what are we waiting for?

Bibi Come on, Ma.

Mother-in-law An adventure. (*She clasps her hands girlishly.*) Where are we going?

Lila Who knows? I will get behind the wheel and let the car take us where it wants.

Scene Eleven

The **Women**, *travelling in the car.*

Fat Auntie Not so fast Lila!

Lila I have slowed down to 30. Nice country, eh.

Mother-in-law I don't know, my eyes are shut.

Bibi Isn't it lovely Lila? It was near here I came camping with the Guides. My first night away from home. I cried so much Akala brought me home the next day.

Fat Auntie And you taught us all that terrible song about goolies.

Mother-in-law With words for idiots.

Sita I thought it was a foreign language, French. I thought it was French.

Sita *sings 'Ging gang gooly'. Everyone joins in.*

Look cows! Stop the car!

Groans from everyone else but **Bibi**.

Bibi Stop the car, Lila. Stop!

Lila *stops the car.*

Mother-in-law Remember the green cross code!

Sita *crosses the road. She runs to the fence, looks into the meadow. Two* **Cows** *approach the fence.*

Sita Hello. How are you?

Both Cows Not happy. We are going to the market today.

Sita Do you know Princess?

1st Cow Princess?

2nd Cow From India?

Sita Yes, that's her.

1st Cow Mummm.

Sita She is looking for me. Will you tell her where I am?

Both Cows Mummm.

Sita Where is the market?

2nd Cow Melton Mowbray, just down the road.

Sita Thank you, goodbye. (**Sita** *crosses the road and gets into the car.*)

Both Cows Morning.

1st Cow } Nice woman.
2nd Cow } Good smell.

Sita We are going to Melton Mowbray.

Lila Where is that?

Sita That cow said it was just down the road.

Mother-in-law Ay ay ay.

Fat Auntie A cow told you? How can you believe a cow? In my experience they are very unreliable. You have heard the expression, 'lying cow'?

Mother-in-law Yes. Better look at the map.

Scene Twelve

The cattle market.

The **Women** *enter the showing area. They look at the ring. An* **Auctioneer** *and a stockman,* **Harold**, *are talking at the side entrance gate.*

Mother-in-law Chi, what a stink! My nose thinks it has been dipped in a sewer.

Auctioneer Now there's a nice one for my collection.

Harold Never had a brown 'un?

Auctioneer Never had the opportunity, Harold. Don't see many Asiatics round here.

Fat Auntie Watch where you're putting your feet, Sita. You're getting cow dung on your sandals.

Harold Look at the arse on that one. (*He goes to whistle at* **Bibi** *but the* **Auctioneer** *stops him.*)

Auctioneer Not so crude, Harold, they're easily frightened.

Lila You belong in a straight jacket, Sita. A day out and you choose to trample in cow shit!

The **Women** *laugh.*

Auctioneer (*to the* **Women**) Morning ladies. (*He tips his hat slightly.*)

Women Morning. (*They are quite pleased at this politeness.*)

Auctioneer Can we be of any assistance?

Bibi No thank you, we're going now. Have you seen enough, Ma?

Sita Yes. I don't like it here. I want to go.

Harold This is a short cut ladies.

He opens the gate. The **Women** *walk towards the gate and are about to pass by the* **Men** *when* **Harold** *grabs* **Bibi**'s *wrist.*

Women Thank you.

Harold Nearly fell din't you?

Bibi No I didn't, let go! (**Harold** *continues holding* **Bibi**'s *wrist.*)

Auctioneer While you're here, I'd just like to say that you've got the nicest pair of tits I've seen in a lifetime's study.

Bibi, *shocked, instinctively covers her breasts with her free hand.*

Lila You dirty bastard!

Auctioneer Foul mouthed cow!

Sita *is chopping at* **Harold**'s *hand holding* **Bibi**'s *wrist.*

Sita Let my daughter go! (**Harold** *fondles* **Bibi**'s *bum.*)

Bibi Mama!

Auctioneer Shut the other gate, Harold. We'll have a good look at 'em.

Harold *closes the back gate, trapping the* **Women**. *The* **Auctioneer** *closes the side gate.* **Lila** *rushes to the side gate, tries to open it.*

Auctioneer Give her a bit of stick, Harold!

Harold *hits* **Lila** *hard. She runs around the ring as a cow.*

Harold Gwaan gwaan, move round you stubborn buggers!

*The **Auctioneer** stands on his podium.*

Auctioneer Get 'em moving, Harold!

Harold *pokes the stick into the group of women. The **Women** move apart a little and run round the ring.*

Auctioneer Separate them out, Harold. Get 'em running. Go on Harold show 'em who's master.

Mr Patel *enters. He stands at the side of the ring appraising the **Women**.*

Harold Geed up! Geed up! Go on run you buggers!

Auctioneer A small herd and a rarity in these parts. Pedigree Indian stock. Good breeders and three guaranteed milkers. What am I bid for a herd? C'mon gentlemen, what am I bid? No bids? C'mon gentlemen, who'll start? Who'll start? No bids? Get rid of the old uns, Harold.

Harold *forces **Mother-in-law** and **Fat Auntie** to the side of the ring. They stand together. The other three **Women** continue round the ring.*

Auctioneer Three milkers gentlemen, fine colour, a rarity. What am I bid?

*This is repeated five times. **Mr Patel** shakes his head slightly.*

No takers. Show us the young un, Harold.

Harold *forces **Sita** and **Lila** to the side of the ring. The **Women** herd together. They make low distressed cow noises. **Bibi** moves slowly making whimpering cow noises. **Mr Patel** takes part in the bidding.*

Auctioneer A youngun. A youngun. Full udders. Fine legs. Good colour. A hundred and fifteen! And twenty! Twenty-five, thirty, thirty-five, *two hundred, two hundred.*Two hundred and fifty-and seventy. Eighty. Three, Three, Three-Three hundred and two, five and fifty. Seven five. Four hundred . . . and fifty. Five. Five hundred. Six hundred. That's more like it. Seven. Eight. A thousand. Two hundred and three. Three, four, five a thousand five hundred! Five hundred. Six, seven, eight. Two thousand five hundred. Sold to Mr Patel! Take her away Harold.

Harold *prods **Bibi**.*

Harold Move you cow!

Bibi *straightens up then tries to run away. But **Harold** pushes her down, pins her to the ground and forces her legs apart. **Bibi** screams.*

Sita *leads the other* **Women** *into Kali sequence. They bear down on* **Harold**.

Auctioneer Settle 'em down, Harold! They're getting out of control.

Bibi *joins the* **Women**.

Use your stick, man!

The **Women** *continue moving in on* **Harold**.

The **Auctioneer** *runs from his podium and through the gate, leaving it open. The* **Women** *continue towards* **Harold**. *He threatens them with his stick.*

The **Auctioneer** *runs into the ring.*

Now get back! Move back! I'm used to being obeyed!

The **Auctioneer** *is knocked out of the way. He runs out of the ring.*

Harold *raises his stick to attack the* **Women** *but* **Sita** *pulls it from him.* **Harold** *falls on the floor.* **Sita** *stands over him threatening him with the stick.*

Harold Don't kill me, please! Please! Please! I'm sorry.

The **Women** *begin to normalise.* **Harold** *takes a chance and jumps up.*

You want locking up! You're fucking mad the whole lot of you.

Auctioneer If you're not out of here in one minute I'm phoning the police.

The **Auctioneer** *and* **Harold** *go.*

Sita Call the police, we'll do the same to them!

The **Women** *jeer and gesticulate at the* **Men**. **Mother-in-law** *makes particularly violent gestures.*

Lila I'll fetch the car round. (*As she exits.*) Don't let Dadima out of your sight eh? She's not safe.

The **Women** *laugh and tidy themselves.*

Sita Are you hurt, Bibi?

Bibi I don't know. I'm too high to care.

Fat Auntie My legs are wobbling. So much exercise!

Mother-in-law But we got rid of the demons didn't we? How they ran!

Bibi They were only men Mam, hardly demons.

Sita Anyone that treats my daughter in that way is a demon. And will get the same treatment.

They start to go.

Fat Auntie Listen to her.

Mother-in-law They got what they deserved.

Scene Thirteen

The mental hospital.

Sita and **Bibi** *enter the ward singing a snatch of 'Ging gang gooly'.*

Bibi (*half laughing*) Don't tell 'em what happened or they will have you in a straight jacket.

Sita I'll say we had a quiet picnic.

Bibi Some picnic!

They laugh. The **Nurse** *enters carrying tea.*

Nurse You're tea, no sugar, aren't you Mrs Prakash?

Sita Yes. (*Pause. She takes the tea.*) Have you put anything in it?

Nurse (*laughing*) So suspicious! (*She looks at* **Sita**.) You're looking well. The fresh air did you good.

Sita Yes, we're leaving soon.

Nurse Oh you are, are you? Where are you going?

The **Nurse** *looks at* **Sita** *and* **Bibi**. **Bibi** *shrugs.*

The **Nurse** *hands* **Sita** *a small pill cup and stands, expecting* **Sita** *to swallow the pill inside.*

Nurse (*kindly*) It's a lower dosage.

Bibi Go on, Ma. You'll be off them soon.

Nurse Yes I'll have a word with the doctor tomorrow.

Sita *pretends to swallow the pill. She does this skilfully, the audience shouldn't notice.*

You're doing very well.

Sita I know.

The **Nurse** *exits.*

Good she's gone. Now we can go to India.

Bibi India! When were you thinking of going?

Sita Tonight.

Bibi I can't come tonight, Ma. In fact I don't want to go at all. I've got my work you see.

Sita Then you must come for a long visit. You and Prem.

Bibi Oh yes. I'd love a holiday there.

Sita I'll be off as soon as I find Princess. She's very near now. Are you sure you'll be all right in England?

Bibi Of course I will. I like it. It's where I live.

Sita Good. Then I needn't worry about you?

Bibi I'll come and see you tomorrow. Do you want me to bring anything in?

Sita But I won't be here. I'll be in India. Goodbye, my darling girl. Give my love to the family. Oh and Bibi, get rid of this.

She hands **Bibi** *the pill.*

Bibi Yes I will. Sleep well.

Bibi *exits.*

Sita Come on Princess, I know you're there.

That's it Princess, this way, look I'm here.

Princess *appears in the window.*

How beautiful you look, not a day older. I've been waiting for you for so long, but now I can go home.

She puts her hand on the window.

Scene Fourteen

The Indian village, early morning as in Act One, Scene One.

Sita *is milking and watching* **Bibi** *and* **Prem** *who are playing a game with a small stick and a block of wood. They are happy.*

Mother-in-law *and* **Fat Auntie** *are mending the photographer's bicycle.*

Mother-in-law We got a bargain eh, sister?

Fat Auntie That crazy photographer, to sell his bike for fifty rupees.

Prem When it's mended can I ride it?

Mother-in-law No, it's too big for you. You will fall off and break your head in half.

Prem But I want to ride it and I will ride it!

Fat Auntie (*sternly*) No! Carry on with your game and move out of our way!

Prem Who's it for if it's not for me?

Fat Auntie It's for Bibi.

Prem Girls don't ride bicycles.

Sita Bibi go and show that boy that he's wrong.

Bibi But I don't know how to ride it.

Fat Auntie Of course you don't know, but you'll have to learn. Now get on it.

Bibi *gets on.*

Bibi But why me?

Fat Auntie You're the eldest. You will need it for secondary school.

Mother-in-law Now we both take a side and support you. Turn the pedals, Bibi. You must do some of the work yourself.

*They support **Bibi** as she wobbles around the compound.*

Prem My sister riding a bike! I am the only boy in the village whose sister can ride a bike! Go on Bibi, do it by yourself now!

Bibi *rides alone.*

Bibi Look Ma, I can do it. I can do it!

The Secret Diary
of Adrian Mole Aged 13¾

The Play

with songs by Ken Howard and
Alan Blaikley

The Secret Diary of Adrian Mole Aged 13¾ was first presented by the Phoenix Theatre Company at the Phoenix Arts Centre, Leicester, on 6 September 1984, with the following cast:

Adrian Mole	Simon Schatzberger
George Mole	Nigel Bennett
Grandma / **Queenie**	Betty Turner
Mrs Lucas / **Matron** / **Doreen Slater** / **Woman on train**	Katy Feeney
Pauline Mole	Sheila Steafel
Bert Baxter	David Davenport
Mr Lucas / **Mr Scruton** / **Rick Lemon**	David Hobbs
Pandora	Sara McGlasson
Nigel / **Barry Kent** / **Mr Singh** / **Electricity Board Official**	Antony Howes

Directed by Graham Watkins
Assistant Director Adrian Bean
Musical arrangements and direction by Mark Warman
Designed by Anthony Dean
Choreographed by Clive Hill
Lighting designed by Mike Seignior
Sound designed by Simon Galton

Musicians: Margaret Gundara (*synthesiser*)
Andrew Huggett (*drums*)
Mark Warman (*piano and synthesiser*)

This production subsequently opened at Wyndham's
Theatre, London, on 12 December 1984, with the following
cast:

Adrian Mole	Simon Schatzberger
Pauline Mole	Mandy Travis
George Mole	Nigel Bennett
Mr Lucas	David Riley
Mrs Lucas	Katy Feeney
Grandma	Sheila Collings
Nigel **Barry Kent** **Electricity Board Official** }	Antony Howes
Pandora	Katharine Schlesinger
Schoolgirl	Louise Catt
Kids in Disco	Michael Arch Louise Catt Ricky Simmonds
Bert Baxter	David Davenport
Doreen Slater	Su Elliott
Mr Scruton	Peter Richards
Queenie	Eileen Bell
Matron	Sandra Fox

Directed by Graham Watkins
Musical staging by Christine Cartwright
Designed by Anthony Dean
Lighting by Mick Hughes
Sound by John Reddie
Musical arrangements and direction by Mark Warman

Musicians: Mark Warman (*piano and synthesiser*)
Charles Hart (*synthesisers*)
Fish (*guitars*)
Andrew Huggett (*drums*)

Author's Note

Staging

The original production had an inspired setting. Anthony
Dean designed a huge cut out dolls' house with a kitchen,
hall and stairs, and living room downstairs; and a bathroom,
Adrian's bedroom and his parents' bedroom upstairs. Gauzes
and lighting effects were used to focus on specific rooms.
Other scenes were played out in front of the house with the
minimum of sets and furniture.

   The play could work equally well with the simplest sets
possible, or even none at all.

The Dog

The Mole dog is an important character. In the first
production three puppets were used. A sitting-up dog, a
lying-down, floppy dog and a show-stopping walking dog on
wheels. The three puppets became unnaturally life-like in
Simon's hands. However, if three puppets are beyond your
budget, then try for at least one. If that's impossible, then go
to the RSPCA and start training a real dog.

Voice-overs

Adrian's diary extracts are often used to link scenes, and
should be pre-recorded. This gives the young actor a chance
to breathe and reminds us that what we are seeing on stage
has just been, or is about to be, written into a 'Secret Diary'.

Music

Ken Howard and Alan Blaikley have written some lovely
songs. In Leicester the musical accompaniment was kept to
the Scrooge-like minimum of two electric pianos and drums.
In the West End it blossomed out into two electric pianos,
drums and guitar. But should Joe Loss be your brother-in-
law, then by all means ask him to play for you and arrange
the band parts.

Style

The actors shouldn't have to break their necks for laughs – providing they go for the truth of what they are saying. Audiences are not thick and are capable of recognising and even laughing at a joke without having it pushed down their throats. Go for a good pace and try not to let it flag. And be warned the dog puppet will get the biggest laughs and receive the most applause as it takes its final bow.

Sue Townsend

Act One

Music: The Mole Overture.

At the end of the Overture, **Adrian** *comes to the front of the stage. He talks directly to the audience.*

Adrian This is just my luck! I've come all the way from Leicester to hear a lecture about George Eliot only to be thwarted at the last minute because the American lecturer missed Concorde. What am I going to do now? I'm doing George Eliot for my English Literature project. I've written him loads of letters, but he hasn't replied to one. Still, with a bit of luck I might be able to mingle with a few intellectuals in the foyer. (*Looking round at the audience.*) There's loads here tonight. But I bet *they* don't live an ordinary life like me. No, they're lucky, they go home to book-lined studies and intellectual families. Perhaps when my diary is discovered people will understand the torment of being a thirteen and three-quarter-year-old intellectual. Until then I'll just have to put up with the charade that is my family life. I bet Malcolm Muggeridge's family didn't carry on like mine did on New Year's Eve.

The lights go up to show the New Year's Eve party. **Grandma** *and* **Mrs Lucas** *are sitting on the sofa.* **Pauline** *and* **Mr Lucas** *are dancing together.* **George** *is drinking from a can of lager.* **Adrian** *joins* **Nigel** *at centre stage. Everyone, including* **Adrian** *is wearing a party hat.*

Nigel I shall be glad to get home, I've been bored out of me skull all night.

Adrian I warned you not to come, Nigel. You should have stayed at home with Andy Stewart . . . Do you want your coat?

Nigel Yeah, I want to split, man.

Adrian Why are you talking like an American?

Nigel Because I'm fed up with being English. I'm searching for a new identity.

Adrian You're never satisfied, Nigel.

Nigel So was that all you got for Christmas, a digital radio alarm clock?

Adrian Yes, that and the new *Beano* annual.

Nigel What's it like this year?

Adrian It's a bit too childish now, for my taste.

Suggestive dancing from **Mr Lucas** *and* **Pauline**. *They go into the kitchen still dancing.* **Grandma** *watches disapprovingly.*

Nigel Is your mum drunk or does she always dance like that?

Adrian She's drunk, I'm afraid.

Nigel It's embarrassing watching adults trying to dance isn't it?

Adrian It's enough to make you sick.

Grandma (*standing*) George! Coat!

George *fetches* **Grandma**'s *coat and helps her on with it.*

Grandma (*to* Mrs Lucas) It was very nice of you to talk to me. I enjoyed our chat about double glazing. Goodnight.

Mrs Lucas Goodnight.

Mrs Lucas *starts tidying up.*

Grandma I shan't bother saying goodnight to Pauline. (*Raising her voice.*) I know she didn't want me at the party. Night, Adrian!

Adrian Night, Grandma!

George *and* **Grandma** *go off.*

In the kitchen **Mr Lucas** *has his hands on* **Pauline**'s *shoulders, talking straight to her face. He is saying how long he has fancied her.*

Nigel You haven't seen my new bike yet, have you?

Adrian No.

Nigel It was made by a craftsman in Nottingham.

Adrian Mine was made by my dad in our back yard.

Nigel Honestly, Adrian, your consumer durables are a disgrace. Where's your mum?

Mrs Lucas She's in the kitchen, I shouldn't go in. I think she's busy.

Nigel Right. (*Shouting.*) Thank you for the party, Mrs Mole. I shall remember it for the rest of my life!

Pauline (*in the kitchen*) 'Night, Nigel pet!

Pauline *and* **Mr Lucas** *separate.*

Nigel You can come round tomorrow and have a go on my Steve Davis snooker table if you like.

Adrian I'm half way through a poem. I'm hoping to finish it tomorrow.

Nigel Suit yourself, Moley. 'Night Mrs Lucas. (*He leaves.*)

Mrs Lucas 'Night, Nigel. Take care walking home. Don't get yourself mugged. (*Pause. She looks at* **Adrian**.) You look tired, love, why don't you go to bed?

Adrian I've got to take the dog for a walk first. It's no wonder I'm short for my age.

Adrian *takes the walking dog out from under the stairs cupboard and goes off as* **Mr Lucas** *comes out of the kitchen.*

Mr Lucas (*to* **Mrs Lucas**) Right, you ready?

Mrs Lucas Have you said 'goodnight' to Pauline?

Mr Lucas Yes, yes, come on. I want my bed.

Mrs Lucas No you don't. You want Pauline's bed.

Mr Lucas What's brought this on?

Mrs Lucas I'm not blind, deaf and dumb. You're going to have an affair with her, aren't you?

Mr Lucas I hardly know the woman.

Mrs Lucas Well, who *are* you going to have an affair with then? You didn't buy yourself three pairs of Pierre Cardin underpants for nothing!

Mr Lucas Look you agreed that we'd have an open marriage didn't you?

Mrs Lucas Yes – open. But not *wide* open. Not the woman next door.

Mr Lucas So it's a matter of geography now, is it?

Mrs Lucas Look, I know that you need other women. It's a sort of hobby with you, isn't it? Like other men go potholing or sky-diving. But *they* don't do it in their own back yards, do they?

Mr Lucas She's wasted on George. My God, he must be the most boring man in Leicester.

Mrs Lucas Well, I'm going home to get some sleep. I'm knocking the kitchen wall down tomorrow. (*She starts to leave.*)

Mr Lucas (*raising his voice*) Look, I'm sorry. It's not my fault I was allocated too many hormones is it?

Mrs Lucas There's no need to shout!

Mr Lucas There's every need. We've got another bloody year to get through.

They go off.

Pauline *comes out of the kitchen singing 'My Way'. She doesn't know the words.* **George** *comes in and watches her for a moment.*

George Come on, duck, time for bed.

Pauline George I've got to tell you. It's my New Year's resolution. (*Pause.*) George, nobody wears flared trousers nowadays. (*Pause.*) Nobody.

George (*looking at his flares*) Jim Reeves does.

Pauline But Jim Reeves is dead, George.

George Jim Reeves will never die.

They go upstairs singing. **George** *sings 'Your Hair of Gold',* **Pauline** *sings 'My Way'.*

Adrian *comes in, carrying the dog. It stil has the lead around its neck.*

Adrian The stupid thing only got to the end of the road before it collapsed. I've a good mind to report my father to the RSPCA. He shouldn't have made the dog drink all that cherry brandy at the party last night. (*He goes to the foot of the stairs and listens to* **Pauline** *and* **George** *singing and arguing in the bedroom.*) There is a chance that my parents could be alcoholics. This time next year, I could be in a children's home. (*To the dog.*) You'd better sleep with me tonight.

Adrian *goes upstairs with the dog. The lights go on in his bedroom. He puts the dog on the bed, and writes in his diary.*

Adrian (*voice over*) Just my luck. It's the first day of the New Year and I've got a spot on my chin where everyone can see it. It's my mother's fault for not knowing about vitamins.

The lights go down in the bedrooms.

The lights are on in the living-room. **George Mole** *is sitting in the untidy living-room fixing his model of the 'Marie Celeste'.* **Pauline** *enters looking rough.*

Pauline George, I'm dying. (*She flops into a chair.*)

George You deserve to be, Pauline. You drank enough Pernod to demolish the Thames Barrier.

Pauline Well it's only once a year.

George And I don't like the way you were dancing either.

Pauline I know I'm a bit out of practice but I didn't think I was that bad.

George You were dancing in a suggestive, not to say wanton, manner. Mr Lucas got all of a doodah, I was watching him.

Pauline We were doing the *tango* George, we weren't Morris dancing. (**Pauline** *gets up and starts to tidy up*.) Is Adrian up?

Lights go up in **Adrian**'s *room to show* **Adrian** *trying to force an asprin down the dog's throat.*

George He's trying to give the dog an asprin.

Pauline Why, what's up with it?

George It's got a hangover.

Adrian *enters.*

Pauline You were the life and soul of the party again, weren't you Adrian? How many times have I told you? If you're not enjoying yourself, then *pretend* that you are. *I* have to do it at your lousy school concerts.

George Have you been at my glue?

Adrian No.

George Well, it's not where I left it. You're sure you didn't take it up to your room for a quick snort?

Pauline As if he would.

George That's what Jack at work said about his lad. Next thing Jack knows, his lad's been arrested for hijacking a Bostik lorry. That's teenagers for you.

Pauline But Adrian's not a normal teenager, George.

Adrian Yes I am!

Pauline Don't be silly, of course you're not. You're polite to me and your dad, you keep your room tidy and you don't play your stereo system at full decibels.

Adrian I haven't got a stereo system, that's why!

George We're not made of money, Adrian.

Adrian I wasn't asking for one.

Pauline What's that on your chin?

Adrian A spot.

Pauline (*shuddering*) Uuugggh!

Adrian It's because I don't get enough Vitamin C.

Pauline Go and buy an orange then.

George Nobody talk to me. I'm rigging the sails.

Pauline Did you make any New Year's resolutions, petal?

George (*shouting*) I said don't talk to me!

Pauline (*shouting*) I'm talking to Adrian!

Adrian Yes, I made ten.

Pauline Oh, what were they?

Adrian Oh, you know, helping the poor, stuff like that.

George I'm glad to hear it. You can help me by turning your bedroom light off a bit earlier. And you left your heated rollers on again, Pauline.

Pauline You're getting obsessive about us using electricity. You know that, don't you? You begrudge us every therm we consume.

Adrian *goes out and sits on the stairs. He listens carefully to the conversation.*

George (*gradually exploding*) Electricity is money, Pauline! Hard-earned money! And until you and him start bringing some money into this house, I shall be as obsessive as I like. I shall stand and watch the little wheel go round, I shall build a bloody shrine around the meter cupboard, I shall . . .

Pauline (*standing up*) Right that does it! I'm getting a job!

George (*standing up*) No wife of mine goes to work!

Pauline How many wives have you got?

George Why can't you be happy to stay at home? You've got it made. A little light housework in the morning. A quiet stroll around the shops in the afternoon. Bit of telly in the evening.

Pauline You have just described a day in the life of a convalescent snail! You sexist pig!

George Here we go, here we go. She's read two chapters of *The Female*-bloody-*Eunuch* and she's already suburbia's answer to Greasy Greer.

Pauline It's Germaine.

George Germane to what?

Pauline Let's not row, George. Not on the first day of the New Year. Adrian will hear.

George (*bitterly*) Adrian, it's always Adrian! He's a disappointment to me, Pauline, I don't mind admitting.

Pauline Just think, fourteen years ago he wasn't even here.

George And then when he was here you wanted to send him back.

Pauline Yes. He was an ugly baby though, wasn't he? . . . I mean I know he's our son but . . .

George Grotesque's the word. I've seen better looking gargoyles.

George *and* **Pauline** *laugh.* **Adrian** *is upset and angry. He puts his raincoat on.*

Pauline I used to dread people looking into his pram. I had to keep the cat net up permanently.

Adrian *comes forward.*

The music to 'The House Where I Live' underplays the following dialogue.

Adrian Bye!

Pauline Where are you going?

Adrian Out. To buy an orange.

George *and* **Pauline** *go upstairs.*

'The House Where I Live'.

Adrian (*sings*)
She doesn't cook me my meals,
Doesn't know how it feels
To be hungry and young:
And he doesn't budge from his chair,
Doesn't care if I'm here – or there!

Yes, this is my family seat,
Eighteen Every Street –
It's the house where I live.

They ought to care if I smoke,
Ask if I'm sniffing coke,
Disapprove of my friends:
I could be in some gangster's pay
Or be wasting away, day by day!

While they sit there sunk in their gloom
I could meet with my doom
In the house where I live.

No cheerful fire in our hearth,
Badedas in our bath,
Aerosol in the loo:
Who sees if we've run out of tea?
Or the dog's done a pee? – It's me!

Yes, here in its bleak monochrome
Is my own broken home,
It's the house where I live,
Yes, this is my own broken home,
It's the house where I live.

During the song, **George** *and* **Pauline** *are seen in the house in
separate rooms. By the end of the song, they are in bed together, in
their bedroom. At the end of the song,* **Adrian** *takes off his coat and
puts a Lurex apron on.*

Adrian My parents have got the flu. This is just my luck! It was cough! cough! cough! last night. If it wasn't one, it was the other. You'd think they'd show some consideration. I've been up and down the stairs day and night with trays of food and drink.

Mr and **Mrs Lucas** enter. **Mr Lucas** is carrying a bouquet of flowers.

Mr Lucas Ah, young Adrian. As you see I bear a floral gift for the invalid.

Mrs Lucas He means he's brought your mother some flowers. (*Pause.*) Are you all right?

Adrian No, I'm a bit worn out to tell you the truth and another worry is that the dog's left home.

Mr Lucas Surely that's a cause for celebration?

Mrs Lucas Bimbo!

Adrian Oh I know it shouldn't have jumped on my father's model ship and got tangled up in the rigging, but there was no need for my father to threaten to have it put down. (*Pause.*) Shall *I* give her the flowers or do you want to see her?

Mrs Lucas He wants to see her.

Mr Lucas (*going towards the stairs*) You go for Lurex in a big way do you, Adrian? . . . (*He laughs.*)

Adrian I bought it for my mother for Christmas, but I haven't seen her wear it yet. (*He takes the apron off.*) My mother told me to warn her if any visitors came . . . to give her time to put her make-up on.

Adrian goes upstairs to his parents' bedroom.

Mr Lucas (*to* **Mrs Lucas**) Why are you still tagging on? Haven't you got a drain to clean or something?

They sit down to wait. Pause.

Mrs Lucas (*casually*) I was lying in bed last night trying to work out ways to kill you.

Mr Lucas I thought you were reading.

Mrs Lucas No. (*Pause.*) I decided on a seaside mishap.

Mr Lucas Go on.

Mrs Lucas (*eagerly*) You know how you make me bury you up to your neck in cool sand when we're on the beach?

Mr Lucas Yes.

Mrs Lucas Well, I thought I'd just carry on and bury your ugly head as well. (*She smiles.*)

Mr Lucas Very nice.

Mrs Lucas I'd bring your body back to England, you wouldn't like to be buried in Benidorm, would you?

Mr Lucas (*shocked*) No.

Mrs Lucas But then I decided against it.

Mr Lucas I'm very pleased to hear it.

Mrs Lucas No. I can't wait for the summer. Why don't we have a winter holiday instead? We could go skiing and I could chuck you over a precipice.

Mr Lucas Wouldn't it be simpler to get a divorce?

Mrs Lucas Oh it would be *simpler* but not half as satisfying. Look, can't you find yourself a young, single girl? The wine bars are full of them.

Mr Lucas I want Pauline.

Mrs Lucas And Adrian. He's part of the package.

Mr Lucas I don't mind. I've always wanted a son and Adrian's past the stage of screaming in the night.

Mrs Lucas If we'd had children it wouldn't have made any difference. We've got nothing in common. (*As she goes off.*) I'm a woman and you're a man!

Mr Lucas *prepares himself to see* **Pauline**. *He combs his hair and sprays breath freshener into his mouth.*

The lights go up in **Pauline**'*s bedroom to show* **Pauline** *sitting up in bed applying lipstick.* **George** *is also in the bed.* **Adrian** *is standing next to the bed.*

Adrian Shall I tell him you're ready?

Pauline (*spraying perfume onto herself and into the air*) Just a minute. I must get rid of the smell of the sick-room.

George You can tell him I'm asleep.

George *pulls the sheet over his head.*

Adrian (*shouting downstairs*) She's ready!

George What's *he* coming round for? I didn't visit him when he had haemorrhoids, did I? I left him in peace.

Pauline He's only being neighbourly, George. Put the sheet back over your head.

Mr Lucas *walks upstairs.* **George** *reads the* Daily Express *under the sheets.* **Mr Lucas** *enters the bedroom.* **Mr Lucas** *and* **Pauline** *stare* **Adrian** *out.*

Adrian *goes to his room to write his diary.* **Mr Lucas** *sits on* **Pauline**'*s side of the bed. He hands her the flowers. He kisses his fingers and transfers the kiss to* **Pauline**'*s lips.* **Pauline** *is conscious of* **George** *awake under the sheets.*

Pauline Mr Lucas, how kind of you! They're beautifully unnatural! They must have cost a fortune!

Mr Lucas No sweat, Mrs Mole. I know a bloke at Interflora.

Pauline George will love them when he wakes up.

Mr Lucas Been asleep long, has he?

Pauline No, he's just dropped off.

Pauline *says 'He's awake' in dumb show.*

Mr Lucas I won't stay long, I just wanted to see you . . . (*He takes* **Pauline**'s *hand and presses it to his mouth, almost eats it.*) . . . and George.

Pauline Well, I'll tell George you came. He'll be sorry to have missed you. (*She grabs* **Mr Lucas**'s *hand and kisses it.*) How's Mrs Lucas?

Mr Lucas She's well, she sends her love.

Mr Lucas *kisses* **Pauline**'s *neck and shoulders.* **Pauline** *tries to wrench his head away. During the following dialogue,* **Mr Lucas** *and* **Pauline** *kiss, cuddle, touch etc.*

Pauline I do admire your wife, the way she installed your gas central heating single-handed! I'm so helpless myself. I have to get George to change the light bulbs.

Mr Lucas You're a very feminine woman, Mrs Mole. You don't want to be messing about with light bulbs. I'm sure you've got other skills at your fingertips. Artistic skills . . .

Pauline Oh I have, I have, but I haven't used them for so long.

George *turns over in bed.* **Mr Lucas** *and* **Pauline** *fly apart.* **Mr Lucas** *picks up* The Female Eunuch.

Mr Lucas Bedside reading eh? (*He reads.*) *The Female Eunuch.* Yes I've heard of that. I read a book once . . .

Pauline Did you? What was it called?

Mr Lucas It was called *I Want You.*

Pauline (*frantically*) I don't think I'm familiar with that title. *The Female Eunuch* is *very good*; it's making me re-think a lot about my role as a woman. Fixing my own light bulbs for instance.

George *grunts.*

Pauline He's talking in his sleep.

Mr Lucas Well, there'll be murder done if I don't get home to the wife. So, I'll love you and leave you, Mrs Mole. Any idea when you'll be back in circulation?

Pauline It will be very, very soon.

They blow each other kisses. **Mr Lucas** *goes.*

George I've never heard such a load of silly slobber in the whole of my life.

Pauline Oh stuff some Vick up your nose and shut up!

Adrian *comes downstairs wearing his school uniform and carrying his briefcase. He comes downstage. The lights go up on a school wall and netball post.*

Adrian When Mr Lucas went, my father had an argument with my mother and made her cry. My father is still in a bad mood. This means he is feeling better. I made my mother a cup of tea without her asking, this made her cry as well. You just can't please some people!

Pandora *enters bouncing a netball. She practises shooting at the net.*

Adrian There is a new girl at our school. Her name is Pandora but she likes to be called 'Box'. Don't ask me why. I might fall in love with her. It's time I fell in love. After all, I am thirteen and three-quarters years old.

Adrian *stands staring at* **Pandora**.

Pandora Do you mind? You're ruining my concentration.

Adrian Sorry. I was just admiring the way you handled the ball.

Pandora Netball is a ridiculous game. So one gets the stupid ball in the stupid net. Who cares?

Adrian Well you're very good at it.

Pandora I'm good at most things.

Adrian I'm no good at sport.

Pandora How boring for you.

Adrian Oh, I don't mind. I'm more the intellectual sort.

Pandora *turns to look at* **Adrian**.

Pandora Are you clever as well as being intellectual?

Adrian No. I'm about average really.

Pandora You poor thing. What *do* you excel in?

Adrian I write poetry.

Pandora Juvenile stuff I suppose.

Adrian Well I *am* a juvenile.

Pandora Boring isn't it? Hanging around waiting to grow up. I mean what's the point? One's no longer a child, so why go through this dreary half-and-half stage?

Adrian You used to go to a posh school didn't you?

Pandora Yes, but then Mummy and Daddy got a conscience about it. They're both socialists, so they threw me into the comprehensive system.

Adrian Do you like it?

Pandora One school is very much like another, isn't it? All that shouting and bullying. Teachers are the same everywhere. Fascists.

Adrian What, like Hitler, you mean?

Pandora Oh, yes. Well, perhaps not *quite* as bad as him. But they do rather think that they're the master race, don't they?

Adrian You go to the 'Off the Streets' Youth Club, don't you?

Pandora Yes, there's rather a banal disco on tonight, isn't there?'

Adrian *stares*.

Pandora What are you staring at?

Adrian Your eyes. They're the same colour as our dog's.

Pandora What sort of dog is it?

Adrian It's a mongrel.

Pandora Gee thanks!

Nigel *enters wearing whatever is current teenage high fashion.*

Nigel Hi, Box!

Pandora (*pleased*) Oh hello, Nigel. You look brillo pad.

Nigel Thanks.

Adrian Where's your uniform?

Nigel In the cloakroom. I'm going to town to buy some gear to wear to the disco tonight.

Adrian Why can't you wear your uniform in town?

Nigel I'd sooner die.

Pandora (*to* **Adrian**) Somebody might see him.

Nigel (*to* **Pandora**) Are you having a relationship at the moment?

Pandora No, actually I'm just recovering from one.

Nigel Like me. I've just broken one off. She was three-timing me.

Pandora Still it gives one the chance to draw breath doesn't it? Have a look round, see what's available.

Nigel Well, I'm available.

Pandora Well, we'll have to see what fate has in store for us, won't we?

She goes off watched by **Nigel** *and* **Adrian**.

Adrian Oh God, she's beautiful! She's got hair like treacle.

Nigel What, sticky?

Adrian No! It's the colour of golden syrup.

Nigel You're in love with her, aren't you?

Adrian Yes.

Nigel *puts his arm round* **Adrian**.

Nigel Well forget it, Moley. You're not in the same division. She's a class bird. She won't *look* at a guy unless he's got at least a hundred quid's worth on his back and you've got to have the right brand names – the right labels.

Adrian OK. If you're the expert on clothes tell me what intellectuals wear.

Nigel Why?

Adrian Because I think I'm turning into one. It must be all the worry.

Nigel When did you turn?

Adrian Last night. I saw Malcolm Muggeridge on the telly and I understood nearly every word.

Nigel Well, write to *him* and ask him what to wear.

Adrian I don't know where he lives do I?

Nigel Well write to him care of the British Museum then, that's where all the intellectuals hang out isn't it? See you.

Nigel *goes off.*

Adrian (*with contempt*) The British Museum! Intellectuals don't waste their time looking at old statues and stuff, they're too busy writing poems and appearing on BBC book programmes. Yes! I'll write to Mr Muggeridge care of the BBC. I'd better enclose a stamped addressed envelope because Mr Muggeridge *is* an old aged pensioner and probably can't afford a first class stamp. I'll soon be an expert on old aged pensioners. I've joined a group at school called The Good Samaritans. We go round doing good in the community and stuff. The old people were shared out at break today. I got an old man called Bert Baxter. He's eighty-nine so I don't suppose I'll have him for long.

At the youth club disco. Loud music. Dim lights. **Nigel** *pogos onto the stage. He is dressed as a weekend punk. He dances for a while in a madly exhibitionist style. The music is turned down in volume.* **Nigel** *reacts angrily.*

Nigel Hey! Where's the sounds?

Adrian *enters dressed in shirt, sweater, tie and school trousers.*

Adrian That's better, it was hurting my ears. I asked Rick Lemon to turn it down.

Nigel Haven't you been to a disco before, Mole?

Adrian No.

Nigel Thought not. You look like Frank Bough. Go and stand in the corner. I'm ashamed to be seen with you. Don't you care what you look like?

Adrian No. I don't. (*Pause.*) You look dead stupid. Doesn't your mother mind you being a punk at weekends?

Nigel No. Not so long as I wear my string vest under my bondage tee-shirt.

Adrian You're not a proper punk, are you? I thought proper punks had safety pins in their ears.

Nigel They do. I forgot to put mine in.

Pandora *enters.*

Pandora Oh, it's Adrian Mole. In the half light I thought it was an old Crumblie.

Adrian Crumblie?

Pandora Somebody over twenty-five.

Adrian You look very nice from what I can see. Is it always dark at discos?

Schoolgirl (*to* **Pandora**) It's his first time.

Pandora (*laughs*) Incredible! Never been to a disco before?

Adrian No. And I don't think I'll bother again.

Nigel (*to* **Pandora**) I came out without putting my safety pin in my ear. So I'm just about to do it now. You can watch if you like. (*He takes a safety pin from his tee-shirt.*)

Pandora Oh you are brave – stupid, but brave.

Adrian *watches, horrified, as* **Nigel** *inserts the safety pin.*

Pandora Well done!

Nigel Oh, it's killing me! Get it out!

Adrian It's your own fault for showing off. (*He gives* **Nigel** *a tissue.*)

Nigel I'm bleeding. Look – blood! It's pouring! I'm going to die!

Pandora It *is* gushing out, rather.

Nigel Take me to the hospital. Get an ambulance!

Pandora *comforts* **Nigel** *who is now close to fainting. They go off to loud disco music.* **Adrian** *comes to the front of the stage. He talks to the audience.*

Adrian My father had to take Nigel to the hospital in our car. Nigel's parents haven't got a car because his father's got a steel plate in his head and isn't allowed to drive and his mother is only four feet eleven inches tall so she can't reach the pedals. It's not surprising Nigel has turned out bad really, with a maniac and a midget for parents.

Adrian Today was the most terrible day of my life: I've got fifteen spots on my shoulders, my father is in a bad mood – he thinks his big-end is going, Pandora is going out with Nigel, but, worst of all, Bert Baxter is not a nice old age pensioner!

The lights go up to show **Bert Baxter** *sitting half-undressed in a television chair. Empty beer bottles are under the chair, also an enormous jar of beetroot. A dog's bowl is beside the chair. An alsatian dog barks loudly offstage.*

Bert (*fiercely*) Who's there?

Adrian *is half in the door.*

Adrian (*desperately*) Can I come in, please? I think your dog's trying to bite me.

Bert Bite yer! 'E'll 'ave yer bleddy leg off. He's a pure, thoroughbred, radged-up alsatian, ain't yer Sabre? (*Sabre answers with a bark.*) Quiet, sir! (*Sabre is instantly quiet.*) Who are you?

Adrian (*squeezes in*) I'm Adrian Mole from Neil Armstrong Comprehensive School.

Bert You got me out of bed.

Adrian Sorry, I thought you'd be up.

Bert Why?

Adrian It's the afternoon!

Bert What's that got to do with ought? A man of my age needs his sleep. (*He sticks a Woodbine in his mouth.*) Got a light?

Adrian No. I don't smoke.

Bert (*shocked*) Don't smoke! A lad of your age! You should be ashamed of yourself!

Sabre goes crazy behind the door.

(*Roaring.*) Quiet, sir! (*To* **Adrian**.) He's hungry. You wouldn't have a spare tin of dog food on you, would you?

Adrian No. (*Pause.*) Mr Baxter, the school sent you a letter about me. It was to warn you that I'd be coming round.

Bert Why, what are you – a burglar?

Adrian No. I'm a good Samaritan. I go round doing good in the community.

Bert What for?

A long pause.

Adrian I miss maths.

Bert So you've come round here to do me some good, have you?

Adrian Yes, is there anything you'd like me to do.

Bert Yes, bugger off!

Adrian Then could you sign my paper to prove that I've been?

Bert No. I never sign nothin', that way they can't get you.

Adrian Who?

Bert The Government.

Adrian But it's only for the school.

Bert Schools is run by governments, ain't they? Don't you know ought? (**Bert** *slaps his legs*.) Come on me old beauties! Here, you can go and get me shoppin' in for me. Now concentrate because I'm going to tell you what I want and I 'ate repeatin' myself. Twenty Woodies.

Adrian Woodies?

Bert Woodbines, lad. Concentrate. A jar of beetroot, a tin of Chum, three bottles of brown ale and the *Morning Star*.

Adrian Is the *Morning Star* a newspaper?

Bert What's up wi' you, lad? Are you backward? The *Morning Star* is the only newspaper worth readin'. The others are owned by capitalist runnin' dog lackeys.

Adrian So – Twenty Woodies. A jar of beetroot. A tin of Chum. Three bottles of brown ale. The *Morning Star*. Could I have the money, please?

Bert Tell 'em to put it on my account. On account of how I've got no money left.

Bert *laughs and goes off.*

Sinister music as **Barry Kent** *enters.*

Kent Mole! You weren't at school this morning, Mole.

He sprays 'B.K. OK?' on a wall. **Adrian** *tries to leave without being seen.* **Barry Kent** *has his back turned.*

Kent Stay where you are, Mole! Where you bin, Mole – Skivin'?

Adrian *stands perfectly still with his back turned to* **Kent**.

Adrian No. I've been out, being a Good Samaritan.

Adrian *starts to go off.*

Kent I said, stay where you are.

Kent *puts the full stops on his graffiti.*

Adrian I've got to go. I've got a test on the Norwegian Leather Industry . . .

Kent Who gives a toss about the Norwegian Leather Industry?

Adrian I do. I'm a bit of an expert. I expect to get full marks. Let me go.

Kent I ain't touched you. You could go if you wanted to.

Adrian You know I can't.

Kent *approaches* **Adrian**.

Kent Give me twenty-five pence an' you can go freely on Her Majesty's footpaths.

Adrian I haven't got twenty-five pence.

Kent You got your dinner money, ain't you?

Adrian I haven't. My dad pays by cheque since it went up to seventy pence a day.

Kent *straightens* **Adrian**'s *tie.*

Kent All you poofters have pocket money, don't you? For helping your mummies with the washing up?

Adrian Mine goes straight into the Market Harborough Building Society. All I get is sixteen pence a day – for a Mars bar.

Kent Oh dear, oh dear. Then you're in trouble, Mole, 'cos I need twenty-five pence a day from you, so's I can maintain my present life-style. You seen the price of Doc Martens?

Kent *twists* **Adrian**'s *arm.*

Adrian You're hurting me, a bit.

Kent Sorry, gotta do it. I ain't 'ad your advantages.

Kent *continues hurting* **Adrian**.

Adrian Now you're hurting me a lot.

'*Sorry, Gotta Do It*'. *During which* **Kent** *beats* **Adrian** *up and kicks him in the goolies and generally humiliates him.*

Kent
  Sorry, gotta do it, gotta do it,
  Sorry, gotta do it,
  Sorry, gotta do it, gotta do it, gotta do it:
  Nothing personal – know what I mean?

  What you need is my protection:
  In return I take collection
  Of a paltry pound or three – it
  Makes good sense! Invest in me! Like

  You're the client, I'm the banker:
  I need finance, you're a wanker!
  Things are as they ought to be, now
  I've got you and you've got me – see?

  Sorry, gotta do it, gotta do it,
  Sorry, gotta do it,
  Sorry, gotta do it, gotta do it, gotta do it:
  Nothing personal – know what I mean?

  Breathe a word and you'll regret it!
  Think of squealing? Don't forget, it's
  Me you'll have to answer to – and
  In the end, I *will* get you! I'll

Have your little guts for garters,
Mash your face in – just for starters!
'Cause you know my golden rule is
No holds barred! Go for the goolies!

Sorry, gotta do it, gotta do it,
Sorry, gotta do it,
Sorry gotta do it, gotta do it, gotta do it:
Nothing personal – know what I mean?

The song ends with **Kent** *standing triumphantly over* **Adrian** *who is crying.*

Adrian I've changed my mind. I will give you twenty-five pence a day after all. I'll get a paper round.

Kent Well that's real decent of you, Mole. 'Ere have a tissue. I ain't heartless.

He throws **Adrian** *a Kleenex and goes off.* **Adrian** *wipes his eyes, blows his nose, then stands and tidies himself up.*

Adrian Woke up next day with a pain in my goolies.

Adrian *picks up a newspaper sack. He sees* **Pandora** *crossing the stage wearing her riding hat and jodhpurs. He hides until she's gone. He looks at the papers he is to deliver to her house.*

Adrian (*to the audience*) Pandora lives at 69 Elm Tree Avenue. They have *The Guardian, Punch, Private Eye* and *New Society.* Pandora reads *Jackie* – the comic for girls; so she is not an intellectual like me. But I don't suppose Malcolm Muggeridge's wife is either.

Adrian *crosses to the house, reading* The Guardian. *He stops at the threshold. He turns to the audience.*

It's full of spelling mistakes! It is disgusting when you think of how many people who can spell are out of work.

He goes upstairs to his bedroom and writes in his diary.

(*Voice over.*) Pandora has got a little fat horse called Blossom. She feeds it and makes it jump over barrels every morning before school. She looked dead good in her riding stuff. Her chest was wobbling like mad. She will need to wear a bra soon.

The lights are up on **Adrian**'s *bedroom, and* **Pauline** *is in the bathroom cleaning the loo.*

Adrian (*to the audience*) My mother came into my room this morning and started mumbling on about 'adult relationships' and 'life being complicated' and how she must 'find herself'. She said she was fond of me. 'Fond'!!! and would hate to hurt me, and then she said that for some women marriage was like being in prison.

Pauline *comes downstairs, puts her coat on.*

Adrian Marriage is nothing like being in prison. Women are let out every day to go to the shops and quite a few go to work. I think my mother is being a bit melodramatic.

Pauline Adrian, I'm off to my 'Women's Workshop on Assertiveness Training'. When your father comes home, tell him his dinner is in the freezer. (*Pause.*) At Sainsbury's.

George Mole *enters from work.*

George I'm home! (*Pause.*) Pauline, I'm home! (*Silence. Mimicking* **Pauline**:) Oh, hello George, how lovely to see you. How many storage heaters did you sell today? You sit down there in front of the telly, I'll bring your dinner in to you. (*In his own voice:*) What are we eating, Pauline? (*Mimicking* **Pauline**:) Home-made steak and kidney pie, followed by spotted dick and custard! (*In his own voice:*) Yum, yum! Come here, wife.

Adrian *watches from the stairs.*

George (*mimicking* **Pauline**) Oh, George! Don't! The dinner will spoil! Oh, all right then . . . (*In his own voice, bitterly:*) Some bloody hope!

Adrian *enters.*

George Where's your mother?

Adrian Gone to a women's workshop on assertiveness training.

George *swears under his breath.*

Adrian What *is* assertiveness training?

George God knows, but it sounds like bad news for me!

Adrian She's bought herself some of those overalls that painters and decorators wear.

George Was she wearing her high heels with it?

Adrian Yes.

George So there's still hope. Lipstick?

Adrian Yes, but it was that lip gloss stuff, not her usual orange.

George I knew it. Give her a fortnight and she'll be running around in monkey boots and a bristly haircut. They've no right to interfere!

Adrian Who?

George Those bloody workshop types. They go around stirring women up telling them they're unhappy. (*Small pause.*) Is there a boil-in-the-bag cod-in-butter-sauce left in the freezer?

Adrian No, she hasn't been to Sainsbury's. She's been looking after Mr Lucas.

George What's up with him?

Adrian Mrs Lucas is leaving him. They're getting a divorce. Poor Mr Lucas is dead upset.

George Poor Mr Lucas could *be* dead for all I care.

Adrian You don't like him, do you?

George No.

Adrian Why? He's ever so nice and he really appreciates what Mum's doing for him.

George What *is* she doing for him?

Adrian She's comforting him for his tragic loss.

George *swears under his breath.*

George Is there any bacon in the house?

Adrian There's one slice.

George Where?

Adrian It's on the floor between the fridge and the cooker. It's been there for *three days* to my knowledge!

George It's bloody disgusting how she keeps this house lately, my socks have been in the Ali Baba basket for over a week!

Adrian I can't remember the last time she bothered to wash my PE kit. I have to do it myself or take it round to Grandma's.

George Poor kid. I'm very fond of your mother, Adrian, very very fond. But she's beginning to be a bit of a handful. Perhaps it's hormone trouble . . . (*Flinging his shoes across the floor.*) Switch the telly on, kid.

Television noise. Lights down. The TV closedown tone is heard. They sleep. **Pauline** *enters. Lights up. She holds herself aggressively. Her voice is firm. She addresses* **George** *and* **Adrian** *who are still asleep. She is holding a large piece of card.*

Pauline (*loudly*) Right!

Adrian *and* **George** *wake up.*

Pauline The worm has turned! Things are going to be different around here! I am holding in my hand a chart; as you see, it is divided into three columns. Each column represents a member of this family. This is me, this is you, George, and this is Adrian.

Adrian What's all that writing under my name?

Pauline It is a list of household jobs. The first job on your list, Adrian, reads 'clean lavatory'. I know you think a little gang of fairies come out at night and fly round with the Harpic, but you are wrong. A *person* cleans the lavatory and until now that person has been me. But not any more. (*She pins the chart up.*) We start tomorrow!

There is fast Mole music, then strobe light as **Adrian** *runs around doing housework.*

Adrian (*voice over*) Cleaned toilet, washed basin and bath before doing my paper round. Came home, made breakfast, put washing in machine, went to school. Gave Barry Kent his menaces money, went to Bert Baxter's, waited for social worker who didn't come, had school dinner. Had domestic science – made apple crumble. Came home. Vacuumed hall, lounge and breakfast room. Peeled potatoes, chopped up cabbage. Cut finger, rinsed blood off cabbage. Put chops under grill. Looked in cookery book for a recipe for gravy. Made gravy. Strained lumps out with a colander. Set table, served dinner, washed up. Put burnt saucepans in to soak. Got washing out of machine; everything blue, including white underwear and handkerchiefs. Hung washing on clothes-horse. Fed dog. Ironed PE kit. Cleaned shoes. Did homework. Took dog for a walk.

Adrian *crosses the stage with the dog. He comes back on stage.*

(*To the audience.*) Just my luck to have an assertive mother!

Lights up on **Mr Lucas** *and* **Pauline** *in the kitchen.*

Mr Lucas Paulie, Paulie. What we've got is something very rare and precious. We're like two sunbeams dancing on the ceiling of life. Together we could make a new sun, a new planet. We're cosmic, Pauline!

Pauline Stop it! I can't think straight when you talk like that.

Mr Lucas *I* can't think straight. I'm losing customers. I keep catching myself saying 'Oh why worry about the future?' It's not a healthy attitude for an insurance man to have. Don't think, Pauline. Just act. Come away with me!

Pauline I keep seeing the expression on Adrian's face the day his mouse died. He came home from junior school. I said: 'Hello pet, your mouse is dead.' He took it very badly.

Mr Lucas (*sulking*) Look, I'm not here to chat about dead pets. Pauline. (*He turns away.*)

Pauline Oh come on, love! Since you moved next door, I've had colour in my life; excitement. I couldn't wait to hang my washing out in the morning. 'Will he be in the garden?' I used to get through a Euro-sized packet of Ariel a week.

Mr Lucas Did you? Did you really?

Pauline Yes, not to mention the Comfort.

Mr Lucas I'll be your comfort, and your joy, and your support. Your bodily lover, your spiritual helpmate, your companion in old age. I'll be your true, true love. Tell him tonight, Pauline, or I'm going to Beachy Head.

Pauline Have you got relations there?

Mr Lucas No, Paulie, pet. I shall chuck myself onto the rocks! I can't face life without my little sunbeam.

They are now just about to make love on the floor. **Adrian** *comes downstairs and tries to get into the kitchen.*

Adrian Mum, are you in there?

Pauline Yes, me and Mr Lucas are . . . mending the boiler. Can't it wait? Only I've got my hands full.

Adrian Have I got any clean socks? (*Shouts:*) Hello, Mr Lucas!

Mr Lucas (*shouts*) Hello, Adrian!

Pauline I forgot to take them out of the washer. Sorry, sunbeam.

Adrian I'll wear yesterday's again then. (*To himself.*) Sunbeam?

There is a lighting change.

(*To the audience.*) Went to school. Found it closed. What with all the worry I had forgotten that I am on holiday. I didn't want to go home, so I went to see Bert Baxter instead. I asked him if he would like to see a horse again. He said he would, so I took him to see Blossom. It took us ages to get there. Bert walks dead slow and he kept having to sit down on garden walls. Bert said that Blossom was not a horse, she was a girl pony. He kept patting her and saying 'Who's a beauty then, eh?'

Then we walked back to Bert's house. I went to the shops and bought a packet of Vesta chow mein and a butterscotch Instant Whip for our dinner, so Bert ate a decent meal for once. We watched 'Pebble Mill at One', then Bert showed me his old horse brushes.

Lights up on **Bert** *with horse brushes.* **Adrian** *crosses to him.*

Bert I turned into a Communist before it became generally popular. I were one of the first. It happened on August 11th, 1910. At two o'clock. As you know, I were an ostler. That's doin' things with 'osses.

Well, one day, I'd got the 'osses brushed and gleamin'. It were a 'ot day, so I'd got a bit of a muck sweat on myself, when the lady of the house comes round the stables. She had her friend with her, pretty little thing in a blue dress, wi' a lace collar like a collection of snow flakes. Any road up, these ladies are wrinkling their little noses up on account of the smell of the 'oss shit. The lady of the house says: 'I say Baxter, is there nothing you can do about the smell in here?' I says: 'No mum, not unless you can stop the 'osses shitting!' Well, you should have heard the carry on. You'd a' thought I'd said summat rude! I 'ad tuppence docked out o' me wages. Then, later on that night, I seen the lady of the house feedin' chocolate eclairs to one of me best horses. Chocolate eclairs cost thruppence each – it were then I turned into a Communist!

Adrian Why didn't you join the Labour Party, Bert?

Bert You know nought lad. Anyway, we were that poor, we never 'ad one.

'The Bad Old Days'. **Bert** *sings to* **Adrian**. *At various points throughout the song,* **Bert** *and* **Adrian** *march and dance.*

Bert (*sings*)
    When I was just your age, son,
    When I was just a lad,
    Things were far different then
    I can tell you, my friend –
    They were ten times as bad!
    Had me no gilded youth, boy,
    Lit by no sunshine rays –
    We were fourteen in a hovel,
    Takin' lessons how to grovel,
    In the bad old days.

    Lenin's my hero still, boy –
    He was a man of steel:
    If he came back today
    His hair would turn grey
    At the whole lousy deal!
    Paid up and joined the Party,
    Carried the big red flag:
    We were comrades in an army,
    Though they told us we were barmy,
    In the bad old days.

They dance.

    We toiled our youth away, boy –
    No money, no thanks, no praise:
    They say 'Where there's muck there's brass' –
    I say 'Not on your bloomin' arse!'
    They were bad old days.

Adrian *and* **Bert** *go off.*

*Lights go up on the **Lucas**'s garden. A trough of flowers and a gnome decorate the space. **Mrs Lucas** is uprooting trees and putting them into a wheelbarrow. She is wearing wellingtons and overalls. It is twilight.*

Pauline Adrian said that you wanted to see me. (*Pause.*) Do you want any help with that bush?

Mrs Lucas No thanks, I'm stronger than I look. (*Pause.*) I'm leaving Derek tonight. I thought you ought to know.

Pauline Who's Derek?

Mrs Lucas That's your lover's name. He wasn't christened 'Bimbo'.

Pauline I can't think of him as being a Derek.

Mrs Lucas Does he still talk about sunbeams?

Pauline They've been mentioned in passing.

Mrs Lucas 'Two sunbeams dancing on the ceiling of life.' He knows how to get us going does Bimbo.

Pauline I love him.

Mrs Lucas I know, I did once.

Pauline I'm ever so sorry. I like you a lot. Oh – put that tree down!

Pauline *holds* **Mrs Lucas**'s *hand.*

Mrs Lucas I've fallen for somebody myself. I may as well tell you. Make you feel better perhaps.

Pauline Oh, I'm so glad. What's his name?

Mrs Lucas *Her* name is Glenys.

Pauline *drops* **Mrs Lucas**'s *hand.*

Pauline Oh, I see.

Mrs Lucas You're shocked, aren't you?

Pauline Well, I am a bit. You don't expect it in a cul-de-sac somehow.

Pauline *grabs* **Mrs Lucas***'s hand again.*

Mrs Lucas You never know about people. There are things you don't know about him. Will you take Adrian with you?

Pauline I don't know. It's hard to uproot a kid, they're not like trees.

Mrs Lucas But at least I'll see these grow. Goodnight. Good luck with Derek.

She pushes the wheelbarrow off stage. It has got dark.

Pauline Good luck with Glenys.

George *enters the garden, shining a torch.*

George Pauline!

Pauline I'm here!

George What are you doing standing in the dark?

Pauline I've been talking to Mrs Lucas. About trees.

George You're shivering. Come in, love. I've turned the thermostat up. It's lovely and warm at home. And I've got Jim Reeves on the turntable.

Pauline What's Adrian doing?

George He's in his room. Why?

Pauline Do you think he'd miss me, if I died, or went away?

George Have you been drinking, Pauline? Of course he'd bloody miss you. You're his mother. (*Pause.*) You haven't got any health problems you've not told me about, have you?

Pauline No.

George What's all this silly slobber about dying and going away for then?

Pauline I'm just being daft, take no notice.

George You've not been yourself lately.

Pauline (*quickly*) George, I'm in love with another man.

A long pause.

George You mean other than me?

Pauline Yes. I said *another* man.

A small pause.

George What's his name?

Pauline Derek.

George Thank God for that. It's usually someone you know. You'll have to give me a minute, Pauline. My body's stopped working. I can't move it.

George *is motionless.*

Pauline Derek is Bimbo, Mr Lucas. We're standing in his back garden.

George *gives a long anguished moan of despair and anger. He drops to his knees.*

Pauline Don't, love, don't. Oh, I'm so sorry. I wish it hadn't happened.

George *clasps* **Pauline**'s *legs.*

George Don't leave me, Pauline.

Pauline I've got to. I can't live next door to the man I love!

George (*desperately*) I'll build you a car port then you can go and see him without getting wet.

Pauline We'll have to talk it over in a civilised manner, the three of us. We're all intelligent people, we can work something out. Tonight. (*She starts to go off.*)

George Where are you going?

Pauline To tell Bimbo.

George What about Adrian?

Pauline (*crying*) I can't tell him. You'll have to. I told him about his mouse!

Pauline *goes off.*

George (*shouting*) What bloody mouse? (*Pause.*) I'll kill him. I'll ram his policies and his third party fire and thefts down his throat. I'll fully comprehensively break his neck! She's married to me! I've got a paper to prove it! (*Sadly.*) But there's nothing in the small print to say she can't go off with anybody else.

'*Your Hair of Gold*'.

George (*sings in the style of Jim Reeves*)
Your hair of gold, your eyes of baby blue –
How could I ever face a life without you?
Your lips so sweet, your touch so tender –
You know I surrender to everything that you do.

Your glance, your smile – they haunt me all the while:
Sleeping or waking you're always there beside me:
Your laugh, your kiss – my riches forever:
You know that I'll never let you go from my heart.

George *goes off as the lights go up to show* **Adrian** *standing in the hall.*

Adrian My mother has arranged what she called a civilised meeting. Mr Lucas is going to be there. Naturally I am not invited. I'm going to listen at the door.

Adrian *listens at the living-room door. The lights go up in the living-room to show* **Pauline**, **Mr Lucas** *and* **George** *arguing.*

George *paces about, he looks haggard.* **Pauline** *watches him anxiously.* **Mr Lucas** *starts talking.* **George** *hangs his head.* **Pauline** *gets up to comfort him.* **George** *pushes her away. He takes a handkerchief out of his pocket and wipes his eyes.* **Pauline** *talks, her eyes down.*

Adrian The civilised meeting broke up when my father found out how long my mother and Mr Lucas had been in love. And when my mother disclosed that she was leaving for

Sheffield with Mr Lucas, my father became uncivilised and started fighting! In the *front* garden. All the neighbours came out to watch.

Adrian *runs up to the first floor.*

George and **Mr Lucas** *mime fighting.* **Pauline** *mimes trying to break it up.* **Mr Lucas** *escapes into the front garden.* **George** and **Pauline** *run after him.* **Adrian** *hangs out of the window, watching.*

George (*shouting*) You're not having her! She's my wife!

He rugby-tackles **Mr Lucas** *and brings him down.*

Pauline Don't hurt him, George!

George Hurt him – I'll kill him!

Mr Lucas *gets up and hits* **George** *on the jaw.*

Pauline Don't hurt him, Bimbo!

Mr Lucas She belongs to me now!

Pauline *gets between the two but is unable to stop* **George** *head-butting* **Mr Lucas**.

Pauline It was supposed to be a civilised meeting.

George and **Mr Lucas** *stagger in opposite directions.*

Mr Lucas Ah! He's hurt me, Pauline! He's broken my nose. I shall look like Henry Cooper.

Pauline Go on! Finish each other off! Kill him, George! Get stuck in! You're uncivilised, the pair of you!

Mr Lucas Steady on Pauline.

George *chases* **Mr Lucas** *off.*

Pauline (*distraught*) I don't care any more. I'm going to Sheffield, with him or without him. (*Screaming:*) I can see you looking through your net curtains, Mrs O'Leary!

Pauline *runs off.*

Adrian (*from the front bedroom window*) All the people looked up and saw me so I looked especially sad. I expect the experience will give me a trauma at some stage in the future. I'm all right at the moment, but you never know.

The lights go up to show **George** *in the bathroom bathing his face, and* **Pauline** *in the bedroom packing a suitcase.* **Adrian** *is in his bedroom with the dog.*

'*Family Trio*'.

Adrian (*sings*)
Two o'clock in the morning:
Leicester's asleep as sound as a log:
I count sheep in the stillness,
As we lie awake – just me and the dog.

Pauline (*sings*)
Maybe this is the right time to
Find out what I am good for,
And what would be really good for me –
Maybe . . . maybe
I'm more, more than I bargained for,
Braver than I believed I could
Be – I'm free to become . . . who knows?
We'll see, maybe . . .

George (*sings*)
Your hair of gold, your eyes of baby blue –
How could I ever face a life without you?

Adrian (*sings*)
Five o'clock in the morning:
No one's about, not even a mouse:
All peace and quiet on the outside –
Who would believe there's a war in our house?

Pauline (*sings*)	**George** (*sings simultaneously with* **Pauline**)
Maybe this is the right time to Find out what I am good for,	Your hair of gold, your eyes of baby blue –

And what would be really
good for me
Maybe . . . maybe
I'm more, more than I
bargained for,
Braver than I believed I could
Be – I'm free to become . . .
who cares?
We'll see, maybe . . .

How could I ever face a
life without you?
Your lips so sweet, your
touch so tender –
You know I surrender to
everything that you do.

Adrian (*sings, as* **George** *and* **Pauline** *repeat their verses*)
Five o'clock in the morning:
No one's about, not even a mouse:
Nothing moves in the silence –
Who would believe there's a war in our house?

Adrian/Pauline/George (*sing*)
Maybe . . . maybe . . . maybe . . . maybe . . . we'll see.

Blackout.

Act Two

Adrian *is in his bedroom writing in his diary.* **George** *is downstairs in the living-room slumped on the sofa. He is unshaven.*

Adrian (*voice over*) Tuesday March 31st. My mother has gone to Sheffield with Mr Lucas. She had to drive because Mr Lucas couldn't see out of his black eyes. I have informed the school secretary of my mother's desertion, she was very kind and gave me a form to give to my father; it is for free school dinners. We are now a single parent family. Nigel has asked Barry Kent to stop menacing me for a few weeks. Barry Kent said he would think about it.

Adrian *comes downstairs and sits down opposite* **George**.

George I don't know what I did wrong. I never hit her. I was tempted, but I never actually got round to (*Punches the air viciously, landing a blow.*). I put my money on the table every Friday night without fail; not all, but most. I've got a temper (*Losing his temper.*), all right, I admit it! It's a fault I've got *and* I shout a bit, but I mean nothing by it. (*Calmer.*) I thought she'd got used to it. Has she gone because I'm losing my hair? (*Pause.*) I know I've let myself go downhill. – No I've not, she has. She stopped sewing my buttons on and stitching my turnups. And I can't remember the last time she bought me any Cherry Blossom. They've noticed at work; a memo was passed about my shoes. When you tell the punters how much the storage heater'll cost, they look on the floor. You can lose a sale because of the lack of a good shine. (*Pause.*) I know things weren't too hot physically, but it was her fault! She put a barrier between us. She read the *Guardian* in bed at night. Even worse, she even sometimes read bits out! 'Listen to what Jill Tweedie says about men' – she'd say. It was never complimentary. It's Jill Tweedie's fault that Pauline's gone. Her and that Greasy Greer! (*Pause.*) So why's she gone off with *another man*?

Grandma *enters, taking her hat and coat off.*

Grandma Hello, Adrian, you look pale. You're not constipated are you? I've got a bottle of syrup of figs in my bag if you are.

Adrian No, it's all right. I went this morning.

Grandma Good boy. Where's Pauline, George?

George *and* **Adrian** *exchange a glance.*

George She's in Sheffield.

Grandma Who does she know in Sheffield?

George Mr Lucas from next door.

Grandma But Mr Lucas from next door lives next door, doesn't he?

George No, not any more he doesn't. He lives in Sheffield – with Pauline.

Grandma Do you mean that they're living . . . together?

George Yes.

Grandma In sin?

George Yes.

Grandma I knew it! I always said she was wanton. Thank the good Lord your father never lived to see this day. It would have killed him.

She sits. **Adrian** *goes off to fetch the tea things.*

George It's hit me hard, Mum.

Grandma How she could bear to tear herself away from that wonderful boy? It just proves how inhuman she is.

George I keep seeing them together, in Sheffield . . . making love in front of a knife and fork factory.

Grandma You're well rid of her, George. She never cleaned behind the cooker.

George I should have taken her out more. She loved Chinese food. The odd prawn ball wouldn't have hurt me.

Adrian *enters carrying a tea tray with milk carton, sugar bag, mugs and a packet of biscuits.*

Grandma (*to* **Adrian**) What's that supposed to be?

Adrian It's the tea tray, Grandma.

Grandma I'll excuse you this once, Adrian, it must have been unsettling when your mother left home. But it's no good descending to the level of animals. Now, go back into the kitchen and do it properly; milk jug, sugar bowl, doily for the biscuits, cups and saucers and apostle spoons.

Adrian *goes out to the kitchen with the tray.*

Grandma How's *he* taken it?

George I don't know, he's not said. I can still smell her perfume on the sheets!

George *starts to sniffle.*

Grandma Right. I'll have *them* in the wash tomorrow. Now, go upstairs and have a shave. You may think it's amusing to look like a Communist but I don't. I know you've had a bit of a shock . . .

George A bit of a shock! My world has fallen apart! I'm a broken man!

George *cries.*

Grandma You've no gumption, George. Your father shaved every day of his life. Even when he was in the trenches at Ypres. Sometimes he had to stop the rats from eating his shaving soap. He was even shaved in his coffin by the undertaker, so if the dead can shave, then there's no excuse for the living.

George I don't want to go on living, not without Pauline. I love her, Mum.

Grandma Do you want me to smack your bum? You might be forty-one but you're not too old. I won't have you giving way to your emotions like this – it's not healthy. All this silly slobber about *love*. It's decency that counts. Keeping a clean front and paying your bills on time. Where's love got you, eh? I shall leave the room until you've pulled yourself together. (*Pause.*)

Grandma *goes off to the kitchen. Lights on kitchen.* **Adrian** *is pouring sugar into a bowl.*

Grandma I'm sorry to see your father in such a state.

Adrian He found one of my mother's earrings down the back seat of the car this morning. He kept staring at it with a funny look in his eyes . . . Then he asked me if I missed my mother. I said 'Of course I do, but life must go on!'

Grandma Quite right.

Adrian But *he* said: 'I don't see why.' I took this to mean that he was suicidal. So I took his razor and all the sleeping pills from out of the bathroom. Just to be on the safe side.

Grandma Good boy.

They enter the living room.

It's times like this I realise what a privilege it was to be married to your grandad. There was no suicide threats or adultery in *our* marriage. We just plodded on day after day for forty years. I wouldn't say we were especially happy, but then again we weren't unhappy either. Your grandad was a quiet man; he hated noise and disagreements, so there were no rows. But I knew when he was upset; he used to rap his fingers on the mangle outside the back door. (*She demonstrates on the coffee table.*)

Adrian Yes, he used to do that a lot when I came round.

Grandma Yes, well you used to get on his nerves a bit – always asking questions.

Adrian He never answered any.

Grandma How could he? He didn't know anything. I used to read bits out of the newspaper to him sometimes, but he'd say: 'Don't bother me with the outside world, May.' It upset him, you see. I suppose you could say he was a timid man.

'*Your Dead Grandad*'.

Grandma (*sings*)
I don't recall
Just when he popped the question:
I'm not exactly sure he ever did!
He bought a ring – I've still got that:
We hired a hall, he hired a top hat –
He looked a toff, your dead grandad.

Adrian Can I have a biscuit please Grandma?

Grandma (*sings*)
He never had to tell me that he loved me –
We had no use for sentimental chat:
I'd wash the dishes – he would dry,
We dug the garden – time passed by:
I miss him still, your dead grandad.

Adrian Grandma, can I . . . ?

Adrian *reaches for a biscuit.* **Grandma** *slaps his hand.*

Grandma (*sings*)
We never made excuses for bad manners,
No psycho-this or socio-that at all:
Folks were either sane or mad,
We'd no posh words for being bad –
But he was good, your dead grandad.

George!

George Yes, Mum.

Grandma Would you mind driving me up to the Garden Centre in the car? Only I'm running low on poisons.

George (*getting the coats*) No – I don't mind.

Grandma Good, and it'll take you out of yourself, won't it? Do you want to come, Adrian?

Adrian I'd love to but Nigel's coming round to collect a book.

Grandma (*kissing* **Adrian**) Well, bye bye love. And don't fret about your mother. You know what they say: 'The bad penny gathers no moss.'

Nigel *enters as* **Grandma** *and* **George** *go off.*

George Go through, he's in there.

Adrian Oh you're here.

Nigel Yeah, you got it?

Adrian Yes.

He takes a magazine called Big and Bouncy *from under a cushion and gives it to* **Nigel**, *who flicks through it and puts it under his jumper.*

Nigel God, your furniture! It's like reject corner at MFI in here. I get a shock every time I come in.

Adrian I know. (*Apologetically.*) It was brilliant staying at your house last weekend, Nigel. It's really opened my eyes. Without knowing it I've been living in poverty for the last fourteen years. Perhaps if *my* father had built a formica cocktail cabinet in *our* lounge, my mother would still be here.

Nigel I doubt it. Your mum left because your dad went round looking like a scruffbag. You can't expect a woman to put up with it. In fact, Adrian, if you don't do something about your own personal image, you're going to end up sentenced to a life of chastity.

'*Get It Right!*'

Nigel (*sings*)
Adrian Mole, why d'you look such a right arsehole?
I've never seen anyone dress worse!

Your bottoms are flared and your boots curl up like
   they're scared
And your duffel coat positively festers!
Your jumper is straight off the tip –
Do you wear it in bed when you kip?
Oh Moley, you're wholly, completely – words defeat me!
Try Lacoste, Doc Martens, some Farahs you'd look smart
   in –
If you want to wear clothes – get them right!

Your bike's a disgrace – you need a BMX or a racer
With a speedo and ten gears like my one:
This Walkman will surprise you, got a built-in graphic
   equaliser
With these new lightweight 'phones – why not try one?
This digital Seiko's for you
If you want to play chess in the loo:
Oh, Mole-face, it's as simple as squeezing a pimple!
Ask for Raleigh, or Sony, Ticini, Cerutti –
Whatever you get – get it right!

Your taste, I must say, falls far short of a true gourmet –
You live on baked beans and fish fingers:
In a hurry a curry from a tin saves a lot of worry,
But it does have a strong pong that lingers:
The best things are subtle, not loud,
And known to a few, not the crowd:
Not your Tizer from Tesco – Frascati, *al fresco*!
Say Martini, say Campari, say Adidas, say Atari,
Say Honda, Sekonda, aerobics, Jane Fonda –
If you want to get on – get it right!

Anyway, must rush, I'm seeing Pandora at four o'clock.
We're having wholemeal crumpets in front of the log fire.

Adrian You're dead lucky Nigel. What's she like to go out
with?

Nigel To tell you the truth she's not much cop. I'm used to
birds that give it out, talking of which have you heard from
your mum?

Adrian I had a postcard telling me that she'd found a flat – she lives at 69a President Carter Walk, Sheffield. Why can't she write a letter like any normal person? Why should the postman be able to read my confidential business? I've asked my father if I can go.

Nigel What's he say?

Adrian (*imitating* **George**) Yeah, providing she sends the train fare.

Adrian *moves off stage.*

Adrian (*voice over*) It was the first time I'd been on a train on my own. I'm certainly spreading my wings lately. (*Pause.*) Sheffield looks just like Leicester really. I didn't see any knife and fork factories. So I suppose Margaret Thatcher has closed them all down.

Pauline *and* **Mr Lucas**'s *Sheffield flat.*

Adrian *and* **Pauline** *come in with shopping. They are met by* **Mr Lucas**.

Mr Lucas Had a good day?

He goes to **Pauline** *and kisses her, then puts his arms around her from the back. He almost touches her breasts but* **Pauline** *holds his hands firmly.*

Pauline I did. (*To* **Adrian**.) Did you, love?

Adrian Yes, thank you.

Pauline There's no need to be so polite! I'm your mother – remember?

Mr Lucas What did you get up to then, young Adrian?

Adrian *turns away from* **Mr Lucas**.

Adrian We had a Chinese Businessman's lunch, then we went to Habitat to buy a lampshade for . . . (*He looks at* **Pauline**.)

Pauline Our bedroom. Then we saw a Monty Python film – it was all about the life of Jesus.

Adrian (*to* **Pauline**) I felt guilty laughing!

Pauline And I got him some nice new trousers – tight ones!

Mr Lucas *kisses* **Pauline**'s *hair, neck and lips.*

Pauline Don't! (*She pushes* **Mr Lucas** *away.*)

Adrian I'm going to try my new trousers on.

Pauline All right, love.

Adrian *goes off.*

Mr Lucas Did you notice? He didn't look me in the eye once.

Pauline He's bound to feel a bit strange. I do myself.

Mr Lucas *grabs* **Pauline**.

Pauline Oh let go of me! I'm fed up with you mauling me about. I feel like the last chicken in Sainsbury's! How would you feel if a man was messing about with your mother?

Mr Lucas I'd be very surprised. She's been dead for five years.

Pauline There's so much I don't know about you. The false teeth came as a surprise.

Mr Lucas I've only got the four.

Pauline Yes, but at the front. Don't take them out again, will you? Not at bed time.

Mr Lucas I'm glad you brought up the subject of bed time. When do you think we'll be able to – er – get together?

Pauline (*pause*) I can't. I just can't. Not with that child here.

Mr Lucas But it's our honeymoon, Paulie.

Pauline Would you mind not calling me 'Paulie'? It reminds me of childhood illnesses. My name's *Pauline*, Derek.

Mr Lucas Oh, I see. So it's Derek now is it, Mrs Mole?

Pauline Yes and I don't think it will ever be Mrs Pauline Lucas either.

Mr Lucas But you promised to marry me! You said you'd get a divorce. You've been using me. Oh God, I feel dirty!

Pauline Oh try and pull yourself together, Derek. You sound like something out of Barbara Cartland!

Adrian *enters. He is wearing tight black trousers. The labels are hanging off.*

Mr Lucas Who's a super trendy, then?

Pauline Oh you do look nice, Adrian. They really suit you. Turn round. Doesn't he look grown up!

Adrian *turns.*

Mr Lucas Oh yes, the birds will be after you now, eh Adrian?

Adrian *blushes, looks uncomfortable.*

Adrian Can you take the labels off please, Mum?

Mr Lucas (*taking a Swiss army knife out of his apron pocket*) Allow me. Don't know how I survived without my Swiss army knife. Now, where's the scissors? (*He fumbles with the blades.*) 'Course they're wasted on the Swiss – never fought a decent war. (*Still fumbling.*) Very good for emergencies.

Adrian *and* **Pauline** *watch as he fumbles.*

Pauline Slow emergencies.

Mr Lucas Give me a chance, Pauline! (*Still fumbling.*) You can saw through a tree with a Swiss army knife, Adrian. In fact, we'll have a drive out to the countryside tomorrow and I'll prove it to you.

Adrian (*coldly*) It's against the law to saw trees down.

Mr Lucas Bloody bureaucrats!

Pauline Yes, it'll do us all good to get out of here and get some fresh air in our lungs. (*She rips the labels from* **Adrian**'s *trousers with her bare hands.*)

Mr Lucas (*handing the Swiss army knife to* **Adrian**) I want you to have this, Adrian. As a sort of memento of your visit which sincerely I hope will be the first of many. We both want you to regard this as your second home.

Pauline Oh Bimbo, what a lovely thing to do.

Adrian Sorry, but I can't accept it. I've turned pacifist.

Mr Lucas (*martyred*) I don't mind admitting I'm very, very hurt. I would have given an arm and a leg for one of these when I was a lad.

He goes off.

Pauline Adrian – why didn't you accept it graciously? He's trying ever so hard to be nice to you.

Adrian Mum, there's things you ought to know about Creep Lucas.

Pauline What?

Adrian There's a new family moved into his house and the bloke, Mr Singh, he found this stack of horrible magazines under the lino in the bathroom.

Pauline So?

Adrian Well, they belonged to Mr Lucas. He's a pervert! You'll have to come home.

Pauline What were these magazines called?

Adrian *Amateur Photographer*.

Pauline So, Bimbo's interested in photography – it doesn't mean he's Jack the Ripper!

Adrian Mum you'll have to come home soon. Dad's falling in love with another woman.

Pauline What's her name?

Adrian Doreen Slater.

Pauline (*laughs*) Oh – Dopey Doreen! Is she still making the rounds? My God, she's got some staying power!

Pauline *goes off.* **Adrian** *goes to his house. He goes upstairs and looks at* **George**'s *bed.*

Adrian (*voice over*) My father said he had had Doreen Slater to tea. By the state of the house I should think he'd had her for breakfast, dinner and tea! I have never seen the woman, but from the evidence she left behind, I know she has got bright red hair, wears orange lipstick and sleeps on the left side of the bed. What a homecoming!

Bert Baxter's *house.* **Bert** *is in his chair. Toothless.*

Bert (*looking for his teeth*) Where are yer? Where are yer? (*Shouting to* **Adrian** *off.*) I know I 'ad 'em this mornin' but then I took 'em out to give me gums a rest. I've looked in the lavvy but they're not on the window sill where I usually leaves 'em.

Adrian *enters.*

Adrian I wish you hadn't rung me at school, Bert. I got into trouble. Scruton went mad.

Bert Scruton? That the headmaster? Stuck-up git! I told *him* a few things. You haven't found 'em, then?

Adrian No, I've looked everywhere.

Bert I shall have to find 'em. They've got sentimental value: belonged to me father. I've had them teeth since 1946 and besides I shall starve. I can't chew me beetroot. 'Ave another look, there's a good lad. And see how Sabre is will you? He's been quiet all morning. It ain't like 'im.

Adrian He's chewing something in his kennel. He's all right.

Adrian *goes off.*

Bert *is struggling to get out of his chair but can't do it.*

Bert (*to his legs*) Come on me old beauties. Don't let me down! (*He sits back.*)

Adrian *enters with* **Bert**'s *teeth held between thumb and finger.*

Bert You've found 'em! Good lad. Where was they?

Adrian In Sabre's kennel.

Bert (*laughs*) He's a bugger! Give 'em a swill under the tap.

Adrian (*horrified*) Bert, no!

Bert I can't put 'em straight back into me mouth after a dog's been chewing 'em all night, can I? What's up with you, ain't you heard of hygiene?

Adrian *goes out to* **Bert**'s *kitchen.*

Bert Talking of which, ain't it time you came round and did a bit o' cleaning? Tomorrow will be all right.

Adrian *comes back, drying the teeth on a tea towel.*

Adrian I can't come tomorrow, my mother's coming home to talk about who gets custody.

Bert Who gets the custard?

Adrian *Custody*, Bert.

He gives **Bert** *the teeth.* **Bert** *puts them into his mouth.*

Adrian (*to the audience*) This is the most revolting thing I have ever seen, and I'm no stranger to squalor.

Bert Be a good lad an' make me a beetroot sandwich up will you?

Adrian OK.

Adrian *makes a sandwich.*

Bert So, your mum and dad are gettin' a divorce, are they?

Adrian (*sadly*) Yes.

Bert I don't hold with divorce. I was married for thirty-five miserable years, so why should anybody else get away with it? (*Pause.*) Did I ever show you a photo of my wife?

Adrian No, Bert.

Bert Pass us the photo album then. It's in the pouffee.

Adrian *passes the album.*

Bert (*opening the album*) That's her. (*Pause.*) 'Course it were in the days before they had plastic surgery. (*Pause.*)

Adrian She looks a bit like . . .

Bert An 'oss? Yes, I know, funny that. I never realised until I stopped working with 'osses and went to work on the railways.

Adrian I'd better go now, Bert.

Bert No, stay a bit longer, lad. Here – you seen this Bible? Saved my life this did. I had it in me breast pocket when a Jerry sniper shot at me. See that? It's a bullet hole. Saved my life. It was a miracle!

Adrian But this Bible was printed in 1958, Bert.

Bert Well, I said it was a miracle!

Bert *goes out.* **Adrian** *crosses to the Mole living-room.*

George Mole *is hoovering the living-room. He is singing 'Your Hair of Gold'. He is looking cheerful. He's tidied himself up.*

George Adrian, I'm just off to fetch your mother's flowers. Won't be long. Carry on cleaning up.

Adrian *makes sure that his father has gone, then he takes a tape measure and looks round furtively. He takes a tiny notebook out and measures his thing and records the measurement. An Electricity Board*

Official *starts banging on the front door.* **Adrian** *drops the tape measure. He quickly adjusts his dress. He lets the* **Official** *in.*

Official Electricity Board. You owe us £97.79.

Adrian That's a lot.

Official Yes, it is isn't it? And it's obviously more than you can pay. So, I've come to cut you off. (*He enters the hall.*)

Adrian But you can't do that! We need electricity for life's essentials, like the television and stereo!

Official (*opening his tool box*) It's people like you what are sapping the country's strength. Where's the meter cupboard?

Adrian There.

The **Official** *goes to the cupboard and fiddles around. The Mole lights go down.*

Official (*mournfully*) Do you think I enjoy doing this son?

The **Official** *puts his hand on* **Adrian***'s shoulder.*

Adrian No, I'm sure you don't.

Official Well you'd be wrong because I do! Good morning.

George *enters. His arms full of flowers. He passes the* **Official***.*

George Morning. Would you like a cup of tea:

Official No thank you, sir. I never fraternise with the enemy.

He leaves.

George (*laughs*) It's nice to know that officials have got a sense of humour. (*To* **Adrian***.*) Stick these in a milk bottle, I'll finish the hoovering – she'll be here soon. (*He switches the hoover on. No power.*) What the bloody hell's up with this? (*He kicks the hoover.*) Have you been playing at Daleks again?

Adrian No. Dad . . . we've been cut off. You haven't paid the bill. You should have put it away every week, in a jug, like Grandma does.

George She'll be here soon and I've still got bits on my shag pile! You should have refused entry, you stupid . . . (*He swears under his breath.*)

Pauline *enters.*

Pauline (*shouting*) George! Adrian!

George Pauline! Love, you look wonderful!

Mr Lucas *enters.*

George What's he doing here? I thought Adrian's custody was being decided between the two of us?

Mr Lucas Where Pauline goes, I go.

Pauline It's gloomy in here, George. Can't we have a light on?

Adrian No. We've had our electricity cut off.

George Temporarily.

Pauline (*kindly*) Well, I'm not surprised you can't pay the bills, George – these flowers must have cost a fortune.

Mr Lucas If you want to borrow a ton, George . . .

George All I want from you, Lucas, is my wife.

Pauline But apart from having no electricity, you're keeping the house beautifully, George.

Mr Lucas *offers* **Adrian** *a fiver.*

Mr Lucas Here, Adrian, go and buy some candles. This meeting might go on all night. We can't negotiate in the dark.

Adrian Shall I, Dad?

George We've got no choice, son. I'm skint.

Adrian *goes to his room. The lights go down on the living-room and up on* **Adrian**'s *bedroom.*

Adrian (*voice over*) The arguing went on for ages. In fact until it was time to light the candles. Mr Lucas spilt candle wax on his new shoes. It was the only cheerful incident in a tragic day.

Pauline *walks off, followed by* **Mr Lucas**.

George Mole *is talking on the phone to* **Doreen Slater**.

George Doreen, I know I said it was all over. But I can't stop thinking about you . . . Baby. Thanks, warm the bed up.

George *puts the phone down, grabs the flowers and goes out quickly.*

'*Dog*' ('*The House Where I Live*' *reprise*).

Adrian (*sits on the bed and sings to the dog*)
    You are my only true friend,
    Always here at the end
    Of a traumatic day:
    I'm used to your slobb'ring embrace
    And your lop'sided face . . . is okay.

    Oh Dog, never gave you a name.
    Still I'm glad that you came
    To the house where I live.

    You are so easy to please
    And occasional fleas
    Don't detract from your charms:
    I s'pose you're a bit of a mess,
    But I couldn't care less – in my arms,

    Oh Dog, you're so floppy and warm!
    We'll both weather the storm
    In the house where we live.

The candlelit living-room. **George** *and* **Adrian** *are sitting around a small primus stove. They are wearing scarves and gloves.* **George** *is reading* Playboy. **Adrian** *is reading a hardback book, using a torch.*

George What's that you're reading?

Adrian *Hard Times* by Charles Dickens.

George D'you want some more beans, son? (*He hands him a Heinz tin and spoon.*)

Adrian No thanks, I don't like them cold.

George Y'know this is good training for when civilisation collapses. You'll thank me one day.

Adrian Oh, I don't mind. In fact, it's quite nice. (*Pause.*) Dad, what do you think my chances are of becoming a vet?

George Nil. (*a*) You're no good at Science. (*b*) You don't want to be a vet, son, they spend half their lives with their hands stuck up cows' bums.

A noise off.

Grandma *enters the house. She gropes about in the dark.*

Grandma George, are you there?

George Blow the candles out! It's your grandma!

Adrian She's bound to find us, Dad. We may as well surrender.

Adrian *goes to* **Grandma***'s aid.*

Grandma (*trying to switch the lights on*) George! I know you're there, I can hear voices.

Adrian In here, Grandma!

Grandma *gropes into the room.*

Grandma Whose idea was it to sit in the dark?

Adrian The Electricity Board's.

Grandma So, you've stopped paying your bills now, have you?

George Pauline managed the money. I don't know how to do it. Mum.

Grandma It's quite simple. All you do is put it away in jugs. Gas in a pink jug. Electricity in a blue and so on. How much do you owe?

Adrian Ninety-seven pounds seventy-nine pence.

Grandma My God! Ninety-seven pounds. You must have a leak somewhere! I'll call the Board out first thing tomorrow.

Grandma *takes a cheque book out of her bag and writes a cheque by candlelight.*

Adrian (*in a loud whisper*) You shouldn't be taking money from a pensioner.

George *hits* **Adrian** *round the head.*

Grandma Now I shan't be able to re-stock my freezer. You know I like to buy half a cow a year.

Grandma *gives* **George** *a cheque.*

George I'm sorry, Mum. Thank you. I'll pay you back.

Grandma (*to* **Adrian**) Now what's this I hear about Barry Kent beating you up for money?

Adrian Who told you?

Grandma It's all round the Evergreen Club.

George I've been to see his father. But he wouldn't listen. I daren't push it any further, he's like an ape, Mum. He's got more hair on his knuckles than I've got on my head.

Grandma Where does this Barry Kent boy live?

Adrian Number Thirteen Corporation Row. You're not thinking of going are you?

Adrian *stands.*

George Leave it to the police, Mum.

George *stands.*

Grandma (*with contempt*) The police! We Moles fight our own battles! (*She straightens her back and leaves.*)

George *goes off.*

Adrian (*to the audience*) She was gone one hour and seven minutes. She came in, took her coat off. Fluffed her hair out. Took £27.18 from the anti-mugger belt around her waist. She said 'He won't bother you again, Adrian, but if he does, let me know.' Then she got the tea ready, pilchards, tomatoes and ginger cake. I bought her a box of diabetic chocolates from the chemist's as a token of my esteem.

Lights go up in the kitchen where **Doreen Slater** *is making tea.*

Adrian (*voice over*) My father rang Doreen Slater up and asked her to come round. It was quite a shock to see her for the first time. Why my father wants to have carnal knowledge of her I can't imagine. She is as thin as a stick insect. She has got no bust and no bum. She is just straight all the way up and all the way down.

The phone rings. **Doreen** *picks up the phone in the hall.* **Pauline** *in a housecoat on the other side of the stage is holding a phone.*

Doreen Hello, George Mole's residence.

Pauline To whom am I speaking at 7.30 in the morning?

Doreen I'm Miss Doreen Slater. To whom am *I* speaking?

Pauline Mrs Pauline Mole. Could I speak to my son please?

Doreen I don't know if he's up. I've only just got out of bed myself.

Pauline Out of my husband's bed, I presume?

Adrian *comes downstairs.*

Doreen I don't see what it's got to do with you. You're the one that left. You've upset me now. (*To* **Adrian**.) Your mother's on the phone.

Adrian *grabs the phone.*

Adrian Mum?

Pauline What's Doreen Slater doing in *my* house?

Adrian Dad sent for her. Something terrible's happened.

Pauline It's not the dog?

Adrian No, it's Dad. He's been made redundant from his job. He'll be on the dole! Mum – how will we manage on the pittance the Government gives us? The dog will have to go. It costs thirty-five pence a day, not counting Winalot! Mum – I'm now a single parent child with a father on the dole. Social Security will be buying my shoes!

Pauline Calm down, Adrian. I'll buy your shoes. Oh my God, what next? How's he taken it?

Adrian He's having a nervous breakdown I think. He watches *Playschool*!

Pauline That's nothing to worry about. He's always watched *Playschool* when he got the chance. (*Fondly.*) He used to love guessing the shape of the windows. Oh, I wish I were there right now.

Adrian So do I, Mum. Come home.

Pauline I can't Adrian. I haven't found what I'm looking for yet. 'Bye pet.

The lights go down on **Pauline**. *She goes off.*

Doreen Well, what's happening? Is she coming home or what? Only I need to know. I'm having a new fireplace put in at my home.

Adrian She's not coming back. (*He puts the phone down.*)

Doreen So does that mean I'm staying, then?

Adrian I don't know. You'd better ask my dad.

Doreen Only if I knew, I could cancel the fireplace.

Adrian Hasn't *he* said anything?

Doreen No, he doesn't talk. He doesn't do anything and I mean anything. He's been rendered impotent.

Adrian *blanches.*

Doreen He was all right before he was made redundant. He was ever so good at it – you don't mind me talking like this, do you? No, of course you don't. In my day, adults didn't talk about . . . you know . . . (*She mouths 'sex'.*) But now, it's all open and above board, isn't it: You and your mates talk about it all the time, don't you?

Adrian *shakes his head.*

Doreen Have you noticed how much he's drinking and smoking?

Adrian *nods.*

Adrian Yes, I think he's going mental.

Doreen I'm ever so worried about him, he's not sleeping either, he just lies in bed with his arms folded behind his head, staring at the ceiling. People are talking about me you know. Saying I've got no morals. It's because my Maxwell was born out of wedlock. But it's not my fault, is it? I'd give anything to be *in* wedlock. It's just my bad luck that I fall in love with married men. (*Pause.*) Over and over again.

Adrian *looks on with growing distaste.*

'The Other Woman'.

Doreen (*sings*)
   The other woman – *his* other woman:
   I'm another woman in the hours he spends with me:
   'The other woman' – why does it bother me?
   You'd think by now I'd play my old familiar role with
      some good grace.

   Now, for a week or two,
   I'll pretend he'll stay with me –
   Such hurried ecstasy!
   Then she'll reappear, he'll say 'Sorry, my dear, it was
      fun' –
   And out will go the sun.

   The other woman: who *is* 'the other woman'?
   Who has shown concern for him? Deserves his trust and
      love?
   The other woman, *this* other woman,

While she ran out on him, without a thought, without a
  backward glance:

Who came to rescue him,
Soothed away all his pain,
Made him feel brave again?
This other woman, who secretly knew from the start
That he would break my heart.

Doreen *goes upstairs.*

Adrian (*to the audience*) Doreen talks to me as if I was another
adult instead of her lover's son, aged fourteen, two months
and one day. I'm just about sick of so-called adults. You
would think that they would be old enough to manage their
lives a bit better, but oh, no! They go about baring their
sickly emotions to anybody who will listen. All this family
trouble is sending me rebellious. In fact, I wore red socks to
school. It's strictly forbidden but I don't care any more.

Adrian *shows his red socks to the audience then walks to the school
wall.* **Adrian** *stands between* **Pandora**, **Nigel** *and another
schoolgirl showing his red socks.* **Nigel**'s *trousers are tucked into his
socks.* **Pandora**'s *socks are Lurex.*

Pandora You're a true revolutionary, Adrian. When they
come to write the history of school politics – your name will
be in the index under 'M'.

Nigel I was gob-smacked when I heard it was you who led
the revolt – I didn't think you were the revolting type!

Adrian Well, I'm not really – in fact I can't help wishing
that I'd worn my black socks the other day.

Pandora Come on now, Adrian – no revisionism. Stand by
your principles! Why should we be forced to wear the black
socks of oppression?

Nigel Come on then! Let's march on Scruton's office!

Adrian But what if the GCE examiners find out about it
next year? It could jeopardise our 'O' levels!

Nigel He's got a point – a valid one.

Pandora So am I going to face that fascist pig Scruton on my own?

Adrian No, I'll come with you. I've started – so I'll finish. Are you coming, Nigel?

Nigel It's a moral decision, isn't it?

Schoolgirl Yes it is, darling.

Nigel It's a bit hard to know what to do.

Pandora If one's immoral – it's hard. But, if one has principles – then one has no choice.

She starts to sing 'We Shall Not Be Moved'. The **Schoolgirl** *and the boys join in weakly but then with gathering strength. They march towards* **Scruton**'s *office. Enter* **Scruton**.

Scruton Good morning.

Kids (*together*) Good morning, sir!

Scruton Yes. I saw you making your way down the school drive. Very colourful, very foolhardy. What a brave little band you are! Now I should like you to hear the letter which I shall be sending to your parents.
'Dear Mr and Mrs . . .
It is my sad duty to inform you that your son – stroke – daughter has deliberately flaunted one of the rules of this school. I take an extremely serious view of this contravention. I am, therefore, suspending your son – stroke – daughter for a period of one week.'

Pandora But, sir! What about our 'O' Levels . . . ?

Scruton (*roaring*) QUIET!

Everyone jumps.

Nigel Can we wear our black socks with a red stripe, sir?

Scruton (*roaring*) *No!* Your socks must be entirely, absolutely, incontrovertibly dense, midnight, black!

Scruton *exits.*

Pandora *starts to cry.*

Adrian Now look what he's done. Don't cry, Pandora. Aren't you going to try to stop her, Nigel?

Nigel No. She broke it off. She says I'm a philistine.

Nigel *and the* **Schoolgirl** *go off hand in hand.*

Adrian *pats* **Pandora**'s *shoulder.*

Adrian Don't cry. I've had a rejection letter from the BBC. Do you want to see it?

Pandora *nods, she puts her head on* **Adrian**'s *shoulder. He shows her the letter.*

Music: 'Oh Pandora'.

Pandora *and* **Adrian** *walk together.*

Adrian (*voice over*) Pandora and I are in love! It is official! She told Claire Neilson who told Nigel who told me. I told Claire to tell Pandora that I return her love. I can overlook the fact that Pandora smokes five Benson and Hedges a day *and* has her own lighter. When you are in love, such things cease to matter!

Adrian *and* **Pandora** *are sitting on a school bench in the playground. They are not touching, but gazing into each other's eyes. They hold hands.*

Pandora So, you didn't fall in love with me because of how I look – like everybody else?

Adrian Good God, no! That's dead sexist. No, it was because of your personal integrity . . . and your brain.

Pandora But, you don't think I'm ugly do you?

Adrian Ugly? You? You're Brillo pad! You're the most desirable, erotic girl I've ever clapped eyes on!

Pandora Do you want to kiss me?

Adrian Well, of course I'd like to . . . I'm a bit out of practice though . . .

Pandora Do you do French?

Adrian Yes, I'm doing it for CSE.

Pandora French kissing!

Adrian Oh no. I usually just stick to the English!

Pandora *and* **Adrian** *fumble a kiss.* **Pandora** *breaks away.*

Pandora I don't think we're doing it properly. You need to open your lips just a little wider, Adrian.

Adrian Sorry.

Pandora Let's try again. (*They kiss.* **Pandora** *breaks away.*) Well, we've got plenty of time to practise. (*Pause.*) So *when* did you fall in love with me?

Adrian When I saw you playing netball.

Pandora I fell in love with your red socks first!

Adrian (*disappointed*) Oh . . .

Pandora Your socks were enormously significant. You see, I'm a radical and I'm gong to devote my whole life to changing our spiritually bankrupt society.

Adrian I'll help you if you like.

Pandora We can do it together!

Adrian And when we're married . . .

Pandora (*starting away*) Married! But we're only fourteen, darling.

Adrian (*laughing*) I know we can't get married now, thanks to the stupid adults that make the laws, but, in two years' time . . .

Pandora We'll be sixteen.

Adrian So we can get married. I know my dad would give me permission – he can't wait for me to leave home and my mother's left home anyway, so she can't prevent us. Don't worry, I wouldn't stop you working . . . You could get a little job . . . something part-time . . . in a cake-shop, for instance.

Pandora *stands.*

Pandora (*sternly*) *I* am going to Oxford University. While there, I may occasionally enter a cake shop, but I will be *buying* a granary loaf. I will certainly not be *selling* one!

Adrian So you don't want to marry me and have twins?

Pandora I don't want to marry anybody!

Adrian Not ever?

Pandora No! I shall live in sin.

Adrian With me?

Pandora With several people I expect . . . in the course of a lifetime . . .

Music: 'Oh Pandora'. During the song, **Adrian** *behaves like a Latin lover.*

Adrian (*sings*)
    Oh, Pandora, I adore . . . ya:
    From the first day that I saw ya
    I felt destiny called,
    I knew I was enthralled
    By your aura of love – my Pandora!

    Always wondered how it would be:
    This is passion as it should be!
    Your lips smoulder with fire,
    Yours eyes melt with desire!
    Take me higher and higher, my Pandora!

    We'll get married straight away,
    Find a cottage by a stream
    With a private wishing-well
    Where I can dream
    Of my Pandora . . .

Pandora (*sings*)
Haven't done my physics homework:
There's that film I want to see on El Salvador –
It must be Channel Four:
There's so much I have to do
If I am to fulfil my potential –
Mustn't waste a second of my time!

Get my 'O's and 'A's – then Oxford!
Take a double first in Law and Economy –
Dead right for an MP!
Spare an afternoon a week
For a lover or two, but no attachment,
Nothing to deflect me from my course!

Adrian (*sings*)
Two hearts beat in unison,
Two souls joined in perfect
    peace:
Our two bodies cry out loud   **Pandora** (*sings simultaneously*
For release . . .   *with* **Adrian**)

Oh, please Pandora – I   Haven't done my physics
    implore ya   homework:
From the first day that I   There's that film I want to
    saw ya   see on El Salvador –
I felt destiny called,   It must be Channel Four.
I knew I was enthralled   There's so much I have to do
By your aura of love –   If I am to fulfil my potential
    my Pandora!   Mustn't waste a second of my
                                                   time!

My Pandora,   Must go . . .
My Pandora,   Must go . . .
Oh, my Pandora!   Mustn't waste a second of m
                                                   time!

Pandora *leaves* **Adrian** *on his knees.*

Adrian (*voice over*) My precious love leaves these shores
tomorrow. I am going to the airport to see her off. I hope her
plane won't suffer from metal fatigue. I have just checked the

world map to see where Tunisia is and I am most relieved to
see that Pandora won't have to fly through the Bermuda
Triangle.

Adrian *gets up and wanders about looking lost.*

(*To the audience.*) Wednesday July 22nd! Why haven't I had a
postcard yet? What can have happened? Pandora! Pandora!
Pandora! (*He opens his notebook and clears his throat.*)

> Oh! My love,
> My heart is yearning
> My mouth is dry,
> My soul is burning.
> You're in Tunisa
> I am here.
> Remember me and shed a tear.
> Come back tanned and brown and healthy
> You're lucky that your dad is wealthy.

She will be back in six days.

Adrian *writes in his diary.*

(*Voice over.*) Friday August 7th.
Moon's first quarter.
I rang Tunisa whilst my father was in the bath. He shouted
down to ask whom I was phoning. I told a lie. I said I was
phoning the speaking clock.
Pandora's flight left safely. She should be home around
midnight.

'Oh Pandora' music triumphant. Enter **Pandora**. *The lighting
becomes romantic. There is an emotional reunion with* **Adrian**.

Pandora Adrian!

Adrian Pandora!

They embrace.

Did you have a good time?

Pandora No. It was dreadful. Mummy was bitten by a camel. Then the Tunisian baggage handlers went on strike, but I told you that on the phone. It *was* clever of you to ring me at Tunis airport. Didn't your father mind?

Adrian He doesn't know yet. I'm dreading the phone bill coming.

Pandora We're together again – that's all that matters.

They start to leave.

Adrian (*to the audience*) Went to Pandora's house. Had an emotional reunion behind her father's tool shed.

They go off.

Adrian (*voice over*) Monday October 5th.
Bert has been kidnapped by Social Services! They are keeping him at the Alderman Cooper Sunshine Home. I have been to see him. He shares a room with an old man called Thomas Bell. They have both got their names on their ashtrays. Sabre has got a place in the RSPCA hostel.

Bert *is sitting in a wheelchair looking miserable.* **Matron** *enters with* **Queenie** *in a wheelchair: an old lady with red hair and over-the-top make-up.*

Matron Mr Baxter, may I introduce a new guest to 'Smoker's Corner'?

Bert Guest? It ain't an hotel you're runnin', Matron! It's an institution. What's run by the State. If I was a *guest* I could have my dog wi' me.

Matron (*to* **Queenie**) Mr Baxter can be rather difficult, but we're hoping he will settle down. (*Pause.*) Most of our guests do. (*Pause.*) In time.

Queenie Well, I think he's right. We're not guests, are we? None of us are here by choice. (*To* **Bert**.) What's your name, love?

Bert Bertram. What's yours?

Queenie Queenie.

Bert *and* **Queenie** *look away from each other.*

Matron Well, you're getting on like a house on fire, aren't you? So, if you'll excuse me . . .

Queenie *and* **Bert** *stare hostilely at* **Matron** *as she goes off.*

Bert What you doin' in 'ere? You ain't incapable of lookin' after yourself, are you?

Queenie Not in my opinion, I'm not. But I'm told that I'm going a bit doo-lally in the head.

Bert Well, you seem all right to me.

Queenie And to me. I think I've been put away because I like a drink now and again. You see, sometimes, after a drink, I forget where I am and I start singing.

Bert What's wrong wi' that?

Queenie I don't know. But others objected. Bus conductors and people in the library. D'you know what you've been put away for?

Bert Yes. Me legs have gone.

Queenie Shame, you're a fine figure of a man. (*Pause. She looks round.*) I don't like it in here, do you? It's full of old people!

Bert I'm plannin' to escape.

Queenie What, dig a tunnel?

Bert No. I've got friends what are sortin' the paperwork out for me. It's only the paperwork what gets you out a' these places. Ay up there, Adrian! Ay up, Pandora!

Adrian 'Lo Bert.

Pandora *kisses* **Bert**.

Pandora How are you, darling?

Bert I'm not happy and that's the truth.

Adrian Cheer up, Bert. Russia's through to the European Cup.

Bert *cheers up.*

Bert How's my Sabre?

Adrian He's outside in the garden. Matron said he could cause heart failure amongst the guests.

Bert I'm puttin' in an official complaint about *her*. Deprivin' a man of his liberty *and* his dog is unconstitutional.

Pandora (*to* **Queenie**) Your hair is a lovely colour. What do you use?

Queenie I do it it once a week with six ounces of red henna. It's a big slice out me pension but I'd sooner go without food than have white hair. I haven't got the personality to be an old age pensioner. (*To* **Bert**.) Are you the only man in here?

Bert Yes, I am.

Pandora Women live longer than men. It's a sort of bonus because we suffer more.

Queenie I've hardly suffered at all. I've been happily married three times. All dead now, of course. But they died contented.

Adrian *and* **Pandora** *push* **Bert** *and* **Queenie** *in a wheelchair gavotte, during:*

'*The Young Girl Inside You*'.

Queenie (*sings*)
When you look in the mirror
The person reflected
Is a stranger you don't know
And don't care to meet:
But the young girl inside you
Is bright-eyed and flirty,
Not a day over thirty,
Who longs to be loved.

Adrian *and* **Pandora** *dance the gavotte behind* **Bert** *and*
Queenie.

> Why does youth think it odd
> That those older than God
> Should know pangs of desire,
> Feel the flame of love's fire?
> It's not strange, it's not odd –
> 'Cause inside these old bodies
> Our younger selves live
> Just as lusty as you.

Wheelchair gavotte.

Queenie } *(sing)*
Bert

> Why does youth think it odd
> That those older than God
> Should know pangs of desire,
> Feel the flame of love's fire?
> It's not strange, it's not odd –
> 'Cause inside these old bodies
> Our younger selves live
> Just as lusty as you.

Queenie What am I doing in this thing? (*She gets out of her
wheelchair.*)

Pandora You've got something for Bert, haven't you,
Adrian?

Bert Brought me some fags in, have you? Good lad. (*He holds
his hand out expectantly.*)

Adrian No, it's a poem!

Bert (*disappointed*) Oh.

Queenie How lovely! Read it out then.

Adrian It's not very good.

Bert Don't bother then.

Pandora (*to* **Adrian**) Darling, you're too modest – go on.

Adrian All right. (*He reads the poem.*)

Poem to Bert – by Adrian Mole.

Bert, you are dead old.
Fond of Sabre, beetroot and Woodbines,
We have nothing in common,
I am fourteen and a half,
You are eighty-nine,
You smell, I don't.
Why we are friends
Is a mystery to me.

Bert *is offended.*

Queenie (*weakly*) Very nice, dear.

Bert It don't rhyme!

Adrian (*to* **Bert**) Would you mind if I sent your poem to the BBC, Bert?

Bert Yes, I would. They're all a load of drug addicts in the BBC. I've got it on good authority.

Queenie (*impressed*) Oh, shocking! Know somebody high up, do you?

Bert Yes – a window cleaner at Broadcasting House.

Everybody laughs. **Matron** *enters.*

Matron Please! Your laughter is disturbing the other guests! Come along. (*She claps her hands.*) It's way past your bed time.

Pandora *Au contraire*, Matron! We can choose our own bed times.

Matron I was addressing myself to the oldsters, you cheeky young madam.

Adrian *and* **Pandora** *leave.*

Pandora
Adrian } Bye, Bert. Bye, Queenie!

Bert
Queenie } Bye!

Matron Time for bed.

Bert Bed? It's still light – I'm used to staying up till after the Epilogue.

Matron Here, we go to bed at half past nine.

Queenie We?

She looks coquettishly at **Bert**. **Bert** *laughs dirtily.* **Queenie** *pushes* **Bert** *off.*

The Mole house. **George** *is in the hall banging the telephone.*

George Bloody British Telecom! Come on, get your act together! Give me a dialling tone. (*He is getting increasingly enraged trying to get a line. Calling up to* **Adrian**.) Was there a storm in the night? Is the telephone pole still up?

Adrian (*calling down*) Oh no! Dad, I've got something to tell you!

George (*to* **Adrian**) Don't bother me now! (*To the phone.*) Come on. Come on! I want a job. I want some money in my pocket. I want to buy a round in the pub.

Adrian (*appearing with the phone bill*) Dad, we haven't paid the bill!

George Because we haven't *had* the bill, you daft pillock!

Adrian But *I* have Dad. I put it under my mattress.

George Have you gone barmy? The bills go behind the clock. (*Pause.*) *When* did you put it under your mattress?

Adrian Two months ago, Dad. We're not on the phone any more!

George *grabs the bill and reads it.*

George (*stunned*) Two hundred and eighty-seven pounds, thirty-seven pence! (*Amazed.*) Operator calls: two hundred and thirty-one pounds! (*Shouting.*) Who've you been phoning? The man in the bloody moon?

Adrian No, Tunisia. Sorry Dad.

George (*weakly*) Sorry. He says he's sorry! He cuts me off from civilisation and he says he's sorry! I don't know why you don't finish me off completely, Adrian. Put rat poison in me tea. Come home one day and tell me you're pregnant. I give up. That's it. George Mole is no more. What you see is an empty shell.

George *goes out through the kitchen. The dog barks off.*

(*Off.*) Not you an' all!

Adrian *opens a telegram.*

Adrian A telegram! Addressed to me! The BBC? No – from my mother. 'ADRIAN STOP COMING HOME STOP.' What does she mean? 'Stop coming home'? How can I stop coming home? I live here!

Adrian *goes into the house and up to his room to write his diary.*
Pauline *enters on the side of the stage. She is carrying her suitcases.*

'*Coming Down to Earth Again*'.

Pauline (*sings*)
Coming down to earth again
Out of the sunshine into twilight:
Coming down to earth again
From my rocket flight.

Coming down to earth again
Terra Firma out of the sky:
Coming round on earth again –
Touch-down from on high.

I've had my fling: I let my hair right down,
I dreamed that I could survive without ties:
Dreaming was fine but now it's wake-up time
And I'm rubbing the sleep from my eyes.

Hello the life I thought I'd shed for good
And hello people I'd blocked from my mind:
After the wine at last it's own-up time
In the world I left behind.

Coming down to earth again,
I'm back home – coming in – coming home . . .

Pauline *goes upstairs and into the bedroom; she and* **George** *kiss and hug.*

George Adrian! Your mother's home!

Adrian *comes out of his room.*

George Put the kettle on. We'll be down in a bit.

Adrian *comes downstairs and speaks to the audience.*

Adrian My mother threw herself on the mercy of my father. My father threw himself on the body of my mother. They've been in bed for two days – on and off. My mother told me why she left Rat-Fink Lucas. She said: 'Bimbo treated me like a sex-object, Adrian, and he expected his evening meal cooked for him, and he cut his toe-nails in the living-room! And, besides, I'm very fond of your father . . .' She didn't mention me! My only hope for future happiness now rests with the BBC. If they would give me my own poetry programmes on Radio Four I would have an outlet for the intellectual side of my nature. I haven't got enough emotions to cope with the complexities of my everyday life. I rang Pandora and told her that my mother had come back and she came round after her viola lesson. I'm glad I've got her. Love is the only thing that keeps me sane. Goodnight.

This is the end of the play, although the curtain call is done at **Bert** *and* **Queenie**'s *wedding. The cast wear their best clothes and flowers in their buttonholes. When* **Bert** *and* **Queenie** *take their call they are showered with confetti and rice.* **Mr Lucas** *prepares to take the wedding photograph.* **Adrian** *enters last – just in time to be in the photograph.*

Music for
The Secret Diary of
Adrian Mole Aged 13¾

Overture: The Mole Theme

The Mole Theme

This forms a part of the overture
and is also used between a number of scenes,
in varying musical styles, throughout the show
and as a background to the house-cleaning scene (page 274),
starting slowly and getting faster.

The House Where I Live

SHE DOESN'T COOK ME MY MEALS, DOESN'T KNOW HOW IT FEELS TO BE HUNGRY &

YOUNG: AND HE DOESN'T BUDGE FROM HIS CHAIR, DOESN'T CARE IF I'M HERE — OR

THERE! YES, THIS IS MY FAMILY SEAT EIGHTEEN EVERY STREET — IT'S THE HOUSE WHERE I

LIVE.

HOME, IT'S THE HOUSE WHERE I LIVE, YES,

IS MY OWN BROKEN HOME IT'S THE HOUSE WHERE I LIVE.

Sorry, Gotta Do It

The Bad Old Days

WHEN I WAS JUST YOUR AGE, SON WHEN I WAS JUST A LAD, THINGS WERE FAR DIFFERENT THEN I CAN TELL YOU, MY FRIEND — THEY WERE TEN TIMES AS BAD! HAD ME NO GILDED YOUTH, BOY, LIT BY NO SUNSHINE RAYS — WE WERE FOURTEEN IN A HOVEL, TAKIN' LESSONS HOW TO GROVEL, IN THE BAD OLD DAYS.

DANCE BREAK

WE TOILED OUR YOUTH AWAY, BOY — NO MONEY, NO THANKS, NO PRAISE: THEY SAY "WHERE THERE'S MUCK THERE'S BRASS" — I SAY "NOT ON YOUR BLEEDIN' ARSE!" THEY WERE BAD OLD DAYS.

Your Hair of Gold

YOUR HAIR OF GOLD, YOUR EYES OF BABY BLUE — HOW COULD I EVER FACE A LIFE WITHOUT YOU? YOUR LIPS SO SWEET, YOUR TOUCH SO TENDER — YOU KNOW I SURRENDER TO EVERYTHING THAT YOU YOUR HEART.

Family Trio

ADRIAN

TWO O'CLOCK IN THE MORNING: LEICESTER'S ASLEEP AS SOUND AS A LOG: I COUNT

SHEEP IN THE STILLNESS, AS WE LIE AWAKE — JUST ME   AND THE DOG

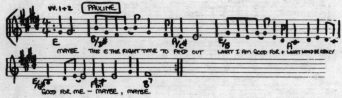

VV. 1 + 2   PAULINE

MAYBE   THIS IS THE RIGHT TIME TO FIND OUT   WHAT I AM GOOD FOR + WHAT WOULD BE REALLY

GOOD FOR ME — MAYBE, MAYBE.

GEORGE

YOUR HAIR OF GOLD, YOUR EYES OF BABY BLUE.   HOW COULD I

EVER   FACE A LIFE WITHOUT YOU?   YOUR

Your Dead Grandad

Get It Right!

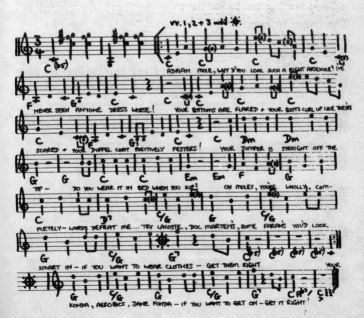

Dog

YOU ARE MY ONLY TRUE FRIEND, ALWAYS HERE AT THE END OF A TRAUMATIC
DAY: I'M USED TO YOUR SLOBB'RING EMBRACE + YOUR LOP-SIDED
FACE ... IS O. K. OH DOG, NEVER GAVE YOU A
NAME, STILL I'M GLAD THAT YOU CAME TO THE HOUSE WHERE I LIVE
STORM IN THE HOUSE WHERE WE LIVE.

The Other Woman

THE OTHER WOMAN — HIS OTHER WOMAN: I'M ANOTHER WOMAN IN THE
HOURS HE SPENDS WITH ME: 'THE OTHER WOMAN' WHY DOES IT
BOTHER ME? YOU'D THINK BY NOW I'D PLAY MY OLD FAMILIAR ROLE WITH SOME GOOD
GRACE. NOW, FOR A WEEK OR TWO, I'LL PRETEND HE'LL STAY WITH ME- SUCH HURRIED
ECSTACY! THEN SHE'LL REAPPEAR, HE'LL SAY "SORRY, MY DEAR, IT WAS FUN"— AND
OUT WILL GO THE SUN. HEART.

Oh, Pandora

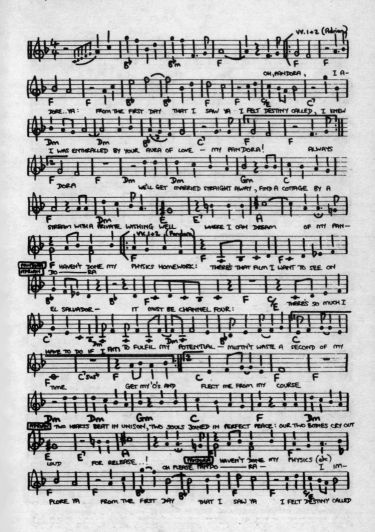

I KNEW I WAS ENTHRALLED BY YOUR AURA OF LOVE — MY PAN'DORA!

(ADRIAN) second of my time

PAN — DO — RA! my PAN — DO

must Go... must Go...

The Young Girl Inside You

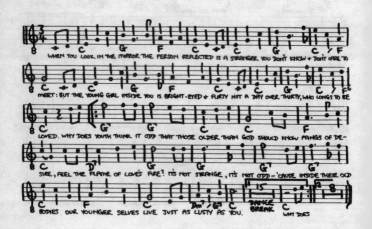

WHEN YOU LOOK IN THE MIRROR THE PERSON REFLECTED IS A STRANGER YOU DON'T KNOW & DON'T CARE TO

MEET: BUT THE YOUNG GIRL INSIDE YOU IS BRIGHT-EYED & FLIRTY NOT A DAY OVER THIRTY, WHO LONGS TO BE

LOVED. WHY DOES YOUTH THINK IT ODD THAT THOSE OLDER THAN GOD SHOULD KNOW PANGS OF DE-

SIRE, FEEL THE FLAME OF LOVE'S FIRE? IT'S NOT STRANGE, IT'S NOT ODD — 'CAUSE INSIDE THESE OLD

BODIES OUR YOUNGER SELVES LIVE JUST AS LUSTY AS YOU.   DANCE BREAK   WHY DOES

Coming Down to Earth Again

Methuen Contemporary Dramatists
include

Peter Barnes (three volumes)
Sebastian Barry
Edward Bond (six volumes)
Howard Brenton
  (two volumes)
Richard Cameron
Jim Cartwright
Caryl Churchill (two volumes)
Sarah Daniels (two volumes)
David Edgar (three volumes)
Dario Fo (two volumes)
Michael Frayn (two volumes)
Peter Handke
Jonathan Harvey
Declan Hughes
Terry Johnson
Bernard-Marie Koltès
Doug Lucie

David Mamet (three volumes)
Anthony Minghella
  (two volumes)
Tom Murphy (four volumes)
Phyllis Nagy
Philip Osment
Louise Page
Stephen Poliakoff
  (three volumes)
Christina Reid
Philip Ridley
Willy Russell
Ntozake Shange
Sam Shepard (two volumes)
David Storey (three volumes)
Sue Townsend
Michel Vinaver (two volumes)
Michael Wilcox